BUSINESS/SCIENCE/TECHNOLOGY DIVISION
CHICAGO PUBLIC LIBRARY
400 SOUTH STATE STREET
CHICAGO, IL 60605

You'd Better Have a Hose

If You Want to Put Out the Fire

REF
HD
49
.H46
2000

HWBI

Chicago Public Library

You'd better have a hose if you want to

Chicago Public Library

C
P L

REFERENCE

Form 178 rev. 11-00

*The Complete Guide
to Crisis and Risk Communications . . .*

You'd Better Have a Hose
If You Want to Put Out the Fire

*Professional Tips, Tactics, Dos, Don'ts
and Case Histories*

Rene A. Henry

GOLLYWOBBLER PRODUCTIONS
Windsor, California

Rene A. Henry, Fellow, Public Relations Society of America, is director of the Office of Communications and Government Relations for the mid-Atlantic region of the U.S. Environmental Protection Agency in Philadelphia. This book is written in Mr. Henry's private capacity, drawing from his more than 35 years of public relations experience, and not in his official role at EPA. No official support or endorsement by the EPA or any other agency of the federal government is intended or should be inferred.

© 2000 Rene A. Henry

Gollywobbler Productions
P.O. Box 1976
Windsor, California 95492-1976

All rights reserved, including the right of reproduction in whole or in part in any form.

Produced by BookMatters, Berkeley
Proofreader: Christine Miklas
Indexer: Ken DellaPenta

LIBRARY OF CONGRESS
CATALOGING-IN-PUBLICATION DATA

Henry, Rene A.
   You'd Better Have a Hose If You Want to Put Out the Fire /
   Rene A. Henry — lst ed.
     p.   cm.
   Includes biographical references and index.
   ISBN 0-9674535-0-x.
1. Crisis management. 2. Crisis communications. 3. Risk
communications. 4. Public relations. 5. Public affairs.
6. Reputation management. I. Title.
                                        99-95476
                                           CIP

Printed on acid-free, recycled paper in the United States of America.

First edition, 2000

10 9 8 7 6 5 4 3 2 1

400 SOUTH STATE STREET
CHICAGO, IL 60605

R0117153956

CONTENTS

Foreword   vii

ONE   Crisis — It Can Strike Anytime,
Anyplace, Anywhere   1

TWO   The Best Insurance — Be Prepared   22

THREE   Managing the Crisis   40

FOUR   Who Said "Silence Is Golden"?   50

FIVE   You Can Fight Back and Win   72

SIX   Even the Government Makes Mistakes   94

SEVEN   The Aggie Pigs and President Bush   123

EIGHT   Natural Disasters — Don't Argue
With Mother Nature   147

NINE   Do the Right Thing — Take Responsibility
and Win Public Support   165

TEN   What Death Means to Healthcare   189

ELEVEN   Foul! Is This Any Way to Play the Game?   202

TWELVE   Institutional Arrogance in the Ivory Tower   234

THIRTEEN   Dealing With Violence in the Workplace   265

FOURTEEN   Profit by Being Green   273

FIFTEEN   Closing the Book — After an Incident   291

Index   297

FOREWORD

I have been helping clients, organizations, companies and others deal with crises most of my professional career—long before the word "crisis management" was coined. This is a subject I cannot emphasize strongly enough to anyone in management. Any organization is vulnerable to a crisis, regardless of how well prepared it may be. Crises strike nonprofit fund-raising institutions and even the church.

Crisis Management, Crisis Communications, Risk Management and *Risk Communications* have become part of the management and communications vocabulary as we enter the 21st century. When I began my professional career, we knew when we had problems, and we knew how we had to deal with them. We hoped that we anticipated problems before they became a crisis, and we did our best to be prepared if and when the inevitable happened.

This book was written for professional communicators, as a textbook for faculty to use with students and as a primer for senior management in for-profit, nonprofit, trade associations and government. I believe this should be a "must read" for all CEOs and anyone on a crisis management committee of an organization. How CEOs handle crises can determine their future. Some have seen crises become career-ending events.

I strongly advocate a course in crisis management being offered in every law school, MBA and executive business program, and curriculum for anyone seeking a degree in public relations, public affairs or communications. In those colleges and universities that do not add this subject as a course, I believe at least a one-day seminar should be required for senior students ready to graduate from law and business schools and enter the real world. However as a former dean of a law school reminded me, from a business viewpoint, lawyers make a little money avoiding crises and a lot of money dealing with them.

It is just as important to understand the communications process as it is the legal process. If senior executives and attorneys had a better understanding of media relations and risk communications, many crises could be contained as incidents. We can anticipate the future by learning from the past.

This book contains numerous case histories from my personal experience as well as from friends, colleagues and reports in professional and general-interest publications. Added to the crisis examples are tips, tactics, and dos and don'ts recommended by many leading practitioners. I deliberately did not review the Exxon Valdez, Bhopal, Three Mile Island, Johnson & Johnson's Tylenol, or Pepsi syringe incident because these crises have been well-documented in numerous publications and other books. I did seek out crises that provide examples to help others avoid similar crises. Every case history example in this book presents a lesson to be learned. The reader should develop his or her own management strategy based on recommendations throughout the book of what and what not to do. The case histories can be used by management teams, professional trainers and professors with their students as departures for discussion.

I have experienced crises all of my professional career. One of the first problems I had involved a client's race car. The car was being prepared for an unprecedented third straight victory at the Indianapolis 500. The week before the race, the driver set a new qualifying speed record and won the coveted No. 1 pole position. The driver, car and sponsor had more pre-race national publicity than any previous Indy car. Arrangements had even been made to fly the car and driver to New York to be on CBS Television's *The Ed Sullivan Show*, if it repeated a third time. However, on Memorial Day, when the race steward announced, "Gentlemen, start your engines," the pit crew and driver could not. They pushed the car off into the pits as the race began.

Several years later, when environmentalists began talking about a national redwood park to preserve forests of the giant Sequoia trees, I was public relations counsel to the largest owner and producer of California redwood lumber. When Cesar Chavez launched his United Farm Workers labor movement, I counseled California agriculture interests who were clients. And over the years other crises have involved product recalls and almost every type of issue imaginable. Some of these are documented in this book as case histories.

I also am very concerned about the increasing crises in sports at all levels — the Olympic movement, players, coaches, owners, officials and even the media. Many incidents look like no one is in control.

One broad field from which I sought case history examples of crises was the Hollywood entertainment industry. Even my close friends could not come up with a single incident. This would lead one to assume that there is no such thing as a crisis in Hollywood. As much as Hollywood condemns the McCarthy-era investigations, it has a unwritten rule about not speaking in vain about the business. Once a rising young star was called by a Congressional committee investigating use of drugs in Hollywood. The actress did what she felt she was obligated to do and told the truth, virtually ending her career.

When award-winning actor Cliff Robertson received an IRS Form 1099 stating he had been paid $10,000 by Columbia Pictures in 1976, he wanted answers. He had not worked for the studio, his accountants had no record of any payment and the check that had cleared the bank for a cash payment had been forged with his signature. Almost every major star, in addition to many directors and writers, has disputed "creative accounting" practices by the studios. This was a different story. The investigations pointed back to David Begelman, head of Columbia Pictures, as being the alleged forger. Robertson went public seeking answers and, on *The Phil Donohue Show,* said, "We're trying to stop a corruption that has become malignant in our industry and grown every year." Robertson, who won an Oscar for *Charly,* was blacklisted for four years. When he did return to work, it was at a salary less than he had been paid in the past.[1]

In Chapter 12, I discuss the institutional arrogance of higher education. But a Hollywood press agent, Pat Kingsley of the publicity firm PMK, has given it a new meaning, which some may simply call *chutzpah*. During the publicity launch of the movie *Eyes Wide Shut*, she tried to place unprecedented restrictions on television coverage of one of the film's stars, Tom Cruise, who also was her client. She demanded to see rough cuts in advance, have a veto option prior to airing and all unused footage destroyed. The waiver included a pledge that the "interview and the program will not show the artist in a negative or derogatory manner." Not understanding the difference between publicity and paid advertising, she backed away from her initial demands.[2]

During the 1988 presidential campaign, George Bush had scores of marquee-name supporters from Hollywood. However, not one would go public with their support of his attacks on the American Civil Liberties Union, even though they agreed with him. They were fearful of being blacklisted.[3] So much for Hollywood.

Simply stated, crisis management and risk communications involve using common sense. It is doing the right thing. There is no magic involved, much less anything illegal about expressing compassion and sympathy to victims and their families when people are injured or killed in an accident or when their property has been devastated. As much as 50 percent of an institution's credibility can be lost by displaying a lack of caring. As Will Rogers said, "People want to know that you care before they care about what you know."

Communicating in times of crisis encompasses all of the broad techniques of public relations, public affairs and media relations. Media training for spokespersons is essential.

Today there is no excuse for any organization not being prepared with an action plan in place. However, even the best laid plans will not prevent a crisis. But a plan certainly could make life easier for all those involved.

RENE A. HENRY, OCTOBER 1999

1. David McClintick, *Indecent Exposure*, Dell Publishing Co., New York, N.Y., 1982, pgs. 1-24, 512, 518.
2. Brian Lowry, *The Los Angeles Times*, "Cruise publicist limits use of talk footage," July 18, 1999.
3. Nikke Finke, "Can Backing Bush Hurt a Celebrity?" *The Los Angeles Times*, October 17, 1988, Part VI, pg. 1.

ACKNOWLEDGMENTS

The author wishes to thank the following people, whose contributions helped make this book possible:

John Argue, Esq., partner, Pearson, Harbison & Meyers, Los Angeles, and former president of the Los Angeles Olympic Organizing Committee and the Southern California Committee for the Olympic Games

Jay Warren Bell, marketing consultant, San Francisco

Sarah Hardesty Bray, senior editor, *The Chronicle of Higher Education*, Washington, D.C.

Judi Brown, acquisitions project manager, Iowa State University Press, Ames, Iowa

Anton Calleia, former deputy mayor to Tom Bradley, Los Angeles

Jeanne Dardini, Northbay Fulfillment, Santa Rosa, California

John DeFrancesco, principal, DeFrancesco·Goodfriend Public Relations, Chicago

Anthony G. Dempster, principal, Consulstrat, L.L.C., Houston

Mike Dodd, sports reporter, *USA Today*, Arlington, Virginia

Dave Erickson, Data Reproductions Corp., Ann Arbor, Michigan

Carla L. Ferrara, Administration for Property & Casualty Communications, CIGNA, Philadelphia

Dr. Edward T. Foote II, president, University of Miami, Coral Gables, Florida

Dr. Thomas A. Graves, Jr., former president of the College of William & Mary and former executive director of the Winterthur Gallery, Wilmington, Delaware

Mildred Howie, Rohnert Park, California

Dr. Marilyn Kern-Foxworth, professor of public relations and journalism, Florida A&M University, Tallahassee, Florida

Anne Sceia Klein, APR, Fellow PRSA, president, Anne Klein & Associates, Inc., Marlton, New Jersey

Dan Lacy, vice president, corporate communications, Ashland Inc., Ashland, Kentucky

Ralph Langer, executive vice president and editor, *The Dallas Morning News*, Dallas

Warren C. Levy, APR, senior vice president and principal, The Gabriel Group, Philadelphia

James E. Lukaszewski, APR, Fellow PRSA chairman and president, The Lukaszewski Group Inc., White Plains, New York

John Maltbie, Esq., staff attorney, Libel Defense Resource Center, New York City

James Gordon Meek, DCi news, Washington, D.C.

John Martin Meek, president, HMI Inc., Washington, D.C.

Judy Lee Munroe, Principal, and Vicki Lewis, senior art director, Munroe Creative Partners, Philadelphia

Dr. Priscilla Murphy, associate professor of journalism and head of the doctoral program in mass media and communications, Temple University, Philadelphia

C. Robert Paul, Jr., former director of public relations and archivist emeritus, United States Olympic Committee, Little Neck, New York

Dave Peattie, BookMatters, Richmond, California

Dr. Albert Schaffer, professor emeritus, Texas A&M University, College Station, Texas

Dr. Ruth Schaffer, professor emeritus, Texas A&M University, College Station, Texas

Brig. Gen. Ron Sconyers, APR, Fellow PRSA, U.S. Air Force Retired, vice chairman, Public Relations Society of America and CEO, K.I.D.S., New York City

James R. Smith, executive director, Building Seismic Safety Council, Washington, D.C.

Andrew Stern, chairman and CEO, Sunwest Communications Inc., Dallas

Frederick G. Thompson, principal, Kerr·Kelly·Thompson, Greenwich, Connecticut, and Earle Palmer Brown, New York City

Margaret Thomson, director, Shareholder & Employee Communications, Ashland Inc., Ashland, Kentucky

Harold Uplinger, Santa Monica, California

Harland (Hal) Warner, APR, Fellow PRSA, Warner Communications Counselors Inc., Vienna, Virginia

. . . and those responsible for the crises that created a need for this book.

CHAPTER ONE

CRISIS—IT CAN STRIKE ANYTIME, ANYPLACE, ANYWHERE

Exxon Valdez. Bhopal. Three Mile Island. Valujet. Watergate. Tylenol. TWA Flight 800. Texaco. Monicagate. Pepsi. Waco. "Mad Cow" disease. E. coli. Atlanta's Olympic Park.

People throughout the world immediately recognize these as major crises. Most are known and studied because of the way these incidents were mismanaged. Tylenol and Pepsi are examples of the right way to manage a crisis. There are lessons to be learned from any crisis.

Crisis management, crisis communications, risk management and risk communications are all closely related. Crisis management is how a crisis is managed and hopefully avoided. Crisis communications, a critical element of crisis management, shapes how the story is told to the public at large, internal publics and the media. Risk management identifies a hazard and anticipates the related risk that could impact public safety, such as the release of toxic chemicals or an explosion. Risk communications is how the public is communicated with before, during and after such a crisis.

The rules a professional communicator follows are virtually the same once an incident happens and is ready to become, or already is, a crisis. Crisis communications is all-encompassing and anticipates and includes all hazards and risk. In effect, risk communications is crisis communications.

What Is a Crisis?

Webster's has a number of definitions for *crisis* ranging from the "turning point for better or worse in an acute disease or fever" and "an emotionally significant event or radical change of status in a person's life" to "an unstable or crucial time or state of affairs in which a decisive change is impending, especially one with the distinct possibility of a highly undesirable outcome."[1]

Depending how it is handled, a crisis can certainly make an executive sick and even create a change of status in employment. The goal of a good manager is to contain the crisis to an incident and get closure as quickly as possible.

How a company, organization, individual or institution responds to a crisis is critical to its public image and reputation. The ultimate cost of a crisis is determined by the way the crisis is managed and communicated and could determine the future profitability and success of an organization.

Two Chinese symbols make up the word for crisis—challenge and opportunity.[2] In fact, the Chinese say there is an opportunity inherent in every crisis.[3] Public relations professionals who are practitioners in crisis management should look at both the challenge and the opportunity. Crisis communicators must consider actions that can be taken that will produce positive results.

There are many types of crises that include natural disasters and even terrorist attacks. Business and government do not have a monopoly on crises. A list would include higher education, sports, public school districts, entertainment, nonprofit associations and virtually every field of endeavor.

Anyone Is Vulnerable

Any CEO who believes he or she is immune from a crisis is most vulnerable. No one is immune from the possibility. Even the church and Mickey Mouse have been under attack.

The most catastrophic of crises happens when people die after using a company's product. People died after contracting botulism from eating Bon Vivant soup. The company couldn't survive the crisis and went out of business. Johnson & Johnson faced a similar crisis when people died after taking tainted Tylenol, but took a positive, aggressive approach to resolving the problem. Nothing impacts harder than an airline crash like the 1996 TWA and Valujet incidents.[4]

In January 1993, three children died and 144 customers were hospitalized after eating hamburgers at a Jack in the Box restaurant. Management first blamed its primary vendor and then addressed the financial impact. It took a week before the company publicly apologized to families and announced it would pay all medical bills. Six months later victims complained the company failed to pay medical bills as promised. Class action suits were filed. The company took a beating in the media for a year. The value of its stock fell 43 percent as Jack in the Box posted a $44 million loss compared to a $22 million profit the previous year.[5]

Resolve the Crisis Before It Becomes Major

The objective of crisis communications is to contain the problem and resolve the conflict as quickly as possible. While some crises are unavoidable, others are exacerbated because of the way they are mishandled. This may be as simple as not returning a telephone call or not taking the time to listen to a customer complaint.

No CEO, director, senior manager, employee, shareholder or customer wants to see negative headlines and stories repeated again and again in newspapers, magazines, and on television and talk radio. A continuing crisis generally will follow with editorials, op-eds, letters to the editor and satirical political cartoons. Depending on the type of crisis, chances are that it will be written into a joke, monologue or skit for *Saturday Night Live*, Jay Leno, David Letterman and Conan O'Brien. If political in any way, it may be further exploited by television's Mark Russell and political cartoonists Paul Conrad and Herb Block. Garry Trudeau, creator of the "Doonesbury" comic strip, took Nike to task for its overseas manufacturing and labor practices and domestic marketing practices. Millions of daily newspaper readers saw the satire criticize Nike for several months. Jokes and other uncontrollable gossip and rumors will flourish—especially on the Internet with its myriad of bulletin boards and chat rooms.

There is always the probability the crisis could become a television "movie of the week" or a feature film, either in a true sense or one where the incident is fictionalized for legal purposes. In the case of a film, the crisis will be replayed for as many as 7 to 10 years—first in movie theaters, then followed by video sales, rerun theaters, television, foreign distribution, primary cable networks and then secondary cable networks.

A best-selling book, *A Civil Action*, and a film based on that book, again made public a 1980 environmental lawsuit against W. R. Grace. Although neither proven in court nor supported by scientific research, the lawsuit alleged that Grace and Beatrice Foods had contaminated the municipal wells and drinking water that caused illnesses to the residents of Woburn, Massachusetts. The Disney/Touchtone film was released in December 1998 with a $25 million promotional budget. While Grace had taken significant steps to improve its environmental policies and programs during the past 10 years, it felt the movie painted an inaccurate and misleading picture of the company.[6]

How Situations Become Crises

Hurricanes, floods, earthquakes, typhoons, tornados and other natural disasters happen. There is no way to prevent Mother Nature from releasing her forces. There is no defense against terrorist attacks. These should all be anticipated and plans made how a crisis will be managed and communicated. Some of the major reasons incidents turn into crises include:

1. Not being prepared with a crisis management and communications plan. Organize all resources and be ready to respond if and when needed.

2. Stonewalling—not being responsive to the media and the people who need to be informed, or responding with "no comment." The media will get information which may be inaccurate from unreliable sources. In a crisis, perception

is stronger than reality and emotion stronger than fact. When those responsible do not communicate concerns directly to those affected, the crisis gets played out in the media and possibly even the courts.

3. Just the reverse of the "no comment" syndrome is talking too much, overtalking or giving too much information without having all of the facts. Be sure to analyze the situation for its newsworthiness. The situation may not warrant media attention. Former White House Press Secretary Marlin Fitzwater said, "You don't have to explain what you don't say."[7]

4. Not telling the truth — lying or deceiving the media and public with misinformation. Always tell the truth. Don't speculate on facts. The media and general public will respect an "I don't know" answer.

5. The "ego syndrome" — too many people getting into the act and wanting to talk to the media. Often the wrong people speak publicly. A central spokesperson is critical. The other problem is the individual who always wants to get in the last word rather than closing the issue.

6. Information or misinformation being leaked to the media by an employee or adversary.

7. Waiting too long to get the story told to the public. The Internet can spread a story worldwide in a matter of minutes.

8. Showing no compassion, concern or empathy for injured parties, victims or their families. There is nothing illegal about saying "I'm sorry."

9. Being defensive, passive and reactive rather than offensive, proactive and aggressive.

10. Spokespersons who are neither trained in media relations nor believable to the public.

11. Not stopping rumors or mistakes when they occur. Mistakes and errors, once reported, can be repeated by the media and even become accepted as fact.

12. Not accepting responsibility.

Ask Three Questions

Fred Thompson, managing partner of the Earle Palmer Brown public relations firm, says when you think you are in a crisis, ask yourself three questions.[8]

1. "Who has the most to gain or lose in this situation?" Polarize the issues.

2. "Is there a fundamental misunderstanding?" A basic misunderstanding might be resolved by an explanation or presentation of the facts.

3. Can this be ended with an apology, admission of wrongdoing or simply saying "we just screwed up." This could create conflict with the legal counsel who may want to avoid any such admission or statement of regret.

Thompson believes answers to these three questions will define the strategy to best deal with a situation before it turns into a crisis.

In *Love Story,* author Erich Segal wrote, "Love is never having to say you are sorry."[9] University of Missouri-Columbia communications professor William Benoit says that may work for people in love, but if you make a mistake, apologizing is the best way to restore your image. "To maintain your credibility, say you're wrong and you're taking steps to ensure the problem never happens again," he advises.[10]

Who Is Responsible for the Crisis?

How responsible the organization was for the crisis influences its response according to Harland (Hal) Warner, APR, Fellow PRSA, of Warner Communications Counselors, Vienna, Virginia. He cites three areas:[11]

1. When the organization is the victim such as with product tampering, threats, protests, kidnaping or extortion. He cites Johnson & Johnson with Tylenol and Pepsi with the syringe incident as situations where the companies knew in the final analysis that facts would clear them of wrongdoing. "This frees you to take positive action without fear that it will backfire on you," Warner says.

2. When the organization is responsible or at fault with product recalls, contamination, environmental spills or discrimination.

3. Or when the responsibility is not clear as with a fire/explosion, product misuse, sexual harassment, product liability or a lawsuit.

"In situations where the responsibility is not clear [McDonald's and the drive-in customer who burned herself by spilling hot coffee], you need to show understanding and concern, and announce what actions you will take to reduce the chances of similar incidents," Warner adds.

Win Forgiveness in a Crisis

James E. Lukaszewski, APR, Fellow PRSA and head of The Lukaszewski Group Inc., White Plains, New York, helps his clients regain public credibility following a damaging situation by using an aggressive seven-step process.[12]

1. Using candor, acknowledge a problem exists, or even apologize, and say that something will be done to remedy the situation.

2. No matter how silly, stupid or embarrassing the problem-causing error was, explain why it occurred and the reasons that led to the situation, even if there is only partial information. Talk about what you learned and how it will influence future behavior and commit to regularly report additional information until it is all out, or until no public interest remains.

3. Declare a public commitment and discussion of specific, positive steps to be taken to *conclusively* address the issues and resolve the situation.

4. Verbalize regret, empathy, sympathy, even embarrassment. Take responsibility for the situation, whether by omission, commission, accident or negligence.

5. Directly involve and ask for the participation of those most affected to help develop more permanent solutions and more acceptable behaviors, and to design principles and approaches that will preclude similar problems from recurring.

6. Publicly set your goals at zero—zero errors, zero defects, zero dumb decisions, zero problems. Promise unconditionally to the best of your ability situations like this will never occur again.

7. Make or require restitution. Go beyond community and victim expectations to remediate the problem. Adverse situations remediated quickly cost a lot less and are controversial for much shorter periods of time.[13]

Understand Why People Get Angry

Consensus builders and dispute mediators Lawrence Susskind and Patrick Field write in their book, *Dealing with an Angry Public*, that there are many reasons for the public to be angry. "Business and government leaders have covered up mistakes, concealed evidence of potential risks, made misleading statements, and often lied. Indeed, our leaders have fueled a rising tide of public distrust of both business and government by behaving in these ways."[14]

Susskind, a professor at MIT and Harvard Law School, says there are three basic reasons the public gets angry:

1. Because they have been adversely affected by something a company, organization or institution has done.

2. Because they fear being adversely affected by something you are proposing to do.

3. Because they disagree in principle with something you stand for.

He says the traditional response is to prove the public has not been or will not be adversely affected by something you have done or plan to do and to downplay value differences.[15]

According to a survey conducted by the Porter/Novelli public relations firm, in the heat of a crisis many people do not believe everything being told them even if it is the truth. The survey revealed that the public gets angry:[16]

- 75 percent of the time when a company refuses to accept blame or responsibility.

- 72 percent of the time when they believe the crisis could have been avoided.

- 71 percent when the company supplies incomplete or inaccurate information as a response to the problem.

- 70 percent when the company places corporate profits ahead of public interest.

The poll also indicated that 95 percent are more offended about a company lying about the crisis than about the actual crisis itself, and 57 percent believe that companies either withhold negative information or, worse yet, lie.

The public's anger is often translated into lawsuits. In 1991, *Fortune 1000* companies were defendants in 95 percent of personal-injury cases. Attorneys focus on who has the most money. The United States has become an extremely litigious society.

Sexual Harassment—A Major Problem of the Times

Sexual harassment incidents are magnets for media coverage and one of the fastest-growing crisis categories affecting organizations today. The Equal Employment Opportunity Commission received more than 15,000 complaints of sexual harassment in 1995, nearly double that of 1991.[17]

Military service academies and schools with cadet corps repeatedly have problems with sexual harassment or gender discrimination. The U.S. Naval Academy, the Citadel, Texas A&M and Virginia Military Institute could have taken a page out of the "how to do it right" book of the U.S. Military Academy at West Point. When several female cadets reported they were groped by football players during a pep rally, officials immediately investigated and decided to go public with the story. During a previously scheduled meeting with reporters of *The New York Times* only 11 days after the incident, West Point officials publicly disclosed what happened.[18] Because of the prompt and open response to the media, the coverage was positive. One day after the meeting with its editors, the *Times* published an editorial, "Wisdom at West Point."[19]

The institutional culture of an organization and its management often dictates its crisis policy. In the area of sexual harassment, two companies could not have been as different in their approach to conflict resolution as Astra USA, the U.S. subsidiary of a Swedish pharmaceuticals company, and Mitsubishi Motor Manufacturing of America. *Business Week* magazine first exposed widespread harassment at Astra's U.S. subsidiary in suburban Boston—a decade of incidents ranging from gropings at company retreats to suggestions that female sales representatives could advance their career by having sex with their bosses. The company had no adequate mechanism for reporting incidents and failed to deal with problems before they became public. Astra suspended Lars Bildman, its chief U.S. executive, and two of his top assistants. It is overhauling its corporate personnel policies and plans to train managers how to handle issues of sexual discrimination. This strategy might help the company avoid thousands or millions of dollars in punitive damages if any of the cases go to trial.[20]

Some 80 women and one man will share Astra's payment of $9.85 million to the Equal Employment Opportunity Commission, the largest sexual harassment settlement negotiated by the commission. The firm admitted its U.S. headquarters in Westborough, Massachusetts, was a hostile workplace environment for women, who claimed they were pressured for sex by company officials, urged to wear bikinis at a beach function and required to attend after-hours parties of drinking and dancing. Bildman, who has pleaded guilty to filing false tax returns, is being sued by Astra for more than $15 million to recover costs related to the EEOC's investigation. Astra's ulcer medication, Prilosec, the best-selling prescription drug in the United States, is probably being widely used by its current and former executives.[21]

Being Too Aggressive Backfires

Mitsubishi took an in-your-face approach when it decided to discredit a sexual harassment suit brought by the EEOC.[22] The company counterattacked and sent busloads of its men and women plant workers to picket the commission's offices in Chicago. More than 2,000 employees who protested got a day off with full pay. The company had mixed reviews in the media. The women workers complained about sexist remarks, fanny patting and sexual drawings that covered walls and equipment.

The editors of *PR News* wrote, "Had the company heeded the most basic of PR principles — responsiveness and a willingness to explore the allegations — it would have been a far gentler and kinder media, and public, it faced."[23]

Gary Shultz, the company's general counsel and also its manager of public relations, denied the charges and fought back.[24] Workers were told that if the allegations adversely affected sales, they could lose their jobs. The company installed phone lines at the Normal, Illinois, plant so employees could call their congressmen to protest the charges. Mitsubishi attorneys insensitively accused the women of "Japan bashing."

These actions prompted Jesse Jackson and the National Organization for Women to call on car buyers to boycott the company. Several weeks later Mitsubishi reversed its course and declared it was going to become the model in handling sexual-harassment and discrimination cases. It retained former Labor Secretary Lynn Martin as an adviser.[25] Unfortunately, the negative press coverage received far more attention than did Martin's recommendations.[26]

Mitsubishi's initial response could be attributed to the institutional culture of its headquarters in Tokyo. Because the awareness of sexual harassment is very limited among Japanese companies, the Japan Overseas Enterprises Association published a guidebook to warn Japanese employees that remarks and attitudes often accepted at home could be considered offensive elsewhere. Examples included "Don't call female colleagues 'babe,' keep straying hands off the shoulders, hips and thighs of women and take down offensive pictures."[27]

Mitsubishi became the big loser. It agreed to pay $34 million to settle the lawsuit, the largest sexual harassment settlement for the EEOC. The money will be shared by more than 300 current and former female employees with a maximum individual award of $300,000.[28]

Frank Swoboda of *The Washington Post* cited this as one of the worst crises he has covered in 20 years with the newspaper. He said the company lied and threatened reporters in an effort to prevent them from getting details about the EEOC's sexual harassment suit against the company. Swoboda said he used the Internet to locate some of the women who said they had been harassed and the *Post* ran a two-page story detailing their allegations.[29]

But What About Six Year Olds?

Probably the most ludicrous example of "sexual harassment" was when 6-year-old first-grader Johnathan Prevette was suspended for kissing a female classmate. The administrators of Southwest Elementary School in Lexington, North Carolina considered this might be a "hostile political act" and were soundly ridiculed by the media worldwide for overreacting. The offending Prevette also missed coloring, playtime and an ice cream party.[30]

The best and most obvious way a company, organization or institution can head off sexual harassment is to require annual EEO and diversity training for all of its managers, supervisors and employees. Leadership also must begin at the top and be reinforced through every level of management. Only training in nursery school and kindergarten could have helped avoid the first-grade problem in North Carolina. Is that really what society wants?

Other Leading Crises

Airlines, tobacco, education, baseball and insurance were on the list of 1996 public relations "Blunders of the Year" picked by Fineman Associates Public Relations in San Francisco.[31] The Lexington school officials were on this list. Some of the crisis makers were fortunate to have had only regional media exposure. But few will forget baseball in a year when George Steinbrenner was not leading the list. Roberto Alomar of the Baltimore Orioles spit in the face of an umpire and later implied the umpire was to blame. Executives at Major League Baseball were not as responsive as their professional sports cousins at the National Basketball Association in dealing out punishment. Rather than suspending Alomar immediately, which would have taken him out of the play-offs, baseball's leadership chose to suspend him for five days at the start of the following season.

On opening day in Cincinnati, the Reds' owner, Marge Schott, couldn't understand why the baseball game was postponed after umpire John McSherry collapsed and died of a heart attack in the first inning. She responded, "Why can't they play with just two umpires?!"[32]

You wonder who advised Charles Harper, chairman of R. J. Reynolds. At the annual meeting when he was asked about children and secondhand smoke, Harper responded by saying that if children don't like to be in a smoky room, they will leave. Told that infants can't readily leave, he said, "At some point, they will learn to crawl."[33]

Nationally, the media and public supported the Girl Scouts and Boy Scouts when the American Society of Composers, Authors and Publishers (ASCAP) informed the scouts that a fee was required to use any of its members' copyrighted songs. The organization wanted licensening fees when the girls sang songs that included "God Bless America" and "This Land Is Your Land." Camps that couldn't pay the fees stopped singing songs around the campfire.[34]

ASCAP claimed the national story in *The Wall Street Journal* in August 1996 was invented and pushed by an "unholy alliance" of the American Restaurant Association and the National Religious

Broadcasters Association who were lobbying for legislation to reduce copyright protection for artists and composers. ASCAP CEO John Lo Frumento was quoted as saying of the Girl Scouts, "They buy paper, twine and glue for their crafts . . . they can pay for the music too." ASCAP's spokespersons refused to take reporters' phone calls. Sunshine Consultants did issue a one-page news release for its client to clarify what it characterized as false reports regarding attempts to license the Girl Scouts of America. To recover from an all-out media attack, ASCAP took out full-page advertisements in major metropolitan newspapers denying it had ever intended to strong-arm the scouts and prevent campfire singing.[35]

The editors of *PR News* said ASCAP made a mistake by not having a well-briefed spokesperson out front to answer questions. They also noted that it's a general PR rule not to criticize the media and that Lo Frumento blundered by lashing out at *The Wall Street Journal* and other papers, leading to further news stories that convinced the public that ASCAP members can be greedy musicians.[36]

Georgia Pacific made a point of being socially responsible after an ice storm hit New England early in 1998. The company delivered truckloads of paper products, including toilet paper and tissue, to the American Red Cross command center in Portland, Maine.[37]

Sears was exposed for aggressive debt collecting but responded well by admitting its flawed legal judgment in handling debt collections. The company offered refunds to consumers and even wrote off 9.23 percent of delinquent charges as customers fell further behind on credit card payments. By contrast, Radio Shack was exposed for aggressive debt collecting but refused to comment and profits were up despite lower sales.[38]

Mattel was another company that did the right thing when its pulled its Cabbage Patch Kids' Snack Time Kids from the market after these dolls chewed the hair and fingers of several little girls.

Athletic-shoe companies had their problems. Reebok named one of its shoes Incubus, the name of a mythical Greek figure who raped sleeping women. It discontinued the shoe.

Truth in Advertising? An Oxymoron?

Nationwide Mutual Insurance in Columbus, Ohio, was sued because it offered two Mercedes and a trip for two around the world to the creator of the best slogan for one of its regional conventions. When David Mears won, he was told the prizes were just a joke. The joke is on Nationwide. Mears is suing, and the insurance company has lost credibility.[39]

As well as Pepsi handled its syringe crisis, it mishandled a contest that advertised a $23 million Harrier jet as first prize. Contestants could win various merchandise for points by saving coupons from bottles and cans of Pepsi or by buying extra points at 10 cents each. A T-shirt was worth 80 points ($8), sunglasses 125 points ($12.50), a leather jacket 1,200 points ($120) or the Harrier jet, worth 7 million points. John Leonard, a Seattle college student, presented Pepsi with a check for $700,008 for the value of the 7 million points and asked for the jet. Pepsi said that the commercial was only a joke and offered Leonard three cases of Pepsi in lieu of the jet that was ironically featured in the film "True Lies." The crisis received national wire-service and television coverage. Leonard and his backers retained a public relations firm and an attorney and filed suit in Florida where laws are very strict about companies living up to promises in contests.[40]

Who Would Boycott Mickey, Donald and Goofy?

Who would ever think that Mickey Mouse would be vulnerable to a crisis? Officials at Walt Disney Co. found out when the Southern Baptist Convention approved a boycott to protest Disney's "overly permissive stance toward homosexuality." Richard Land, president of the Baptist's Commission on Christian Life says, "You can't walk on the family side of the street and the gay side of the street in the Magic Kingdom at the same time." With 15.3 million members, the nation's biggest Protestant denomination and one of the mainstays of the militant Christian right declared war on Disney.[41]

The Baptists' objections included the fact that Disney extended health benefits to the partners of its gay and lesbian employees; it owns ABC which aired Ellen DeGeneres' coming-out episode;

Disney World in Orlando has a "Gay Day" at its park each June; and produced and distributed the animated feature movie *Hunchback*. A number of Baptist pastors questioned whether the boycott could succeed against all of the Disney enterprises.[42]

One minister who disagrees is Rev. James M. Watkins who has been pastor of six churches, four of which were Southern Baptist. "American culture has its problems. But having spent the first 20 years of my ministerial career as a Southern Baptist, I can assure you that fundamentalist Christian culture has plenty of demons of its own," he wrote in a newspaper opinion piece.[43]

Morality and the Church

During a time when the church is trying to build membership, it is going through its worst crisis in centuries. Various surveys suggest that as many as 30 percent of male Protestant ministers have had sexual relationships with women other than their wives, and in recent years the divorce rate for Protestant clergy has risen to match that of the general population.[44]

The General Synod of the United Church of Christ, the General Assembly of the Presbyterian Church (USA) and the General Convention of the Episcopal Church all had debates defining sexual standards expected of its clergy. While all three denominations have clergy who are living with members of the same sex, ordination of sexually active homosexuals was one key issue. In a 1993 survey of Southern Baptist pastors, 14 percent acknowledged they had "sexual behavior inappropriate for a minister," and 70 percent said they counseled at least one woman who had sex with another minister.[45]

In one of the costliest sex-abuse judgments ever levied against a church, a jury in Dallas, Texas, ordered the Roman Catholic Diocese of Dallas and a defrocked priest to pay $119 million to 10 men and the family of a suicide victim who were molested when they were altar boys. The award ended an 11-week civil trial in which the church was accused of covering up the conduct of an alleged pedophile priest. During an 11-year period, the diocese repeatedly ignored complaints about Rudolph Kos and a "mountain of evidence" regarding his behavior. Kos served at three Dallas parishes.[46]

Intel—A "Chipwreck" in Cyberspace

Intel, the world's leading maker of computer chips, spends millions of dollars advertising the advantages of buying a computer with "Intel Inside." In 1994, with more than 4 million Pentium chips in use, it tried to hide a flawed chip rather than go to the expense of a recall. The issue began June 13 in Virginia when a Lynchburg College math professor noticed his Pentium-based PC made mistakes. Then a high-tech reporter for *The Washington Post* found incorrect division answers on an Intel 486-based PC. The problem became a publicity nightmare after the flawed chip was reported by *Electronic Engineering Times* in its November 7 issue and was followed by stories by CNN, *The New York Times*, *Boston Globe* and *The Washington Post*.[47]

Intel used no outside public relations help and its president and CEO, Andrew S. Grove, made no public appearances to give any supportive assurance to the general public. Instead, the company established a toll-free 800 telephone number that people could call to talk to an Intel technical specialist and Grove sent an apology letter over the Internet to the computer industry.[48]

Instead of immediately announcing the flaw and offering replacement chips, the company stated that only those customers who could prove that they might be affected by the defect would be given new chips. IBM, its biggest corporate customer, forced Intel to change its policy. During the short time Intel was reluctant to change, 15 lawsuits were filed in three states alleging everything from securities fraud to product liability to false advertising.[49]

On December 20 Intel ran full-page ads in newspapers and magazines to announce that it would replace the defective Pentium chips at no cost.[50] The poorly handled crisis not only took a big bite out of Intel's reputation but produced a $475 million loss for its fourth-quarter earnings. Shareholders suffered as the stock price tumbled. There was negative press for three months and loss of credibility and brand loyalty.

According to Jack O'Dwyer, several crisis management special-ists believed that Intel's Grove acted too unconcerned about the problem and the company's big public relations mistake was trying to minimize the problem with technical explanations that catego-rized the flaw as "extremely minor."[51]

Intel's CEO Speaks Out

"Most CEOs are in the center of a fortified palace, and news from the outside has to percolate through layers of people from the pe-riphery where the action is. . . . I was one of the last to understand the implications of the Pentium crisis," writes Intel's Grove. "It took a barrage of criticism to make me realize that something had changed and that we needed to adapt to the new environment. We could change our ways and embrace the fact that we had become a household name and a consumer giant, or we could keep our old ways and not only miss an opportunity to nurture new customer relationships but also suffer damage to our reputation and well being."[52]

In how the company dealt with the problem Grove also writes, "In a matter of days, we built up a major organization practically from scratch to answer the flood of phone calls. We had not been in the consumer business in any big way before, so dealing with consumer questions was not something we had ever had to do."[53]

Sometimes Well-Intentioned Plans Get Stonewalled

Warren Anderson, Union Carbide's chairman, rushed to Bhopal telling his colleagues at headquarters, "We can't show our concern about this tragedy by me staying in Danbury." However, three days after the the incident, December 7, 1984, the media reported that the company had repeatedly refused to provide a detailed description of the system used to store and process the lethal gas. For all the good that Anderson wanted to do, here is how his di-rector of Health, Safety and Environmental Affairs handled a press conference:[54]

> REPORTER: "I think you've said the company was not liable to the Bhopal victims?"

DIRECTOR: "I didn't say that."

REPORTER: "Does that mean you are liable?"

DIRECTOR: "I didn't say that either."

REPORTER: "Then what did you say?"

DIRECTOR: "Ask me another question."[55]

Reputation Going Into a Crisis Is Important

Establish a reputation of being a credible and believable source of information before any crisis. Build relationships with the media so they know you are telling the truth in the face of challenges from adversaries.

The degree to which a company will get the public to believe its story will greatly depend on the company's reputation before a crisis. The results of a national survey commissioned by the Porter/ Novelli public relations firm in 1996 with a sample of 1,100 individuals revealed that the credibility of government, business and the media has deteriorated over the past five years.[56]

Only 8 percent considered the government and 2 percent considered political parties to be believable sources of information; 68 percent said elected officials are less credible than in 1991; and political reporters were deemed less credible by 45 percent of those polled.

Of 11 industries listed, the tobacco industry rated lowest for its trustworthiness with only 6 percent finding it believable, followed by the managed-care industry with 10 percent. The computer and software industry was rated credible most frequently with a 37 percent response, followed by pharmaceutical manufacturers with 28 percent and public utilities, 22 percent.

Americans also are less trusting of the news media — 42 percent responded that the media are not credible in general. Television news was rated 25 percent less credible than five years before, followed by newspapers (20 percent) and magazines (19 percent). Radio was the only medium increasing in credibility.[57]

Endnotes

1. *Merriam-Webster's Collegiate Dictionary*, Tenth Edition, Merriam-Webster, Incorporated, Springfield, Mass., 1993, pg. 275.

2. Council for Advancement and Support of Education, promotional flyer for "Crisis Management" seminar March 10-11, 1994, Atlanta, Georgia, pg. 2.

3. Raymond J. O'Rourke, "Learning from Crisis: When the Dust Settles," *The Strategist*, Public Relations Society of America, Summer 1997, pg. 35.

4. Ibid. "Rebounding From Tragedy," pg. 6.

5. Ibid. Robin Cohn, "Learning from Crisis: As the Curtain Rises," pg. 28.

6. International Conference of the Public Relations Society of America, Boston, Mass., October 19, 1998, presentation by Katherine Tynberg, president, The Tynberg Group, Inc., and Mark Stoler, assistant vice president for health and safety and Jane McGuineness, director of corporate communications, W. R. Grace.

7. Judy A. Smith, "Learning from Crisis: In the Heat of Battle," *The Strategist*, Public Relations Society of America, pg. 32.

8. Fred Thompson, Earle Palmer Brown, New York, N.Y., personal interview, February 1997.

9. Erich Segal, *Love Story*, Harper & Row, New York, N.Y., 1972.

10. *Currents*, Council for Advancement and Support of Education, September 1995, pg. 12.

11. Harland Warner, "Level of Responsibility Sets Tone of Actions," *Crisis Counselor*, Volume I/Issue III, Fall 1995, Capitoline/MS&L, Washington, D.C.

12. James E. Lukaszewski, The Lukaszewski Group, White Plains, N.Y., *Communications Standards: The Principles and Protocols for Standard-Setting Individual and Corporate Communication*, pg. 7, (c) 1995, James E. Lukaszewski. All rights reserved. Used with permission of the author.

13. Ibid.

14. Lawrence Susskind and Patrick Field, *Dealing With an Angry Public*, The Free Press, a division of Simon & Schuster Inc., New York, N.Y., 1996, pg. 1.

15. Lawrence Susskind, "Dealing With an Angry Public," seminar by the MIT-Harvard Public Disputes Program, November 13-14, 1997, Cambridge, Mass.

16. *Public Relations Journal*, September 1993.

17. Michael Meyer, "School for scandal — How to handle sexual-harassment charges," *Newsweek*, May 20, 1996, pg. 44.

18. *PR News*, October 2, 1995, pg. 4.

19. Ibid.

20. Ibid.

21. Stephanie Armour, "Record $10 million payment OK'd in sex harassment case," *USA Today*, February 6, 1998, pg. 1.

22. *PR News*, "Sexual Harassment Suit Puts Media In Driver's Seat," *The 12 Hottest (And 7 Not So Hot) PR Campaigns of 1996*, Phillips Business Information Inc., pg. 37.

23. Ibid.

24. Michael J. Major, "Mitsubishi's PR Strategy Stalls," *Public Relations Tactics*, June 1996, pg. 1.

25. Ibid.

26. *PR News, op cit.*

27. Mari Yamaguchi, Associated Press, "Sexual harassment starts to draw attention in Japan," *The Philadelphia Inquirer*, April 22, 1997, pg. A26.

28. Stephanie Armour, "Mitsubishi settles suit for $34M," *USA Today*, June 12, 1998, pg. 1.

29. "Honest Is Best Policy in a Crisis," *Jack O'Dwyer's Newsletter*, June 30, 1999, pg. 2.

30. *Public Relations Tactics*, February 1997, pg. 1.

31. *Public Relations Tactics*, "The Best of the Worst," February 1997, pg. 4.

32. Ibid.

33. Ibid.

34. Ibid. and *PR News*, "Association Loses Major Brownie Points," *The 12 Hottest (and 7 Not So Hot) PR Campaigns of 1996*, Phillips Business Information, pgs. 33-34.

35. Ibid.

36. Ibid.

37. Katharine Paine, "A Look Back At Companies & How They Weathered Crises," *PR News*, February 9, 1998, pg. 6.

38. Ibid.

39. Ibid.

40. *Jack O'Dwyer's Newsletter*, September 4, 1996, pgs. 7-8.

41. Tom Morganthau, "Baptists v. Mickey," *Newsweek*, June 30, 1997, pg. 51.

42. Ibid.

43. James W. Watkins, "Disney joins a long Baptist enemies list," *The Philadelphia Inquirer*, Commentary, July 29, 1997, pg. A11.

44. Kenneth L. Woodward, "Sex, Morality and the Protestant Minister," *Newsweek*, July 28, 1997, pg. 62.

45. Ibid.

46. Larry B. Stammer and Lianne Hart, *Los Angeles Times*, "Diocese loses abuse suit, must pay $119 million," *The Philadelphia Inquirer*, July 25, 1997, pgs. A1, A24.

47. *Jack O'Dwyer's Newsletter*, January 10, 1996, pg. 2.

48. Ibid.

49. Susskind and Field, *op cit.*, pg. 102.

50. *Jack O'Dwyer's Newsletter*, January 10, 1996, pg. 2.

51. Ibid.

52. Andrew S. Grove, *Only the Paranoid Survive*, Copyright by Andrew S. Grove, A Currency Book to be published by Doubleday, a division of Bantam Doubleday Dell Publishing Group, Inc., from *Newsweek*, Book Excerpt, "How WE Miscalculated," September 2, 1996, pg. 62.

53. Ibid.

54. Susskind and Field, *op cit.*, pg. 9.

55. Ibid. and Thomas J. Lueck, "Crisis management at Carbide," *The New York Times*, December 14, 1984, pg. D1.

56. *Jack O'Dwyer's Newsletter*, August 7, 1996, pg. 2

57. Ibid.

CHAPTER TWO

THE BEST INSURANCE—
BE PREPARED

Be prepared. Anticipate every possible crisis. Then develop a communications plan for each potential crisis. Be prepared to respond immediately. This is essential if one hopes to avoid a crisis or be able to manage one if the inevitable happens. "Prepare, prepare, prepare" is the first sentence of the chapter on planning in the crisis management guide of the public television's PBS.[1] Many companies, organizations and institutions are not fully prepared for a crisis because they have a philosophy that "it won't happen to me."

The best time to be prepared is when there is no crisis. It is almost impossible to respond to a crisis without a plan. This is when mistakes happen. Public relations and crisis communications consultant Hal Warner says it takes six to eight months to develop the first draft of a crisis plan, which then needs review and testing, ideally through simulation of an actual crisis.[2]

He uses a 10-question test for companies to self-assess their crisis vulnerability and determine their level of crisis preparation.[3]

1. Does your organization have a crisis management plan in place?

2. If yes, is it up-to-date?

3. Has it been pre-tested?

4. Do you have a designated spokesperson?

5. Has the spokesperson had media training?

6. Do you have backup spokespersons?

7. Has management discussed a "desired result" philosophy for handling crises? Does it know whether a legal, economic or corporate-reputation result is top priority?

8. Does your organization see the media as villains?

9. Do you have a crisis management team authorized and trained to take responsibility in a crisis?

10. Has your organization evaluated what types of crises are most likely to occur and which kind will have the most severe impact?

ANSWER KEY (according to number of YES answers): 9 or 10: Probably in good shape; 7 or 8: Need improvement; 6 or under: Act now. You have a problem.

Here are questions the Institute for Crisis Management, a public relations firm, suggests asking at the next management meeting:[4]

1. What kind of management notification system do we have in place if a crisis occurs during nonbusiness hours? How long would it take to reach everyone on the management committee if we had a crisis at 3 P.M. on a Saturday?

2. What is our corporate emergency-response plan like? When was it last updated? Has it ever been used or tested to see if it works? How well does it tie in with the response plans of our other facilities?

3. What internal problems or other vulnerabilities do we have that could be damaging to our business if they went public? What would be the public reaction if one of them was disclosed by a disgruntled employee or in a stockholder lawsuit, government investigation or investigative news report? How would we explain or justify the situation so

it would have minimum business and financial impact on our company? What is being done to minimize the chances of that problem occurring?

4. Who would be our spokesperson(s) in a crisis situation? Who would be the alternate if they were not available or not appropriate for that kind of crisis situation? How good would they be in handling tough questions from reporters? How much confidence do we have that they will be credible and convincing in a confrontation with reporters, neighbors, customers? How would disclosures be handled at one of our facilities if they had a crisis? Who would be the designated spokesperson?

5. How much information would we give out if we had a crisis? Who would decide what to say? What would be the approval process? How long would it take?

6. How would we contact our management and employees so they would hear from us before learning about it from the news media? How about our customers, suppliers and other key audiences? How would we do it, and how long would that take?

7. What crisis situations have similar organizations had in the past year that went public? How well would we have handled those crises? How much management time has it taken? How much has it cost them so far in expenses, lost business? What are the prospects for lawsuits, government investigations? How long will it be before they get the problem behind them? How would we have done if it had happened to us instead of them? What can be learned from their experiences? Have we made any changes in the way we do business as a result of what happened to them?

Establish Credibility Before a Crisis

It is too late to establish credibility with the media and the public once a crisis happens. Credibility and reputation management needs to be done as part of the overall communications plan of the organization. If the organization lacks credibility before a crisis, its public statements will lack credibility and believability. Having an established reputation generally will make things much easier during a crisis. Reputations are hard to come by but easy to lose.

More and more public relations agencies are helping clients with strategic communications and reputation or perception management. Harold Burson, APR, Fellow PRSA of Burson-Marsteller, the world's largest public relations firm, says his firm's work, now 35 percent strategic, will rise to 65 percent. Thomas L. Harris, APR, Fellow PRSA, now head of the counseling firm bearing his name and co-founder of Golin/Harris Communications, says strategy is the fastest growing element of internal departments.[5] Companies and organizations must be sure not only that the right message is being communicated, but that it is being received, understood and believed by the intended audience. The reputation, perception or image factor must be strategically in place before a crisis.

No one should be without a crisis management plan. No company, organization or institution is immune from a crisis. It doesn't take a Ph.D. to know that if you are in the oil business and have storage tanks or tankers transporting oil across oceans that the single biggest crisis could be an oil spill. Or if you are in the food or restaurant business you want to worry about E. coli bacteria, salmonella or other forms of contamination. If you operate an amusement park, you worry about someone being injured or killed on a ride. Those are obvious.

There is risk associated with every product or service. Do a self-audit and look at the possible situations and problems that could happen to your company. If you have laboratories dealing with toxic substances, there should be concern about a spill. Or at a chemical manufacturing plant, about a potential leak. Do you use, store or manufacture hazardous or flammable substances? Are you prepared if there should be a natural disaster? Or violence in the workplace? A product boycott?

Common sense often can avoid a crisis. Tourism is the leading economy in Branson, Missouri. Without tourist dollars the town would be in a depression. So in the spring of 1997 when a food worker in one restaurant was found to have hepatitis A, it was decided to innoculate more than 4,000 of the town's food workers. The cost was $15 for each person. This was great insurance against a possible outbreak that could impact the economy.

In some organizations different plans need to be prepared for different types of possible crises. A research university needs to look at several areas, including date rape, campus crime and athletic scandals as well as spills of toxic chemicals in its laboratories or a protest by animal rights activists against the use of animals in laboratories.

Do You Want Repeat Business?

While cruise lines have had a remarkably safe and positive image, they are vulnerable to a number of possible crises — an engine room fire, an outbreak of Legionnaires' disease, a food-related illness or striking a submerged object. And then there is the possibility of severe weather such as a Caribbean hurricane. How cruise lines handle problems varies considerably. When Carnival Cruise had a minor fire on one of its ships, it rewarded passengers on the planned three-day cruise with a full refund as well as a free future seven-day cruise.[6]

Royal Majesty had a problem with an unexpected grounding off Nantucket Island, leaving passengers waiting to sail to Bermuda stranded in Boston and giving passengers on board an unplanned extra day at sea. The ship then got caught in Hurricane Felix, sending passengers to the Bahamas rather than Bermuda, followed by a return to New York rather than Boston and a four-hour bus ride home. Reporter Jerry Morris of *The Boston Globe* wrote that while no problem was life-threatening, most of Royal Majesty's problems were because of poor communication and compensation which the passengers felt was inadequate.[7] How Royal Majesty handled its crisis was a contrast to Carnival, whose revenues and profits continue to increase.

Problems Common to All Organizations

There are protential crises common to all organizations — natural disasters, a terrorist attack, a bomb scare, a mail bomb, and sexual harassment or violence in the workplace. How natural disasters are dealt with should be a major concern to any organization, including how employees and customers are notified of an impending hurricane, twister, winter storm or flood.

Workplace violence is increasing. Figures released by the Bureau of Labor Statistics found that homicide ranked as the second-leading cause of death on the job. In 1995, 6,588 people were killed, an increase of 4 percent over 1993. The majority of violent acts committed in the workplace are done by strangers and not by co-workers or are an extension of domestic violence.[8] According to former Postmaster General Marvin Runyon, murder is the No. 1 cause of death for women in the workplace.[9] In 97.5 percent of the cases, men, with an average age of 36, were responsible for workplace murders. Firearms were used in 81 percent of the cases, and in one-fourth of the incidents the person perpetrating the violence committed suicide.[10]

While the tragedy of a workplace homicide is terrifying enough, the Crisis Database of the Institute for Crisis Management showed a 44 percent increase in news coverage of work-related violence from 1990 to 1995.[11] Ways to deal with crises involving violence in the workplace and case histories are further detailed in Chapter 13.

Many Companies Have Not Yet Learned

It would seem inconceivable that an organization would not be prepared. However, in a survey of the Fortune 500 companies by Wixted Pope Nora Associates, a Chicago-based public relations firm, only 150 companies responded as having a plan.[12] No good reason can be offered for not being prepared. Many executives who have risen to the top in their organizations believe they can weather any kind of storm. Crisis management and crisis communications are not taught in business schools but should be required for all graduates. All too often the lesson has to be learned the hard way. Even then, some executives still don't get the message.

"In today's media environment, a company can become a household name in two hours," said Wayne Pines, president of the health-care practice at APCO Associates, the public affairs/lobbying unit of

GCI Group, Washington, D.C. "Companies without crisis teams are being 'shortsighted.' The investment that you make in setting up a team will pay off dramatically if and when your company faces a crisis."[13]

Coca-Cola's European Nightmare

In June 1999, after scores of Belgian children became sick after drinking Coca-Cola, the governments of France, Belgium, Luxembourg and the Netherlands ordered bans on the world's most famous brand. It led to the biggest recall in the company's 113-year history. Crisis communications professionals gave Coke mixed reviews for the way it responded, many saying it did too little, too late. The company's established reputation for quality became its greatest asset.

Unrelated problems at two plants produced colas that smelled and tasted badly. M. Douglas Ivester, chairman and CEO, first said there could have been a problem with the handling of the Swedish carbon dioxide used to make the bubbles in the sodas. He then attributed the "smell" to transporting cans of the product on wooden pallets contaminated with creosote. In a letter printed in June 22 Belgian newspapers, two weeks after the first incident, Ivester apologized for not speaking to them earlier and stressed that "for us, health and safety issues always have come before business issues." Ads also were published in Italy, Spain and France.

The Coke crisis followed a nationwide food crisis in Belgium that forced the recall from store shelves and an export ban of chicken, meat and eggs. It contributed to bringing down the government of Prime Minister Jean-Luc Dehaene and helps explain why Luc Ven den Bossche, Belgium's interior minister who also is in charge of public health, publicly criticized Coca-Cola and Ivester for not responding sooner.

The company's production facilities in France and Belgium were given a clean bill of health and Coke was in full production three weeks after the first incident. Coca-Cola stock fell almost three percent to $61.56, partly on concern about the ban's effect on sales, and Coca-Cola Enterprises, its biggest bottler, lost $3.4

million in revenue daily. "Any time the government bans your product, it sends a very, very strong signal to the public," said Steven Fink, president of Lexicon Communications Corp., Los Angeles.

"Coke's inability to contain the growing alarm shows how quickly a global icon can be knocked off center," wrote *The Wall Street Journal* on June 17. There was sympathetic coverage the same day in *The Los Angeles Times*: "The way you're perceived to have reacted to a crisis like this is determined by how upfront you address the problem. And Coke is in a good position to deal with it upfront." In a June 25 editorial, *The New York Times* wrote that "Coca-Cola reacted slowly but adequately" and that "Doctors say the numerous reports of illness may have had more to do with mass hysteria than with the defects in the products."[14]

Some professionals noted that Coca-Cola was not as prepared as it should be since the company had never before experienced a major crisis. No doubt it will be if there is a next time.

Questions to Ask

In Chapter 1, Fred Thompson asks three basic questions when a crisis happens. Andrew Stern, chair of Sunwest Communications, Dallas, believes in asking a number of questions before a crisis as part of being prepared. "If a crisis is ready to happen, you don't have time to go through steps one through four. You must be prepared in advance. The plan should have a scenario so that when a potential crisis is ready to happen, every member of the team knows instinctively what to do," says Stern.[15]

Stern asks: Does the situation stand the risk of escalating in intensity? How intensive can it become and how quickly? What can we endure? Does it present hazards to people off-site (away from the workplace)? To what extent will the situation be reported by the news media? To what extent will the media coverage be monitored by government agencies? Will local news media call to inquire? Will there be regional, national or international coverage? Does the organization typically report whatever kinds of incidents occur to local, state or federal government agencies or officials?

Are injuries or deaths involved? Will the crisis interfere with operations? Will business be conducted as usual despite the situation? Will people be interrupted in doing their normal duties?

Will work come to a halt? Will outside organizations be affected? Will this crisis affect the reputation and good image the company has with customers and the public? Will it affect the confidence people have in the institution? Will sales or products or services be impacted?

Did the crisis happen because of anything the company did? Or did it just happen? Is the company the victim of external forces and events beyond its control? What extent could the company be injured financially? Politically? Sales and profits?

Preparing the Plan

After identifying all of the crises that could conceivably happen, the next step is to write the crisis management/crisis communications plan. The plan outlines the operations and procedures to follow and names the people responsible in the event a situation becomes a crisis. Every plan should include the following:

1. The organization's philosophy statement regarding crisis management and the purpose of the plan.

2. A list of all team members with direct-dial telephone, e-mail, and fax numbers at home and office and cellular and pager numbers. This information also should be on a laminated wallet-size card given to every member of the team.

3. The phone tree of who is to be called by whom and how e-mail and voice mail can be used to notify employees.

4. A policy statement regarding the spokesperson.

5. Phone numbers and contact names of all local and regional authorities who will be contacted or dealt with regarding the crisis, including police, fire, emergency medical, utility companies, emergency response-preparedness agencies and others.

6. Guidelines for releasing news and information to the media.

7. Location of the sites and facilities for the media briefing room and media operations room. In some cases the rooms should be prepared with telephone jacks where lines for telephones, faxes and computers can be connected.

8. A media communications and operations plan that includes lists of all key media, credentialing procedures, emergency parking, location for television and satellite uplink trucks, and electric power. Lists with phone numbers, addresses and brief descriptions of restaurants and hotels and other service businesses should be in the package for media. Alternate locations and plans should be prepared.

9. Lists of other target publics that may need to be notified, such as shareholders, customers, government agencies or special-interest groups.

10. Procedures to follow in the event of loss of electricity, telephone or even access to the facility.

11. An emergency response and rumor-control hot line with trained operators during normal business hours and during the time of the crisis and a voice-mail message for times when the phones cannot be personally answered.

12. If the crisis involves conflict between differing groups, identify and understand the opposition. Build a reference file on the leadership so you know who you are dealing with and can speak with authority when the name of an individual or organization is in a question from the media. The more informed the team, the better it will be able to deal with the situation.

13. Maps of the area with location of buildings. The director of the physical plant should have immediate access to all underground utility service. Floor plans and location of offices should be available for all buildings.

14. Have rosters of all people who would normally be working in each office in the building broken down by time of day. Residential units, such as college dormitories, should have names of all students cross-referenced on computer against class schedules. Should there be a disaster, you need to know the names of the people who might normally be working at that time.

Have Press Materials Prepared and in the Can

When the crisis unfolds, press materials should already be prepared in anticipation of the problem. Fact sheets on the company, its products or services, biographies on the key executives and spokesperson, maps and diagrams and other basic information should be current and ready to be downloaded from a computer to a printer to a copy machine and back to an Internet web page.

For some situations the first news release should already be prepared as part of the plan so there can be an immediate response while looking into all of the facts. This is important in the event the CEO or the spokesperson may not be readily available or if the CEO wants legal counsel to sign off on a news release. Any delay in a response can mean disaster. Where possible, plan on even two or three general news releases that can be prepared in advance, approved by all involved, and then held in a safe place in the event they are ever needed.

You will already be too late if the news release has to be prepared once the facts are gathered related to an incident and then scrutinized or approved by legal counsel, or even worse, by a committee. The delayed response is a negative factor that increases proportionately from the time of the incident to the time of the public announcement.

The same is true if a crisis team is not already in place and familiar with the process. Do not wait to form a crisis team after the crisis has happened.

Notification Priorities

Every plan will have a cascading notification system used to activate the communications plan. This permits one individual to contact several other individuals who in turn contact several others. In an emergency at a plant or nonheadquarters facility, notifications to communications support staff begin with a site communications coordinator. This person may have first-hand knowledge of the situation or may be alerted by safety or security personnel. In turn, the coordinator determines whether the communications plan should be activated and when further notifications should begin. Here is how Andrew Stern believes notifications should be prioritized:

1. Those who must implement and manage the communications response.

2. Those who will be asked to comment on the situation publicly or speak for the company.

3. Those who will support the communications response.

4. Those with a special need-to-know (e.g., senior management, victim's family, off-site response agencies and government officials).

5. The news media and public.[16]

Opposition Research

Know and understand your opposition. If you are in a dispute that could elevate to a crisis situation, opposition research is essential. This could involve employee/labor relations, community relations and issues that could become very political. Identify the key players. Obtain biographical information on your adversaries. Review their speeches and public statements. Do they have the facts? How do they "spin" the truth? If there are several organizations, what are they? What do they stand for? Who provides the funding? Is the organization legitimate or a front for another organization? Who are their media allies?

The more you know about your potential enemy, the better prepared you will be. You need to anticipate what your adversary may say or do, how or when he will take action, and what you can do to prevent being in a defensive posture. Anticipate how the public will react to issues. Focus-group research and public opinion polls will help determine whether you can expect public support. You need to understand different points of view and identify various levels of understanding and misunderstanding. Will the public believe you? Will the media believe you?

A "must read" book in the library of anyone involved in crisis planning is Saul D. Alinsky's *Rules for Radicals*. The book was written in 1971 as a "how to" primer for students and dissenters. "All change means disorganization of the old and organization of the new," wrote Alinsky, who died in 1972. "When there is agreement there is no issue; issues only arise when there is disagreement or controversy. An organizer must stir up dissatisfaction and discontent; provide a channel into which the people can angrily pour their frustrations."[17]

Alinsky's advice for organizers should be understood by all trying to resolve a crisis. He believes that the art of communication is the single most important quality for an organizer. "One can lack any of the qualities of an organizer — with one exception — and still be effective and successful. Communication with others takes place when they understand what you're trying to get across to them. If they don't understand, then you are not communicating regardless of words, pictures, or anything else. People only understand things in terms of their experience, which means that you must get within their experience."

His advice on communication should be followed by any spokesperson. "Further, communication is a two-way process," Alinsky said. "If you try to get your ideas across to others without paying attention to what they have to say to you, you can forget about the whole thing."[18]

Being Prepared With Issues Management

Judy B. Rosener, a professor in the graduate school of management at the University of California-Irvine, believes companies can avert crises through issues management and cites the crash of TWA Flight 800 as an example. "If there had been an issues management process in place . . . airline executives would have anticipated the reaction of the victims' families and immediately provided explanations for the delay in notifying them," she wrote in *The Los Angeles Times*.[19] "Clearly, TWA had not thought through how to react before finding itself in the middle of a crisis."

Rosener believes issues management will reduce or eliminate unwanted surprises, improve the ability to take advantage of anticipated change, concentrate responses on key issues and opportunities and facilitate exerting more control over the future of an organization.

Issues management is part of strategic communications planning. Issues that can affect how a company or organization is perceived and believed must be identified so they can be dealt with during a crisis. Issues that are part of the organizational culture need to be understood internally and externally. A strategic communications plan will identify the most critical issues and the tools, techniques and media to best communicate them.

Building the Crisis Communications Team

A written plan is only as good as the ability of the company and team to execute the plan. This means having a team that is prepared. The team should meet at least annually. If an organization identifies more than one potential crisis, it needs to develop a plan for each crisis. Chances are that different management teams and even different spokespersons will be needed for each. There will be a nucleus on each team with participation most likely involving the president or his designate, the top public relations professional, the head of security and the general counsel.

A chain of command needs to be established in advance so there is no doubt who is in charge during a crisis. In most cases this will be obvious, but it is needed should disagreements arise between the public relations professionals and the lawyers and people responsible for security.

The CEO should appoint a chair for the team. The most appropriate would be the senior individual heading public relations and responsible for crisis communications. This person has the responsibility for keeping the team and plan current, calling meetings of the team and making any changes as required. In the event of a crisis, each member of the team will have an assigned responsibility. There should be backup members of the team who play the role of understudies and must be equally as prepared and capable in the event that any team member is out of town, sick or otherwise unable to do his or her job when needed.

Be Prepared for the Media

It is essential that the team and spokesperson receive media relations training. Even the most proficient and articulate executives realize that they must be prepared before standing in front of the media, many of whom will be adversarial and even hostile. One course in media relations training is not always sufficient and selected spokespersons should be retrained with refresher courses on an annual basis. A number of firms specialize in personalized media relations training and group sessions that can run from $1,000 to $10,000 a day. A novice spokesperson who does not get the message across can mean disaster for a company during a crisis.

Any person who may represent a company on radio, television or in public should be professionally trained. Most executives today in business, industry, associations, nonprofit organizations and government at some time will be in front of a camera; a microphone; a reporter with a pen, notebook and tape recorder; or a public audience.

Be as prepared as possible before the interview by watching the host or interviewer in action to get an idea of his or her style and technique. Is the person aggressive? Does the person interrupt and not let the guest always finish an answer? Is the approach friendly and relaxed? If you are going to be on a panel or with other guests on a talk show, will any be adversaries? If so, have background information on your adversaries and competition. For newspaper and magazine reporters, review other articles they have written to get an idea of their style.

Veteran newsman Walter Cronkite says that the subject of the interview has more control over a news interview than the reporter. He writes this in his book citing a disagreement he had with Pierre Salinger when he was White House press secretary for John F. Kennedy. Cronkite says that at any time during his interview, the president could inject a statement whether the question was asked or not.[20] A CEO in an adversarial position should remember this and be prepared to make an important point even if not asked the question. Dan Rather learned this the hard way when he became hostile with then Vice President George Bush during the 1988 presidential campaign.

For any interview, be candid and brief. The average sound bite is 7.2 seconds. That is what most likely will be used on radio or television of all of your responses. Many newspapers and magazines also use only one or two sound-bite-length quotes. Make your main point in 30 seconds or less or no more than about 120 words.

Keep your language simple. Avoid unfamiliar acronyms, jargon and technical terms that the pubic may not understand. Be simple and talk as if you want an eighth-grader to understand what you say. Do not overanswer or overqualify your answers.

During the rehearsal and pre-interview training, anticipate the questions that may be asked and prepare and practice 30-second answers on subjects you expect to discuss. Know how to turn a tough question into a positive answer.

If the reporter is hostile, do not get argumentative or uncooperative. Be cool and remain in control. Always remember with absolute confidence that you know more about your company and subject than the reporter.

If a question doesn't make sense, come up with an answer that does make sense. Just because a question is asked is no reason you have to answer it. You can always give the answer you want to make your point by talking around the question.

Remember body language and facial expressions. Dr. Vincent T. Covello says generally what you say counts for 75 percent of the message and body language 25 percent. However, in high-concern situations, body language can represent 75 percent of the message and what you say only 25 percent.

Go to the interview prepared with the one, two or three points that you want to make. Then have more than one way to make that point so your answers are not always the same, but you are making the same point.

Always stay in charge of the interview. Never allow yourself to be put in a defensive position.

Summary Preparedness Checklist

Here is a quick checklist to use in developing a crisis management and communications plan:

1. Anticipate the problem.

2. Prepare the crisis communications plan.

3. Assemble the crisis management team.

4. Distribute the plan to all members of the team.

5. Determine the spokesperson and backup spokesperson(s).

6. Media train all possible spokespersons.

7. Where possible, pretest the plan with a simulated incident.

8. Have the team meet at least once a year to review and update the plan.

9. Plan what to do and say after the crisis.

10. Review the crisis; research the publics.

Endnotes

1. PBS, *A Guide to Crisis Management*, June 1992, pg. 3.
2. *PR News*, May 1, 1995, pg. 7.
3. Ibid.
4. Institute for Crisis Management, Products & Services, Louisville, Kentucky, http://www.crisisexperts.com.
5. "Why This May Be the Year It All Comes Together," *PR Reporter*, January 5, 1998, pg. 1.
6. *The Boston Sunday Globe*, "Cruise lines' real problem: public relations" by Jerry Morris, September 10, 1995, pg. A109.
7. Ibid.

8. *USA Today*, August 4, 1995, pg. 1A.

9. *The New York Times*, Associated Press dispatch, December 18, 1994.

10. Ibid.

11. *Public Relations Tactics*, December 1995, pg. 1.

12. *PR News*, July 31, 1995, pg. 1.

13. *PR News*, August 28, 1995, pg. 7.

14. "Coca-Cola Acts Slowly but Credibly," editorial, *The New York Times*, June 25, 1999; Reed Abelson, "In a Crisis, Coke Tries to Be Reassuring," *The New York Times*, June 16, 1999; Sue Anne Pressley, A Bitter Aftertaste," *The Washington Post*, June 24, 1999, pg. E1; Larry Dobrow, "Coke PR too little, too late with contamination issue," *PR Week*, June 28, 1999, pg. 3; Media Watch, "Coca-Cola crisis communications go flat," *PR Week*, June 28, 1999, pg. 3; Constance L. Hays, "Coca-Cola Chairman uses Ads to Apologize to Belgians," *The New York Times*, June 22, 1999.

15. Andrew Stern, Sunwest Communications, Dallas, Texas, interview, April 1977.

16. Ibid.

17. Saul D. Alinsky, *Rules for Radicals*, Vintage Books, a division of Random House, New York, 1971, pg. 117.

18. Ibid., pg. 81.

19. *Jack O'Dwyer's Newsletter*, September 11, 1996, pg. 7.

20. Walter Cronkite, *A Reporter's Life*, Alfred A. Knopf, New York, 1996, pg. 247.

CHAPTER THREE

MANAGING THE CRISIS

Being prepared is only part of the public relations and communications challenge during a crisis. How a company or organization responds when a crisis actually happens is the ultimate measure of success or failure.

Was the plan effective? Was the right spokesperson chosen? Was the response timely? Was the response believable? As soon as possible after a crisis, it is important to bring the team together for a critique.

You have to be flexible because every aspect of every crisis cannot always be anticipated, even with the best of planning and "What if?" sessions. Members of the crisis team and their principal deputies need to be empowered to know they can act on their own. They must be entrepreneurial and know when to take the lead.

The rooms you had planned to use for media briefings and a working pressroom may not be usable because of an explosion or fire. You planned for a backup facility, but is it available?

Communications is your key to coordination. But what if your telephone system, which provides not only your regular service but your cellular phones, computers and faxes, is out? An Illinois Bell System fire knocked out phone service to tens of thousands of Chicago-area customers for weeks. A similar problem occurred in New York City several years earlier. In 1959 the U.S. Army Corps of Engineers projected that a high-tide hurricane affecting New York harbor would shut down phone service for a month or more in Manhattan. The communications plan for a catastrophic California earthquake anticipates that land-based telephone service will be disrupted during the first 24 to 36 hours of the emergency period.[1]

Radio is the communications mode of choice for emergency managers because it is portable, available and versatile. Battery-powered radios are not susceptible to downed wires, loss of power, damage to switching stations or inundated switchboards.[2] How the communications system works depends on how it links to other essential parties — your own team, emergency response, fire, police and media.

Timing Is Everything

A system to notify the team responsible for implementing communications is critical to the success of the crisis plan. Generally, notifications should be carried out in this order:[3]

1. Those who implement and manage the communications response.

2. Those who will be asked to comment on the situation publicly or speak for the company.

3. Those who will support the communications response.

4. Those with a special need-to-know (e.g., senior management, family of the victim(s), off-site response agencies and government officials).

5. The news media and public.

A cascading notification system that permits one individual to contact several other individuals, who in turn contact others, is the best method for activating the plan. If the incident happens away from headquarters, such as at a plant or other facility, getting the communications team immediately involved is critical. There will be an on-site coordinator who will most likely be the initial spokesperson for the media and who will determine whether the communications plan should be activated and when further notifications should begin. The notification process can originate at the site, region or headquarters level.[4]

The First Minutes Are Critical

Robert J. Stone, vice president of The Dilenschneider Group, New York, says a response must come in the first 10 to 15 minutes of a crisis or credibility can be lost. His crisis rules are as follows:

- Take charge or take it on the chin.

- Don't follow your first impulse to minimize the situation.

- Assume the worst so you will extend yourself to maximum effort.

- Don't wait for all the facts; full details won't be available early on.

- Head for the scene to assess damage.

- Be the source for bad news, not the victim of it.[5]

In a crisis, the CEO or top executive of the company or organization must be available according to Ed Turner, executive vice president of CNN. "With the technology we have today, people can be instantly available anyplace in the U.S. or the world. Have your most credible authority front and center. A 'no comment' is 'guilty' and dumb," says Turner. "Credibility is all you have to offer. Build this trust over time." He also says it is all right to say "I don't know" or "I can't talk about it."[6]

What you say, when you say it and who says it are critical. Preferably your CEO should be the spokesperson. You do not want the organization's attorney as a spokesperson and under no circumstances should any outside lawyer speak for you. Be sure a competent, experienced professional is in charge of media relations during a crisis. This is no time for novices or amateurs. Some overanxious, well-meaning people starting talking before thinking.

"Don't duck the press in the hope that we will leave you alone," said Margo Slade, assistant national editor of *The New York Times*. She said companies in crisis tend to treat reporters as though they are "armed and dangerous."[7] "The job of reporters is to get the story. They'll do that with or without your cooperation," say John DeFrancesco and Gary Goodfriend of DeFrancesco· Goodfriend public relations, Chicago. "The risk of being uncooperative, however, is that the story can be based on hearsay, rumor and misinformation from outside sources. Such a story can be damaging to your company and its reputation. Conversely, when informed in a timely, honest manner, reporters will tend to write the facts, and the attention to the crisis in the press can subside quickly."[8]

"If the first time you're speaking to a reporter who covers your business is when there is a crisis or negative news event, then the reporter's worst instincts are bound to take over," says Andrew Gilman, president of CommCore Consulting Group. Speaking at the National Law Firm Marketing Association, he said that: "One of the best ways to prepare for the inevitable is to get to know your media. If the reporters know you, your products and have a sense of your personal credibility, you may get the benefit of the doubt when they make judgments in articles and news stories."[9]

PR/Crisis Communications Counselor and Lawyers May Not Agree

What is said and when it is said may polarize the public relations counselors and the attorneys. The CEO will have to decide whose recommendation will be accepted. The public relations counselor will be concerned with the image, reputation, credibility, trustworthiness and believability of the company. These are not areas of concern for a lawyer because few have had training or experience in public relations or public affairs disciplines. The most important advice the attorney can give is whether or not what is being said and done is legal.

Most lawyers have little understanding of the media and will want to move slowly and cautiously and delay any announcement as long as possible. "Companies are foolhardy when they follow legal advice to dodge the media," said James Cox, executive vice president of Edelman Public Relations Worldwide and head of its litigation unit.[10]

Manage Release of Information, Be in Control

If the crisis has been anticipated and an approved news release already prepared, it should be on its way to the media the minute all the facts have been evaluated and confirmed. If not, the spokesperson should be briefed and a statement made as soon as possible. As soon as you have all of the facts, disclose them.

You want to manage the release of information and be in control. You want the media to depend on you for the story and updates. This will happen only if trust, credibility and believability have been established. The last thing you want is for the media to seek out sources who may be uninformed or to follow up on unfounded rumors or interview adversaries.

The media center is the operations or control center where communications with the media take place. It should be a central site with easy but secured access, with necessary electronics support for telephones, computers, faxes and electrical outlets for camera lights. The media center can be all-inclusive or separate and adjacent rooms that provide space for the working press, a site for interviews and media briefings and the spot where the crisis communications team will be working. Backup media centers should be considered in the event of a natural disaster or other reasons the primary center could not be used. Be sure to plan for parking and access for television remote trucks as well as convenient parking for all journalists.

Optional entries and exits are important and ideal if possible. They can be protected by security and used primarily for spokespersons making announcements who cannot be trapped when leaving.

When the center is established, let the media know when you are going to make an announcement. Tell them what you know, distribute background information and fact sheets and set a time for an announcement within a stated period of time (such as within the next 45 to 90 minutes). Come back on time and with answers to questions they have asked. If you keep giving the media updated reports, and in the time you specified, they will be less apt to leave the media center.

Take advantage of all communications tools you have at your disposal. Internet. Intranet. Compressed video. Satellite. The Internet and Intranet provide a means to quickly and broadly distribute information. Compressed video is an inexpensive way to link to media sources if you are based in a remote location. One-on-one or simultaneous media interviews can be conducted using this inexpensive but nonbroadcast-quality system. If a satellite facility is available, that could be used for periodic updates for broadcast quality.

The basic principles always apply — be honest, tell the truth, never lie, do not mislead, tell it quickly, do not stonewall, show compassion, don't hide behind a "no comment," be on the record with all statements and don't give the media a chance to speculate or get comments from unreliable sources. If there is some information you cannot disclose, such as withholding a name until a family member has been notified, let the media know the reason. If just don't have the answer to a question, say, "I don't know," and let the media know you will seek to get the answer. If information can be made clearer to the media by the use of charts, graphs, maps, etc., use them wherever possible.

A policy difference can be expected between the public relations counselor and the attorney over whether or not to accept responsibility for the crisis and even publicly apologize or say "I'm sorry." Attorneys may fear this opens the door for lawsuits, but many can be mitigated by winning public favor.

One of the best examples of taking the advice of public relations counsel over legal counsel is what John Hall, CEO of Ashland Oil, did in 1988. When a company's storage tank exploded and released one million gallons of diesel fuel into the Monongahela River near Pittsburgh, Hall took full responsibility for the accident, admitting actions that had clear legal implications. The company won support from the public, the media and its employees.[11] The case study on Ashland Oil is detailed in Chapter 9.

Spinning Doublespeak

Be clear and concise if you want the message understood. Truthfully position your organization and its message and give both the public and media credit for being able to understand what they are being told. Avoid what an English professor and nonpracticing attorney at Rutgers University-Camden calls doublespeak. "The purpose of doublespeak is to *not* say something while pretending to do so," says William Lutz. He notes that the government is the worst offender, but that corporate America is only a half-step behind. He gives these examples:[12]

- Negative gain in test scores v. Test scores dropped.

- Meaningful downturn in aggregate output v. Recession.

- Normal payroll adjustment v. Layoffs.

- Volume-related production schedule adjustment v. Closed down a production plant.

- Repositioned v. Fired.

The Impact of Television in a Crisis

"Television news is truly at its finest moment in the early hours of tragedies and national disasters, be they natural or man-made disasters," says Don Tomlinson, an attorney and professor of journalism at Texas A&M. "Today, we are connected instantly with the world through television, and we turn to that connection for more than entertainment and information."[13]

Echoing his comments is Nick Peters, vice president/operations of Medialink, a video public relations firm headquartered in New York City. He believes successful crisis management requires the impact and immediacy of video. "Surveys repeatedly confirm that Americans get most of their news from television, and believe what they *see* rather than what they *read* or *hear*," says Peters. He points out that video news releases have made a difference in a number of corporate crises, including product tamperings, environmental disasters, airline crashes, mergers and acquisitions, and product recall announcements. "It is the way to insure the maximum number of Americans receive the message quickly and effectively," he adds. [14]

In January 1995, Hasbro/Kenner Products cooperated voluntarily with the U.S. Consumer Product Safety Commission to recall its "Colorblaster 3-D" spray-art toy. It used a video to visually demonstrate what could happen if kids didn't use the toy properly. When used incorrectly, the pressurized air system could cause the pump handle and cap assembly to blow out, possibly hitting the user in the face. There were reports that the toy had caused eight injuries. The company quickly produced a video with a Hasbro executive showing how to properly handle the toy. The video was distributed by satellite and aired on the news within hours.[15]

Don't Forget Internal Communications

Keeping employees informed is critical. You want to dispel any rumors. You also want your employees current on all factual information. They will be asked questions by their family, neighbors and friends, and possibly even the media. You cannot control their message and you certainly want it to be correct. Good investigative reporters will also will contact employees and their families in their homes.

Recent surveys by counselor Tom Harris and Northwestern University-Edelman Public Relations Worldwide indicate that employee relations is now the No. 2 priority as companies are practicing "inreach" before "outreach." Editors at PR Reporter predict that the new direction of public relations will make this primary.[16] In a crisis situation, communicating to employees is even more important.

Internal communications is critical when a crisis has involved violence in the workplace, a terrorist attack or a hostage situation. You need to help your employees heal after such crises and bring normalcy back to the workplace.

Burton St. John III, a public relations consultant for the U.S. Postal Service in St. Louis, notes that it is important to have psychological counselors with excellent people skills on the scene within 24 hours. The leader needs to make face-to-face contact with as many employees and victims as possible. During the second 24 hours, employees move from shock and denial to anger and anxiety. This can last for weeks or months. He believes it is important to cut red tape and move quickly. In the case of a fatality, "Often the simple act of completing a memorial service will bring some closure."[17]

Decisions made during a crisis can impact relationships and trust for years to come according to Don Sherry, manager of communications for Oklahoma Natural Gas in Oklahoma City. The company's headquarters are located less than a block from the site of the bombed Murrah Federal Building, and employees physically experienced the explosion. Because of damage to the building, offices were temporarily moved.[18]

The employee assistance program and counseling were given top priority. A decision to return to the downtown offices was delayed and employees allowed to stay longer in the temporary location. Supervisors were given wide latitude in granting leaves and vacations. Supervisors and employees were encouraged to respect others' feelings.[19]

All of the usual forms of communications were used — publications, e-mail, recorded news hot line. "The most important and effective," says Sherry, "was direct, one-on-one conversation and small group meetings. Our president spent a day meeting personally with as many employees as possible, conveying the company's concern and appreciation for work under the most trying of circumstances." Oklahoma Natural Gas supported the desire of many employees to contribute funds to aid victims by matching employee gifts and making a separate corporate contribution.

Endnotes

1. Robert D. Vessey and Jose A. Aponte, "Needed: The Right Information at the Right Time," *Communication When It's Needed Most*, The Annenberg Washington Program in Communications Policy Studies of Northwestern University, 1989, pg. 9.

2. Ibid.

3. Andrew Stern, Sunwest Communications, Dallas, Texas, interview, April 1977.

4. Andrew Stern, *op cit.*

5. Meeting in Philadelphia with Robert J. Stone, vice president, The Dilenschneider Group, New York, November 7, 1996.

6. Ed Turner, executive vice president, CNN, Atlanta, comments during Public Relations Society of America conference, "Media Relations: The Good. The Bad. The Ugly." June 5, 1996, Nashville, Tennessee.

7. Ibid.

8. "How To Handle Media in Time of Crisis," *Newsline*, Summer 1997, DeFrancesco·Goodfriend, Chicago, pg. 1.

9. *Public Relations Tactics*, May 1997, pg. 4.

10. *Jack O'Dwyer's Newsletter*, November 20, 1996, pg. 7.

11. Robin Cohn, "Learning from Crisis: as the Curtain Rises," *The Strategist*, Public Relations Society of America, pg. 29.

12. Rosland Briggs, "Efforts of 'spin doctors' have professor spinning," *The Philadelphia Inquirer*, November 28, 1996, pg. D-1.

13. Diane Holloway, "TV viewers drawn to exhaustive coverage when a crisis unfolds," *Austin American-Statesman*, Austin, Texas, May 28, 1995, pgs. F1, F11.

14. Nick Peters, "Using Video to Snuff Out a Crisis," *Public Relations Tactics*, May 1995, pg. 14.

15. Ibid.

16. "Progress: Studies Find Employee Relations Now 2nd Priority," *PR Reporter*, January 5, 1998, pg. 4.

17. Burton St. John III, "Recovery Communications — Helping Your Employees Heal After Workplace Violence," *Public Relations Tactics*, May 1997, pgs. 1, 14, 27.

18. "Think It Thru: Crisis Decisions Have Lasting Impact," *Channels*, July 1995, Exeter, New Hampshire, pg. 1.

19. Ibid., pg. 2.

CHAPTER FOUR

WHO SAID "SILENCE IS GOLDEN"?

No one really knows who first said "silence is golden," but more than likely it was an attorney. The lawyer-driven "no comment" could well have evolved from "silence is golden." Both of these phrases could be why the great wordsmith William Shakespeare, wrote the following in *Henry VI*: "The first thing we do, let's kill all the lawyers."[1]

Actually "silence is golden" more recently comes from "Speech is silvern, Silence is golden" from Thomas Caryle's *Sartor Resartus*, where he translates a "Swiss inscription." This also is a common German proverb that has been traced back to the Talmud in ancient Babylonia.[2]

The rules of good crisis communications have been outlined in the previous chapters but cannot be repeated enough—respond quickly, always tell the truth, never lie, never say "no comment," it is all right to say "I don't know," never deceive, never mislead and be open and honest with the media and all of the audiences to whom the story must be communicated.

" 'No comment' or 'no comment because it's in litigation' don't serve the organization's reputation, credibility, or market share very well and rarely protect it against future litigation, or reduce settlement costs," says James Lukaszewski. "In high-profile cases, saying nothing may be the costliest single mistake."[3]

In October 1995 at an Edelman Public Relations Worldwide

seminar, panelists said a "no comment" implies guilt. James Fink of Opinion Research Corp. said 40 percent of the people believe large companies accused of wrongdoing are guilty when they do not respond and that jumps to more than 60 percent when the company refuses to talk about litigation.[4] Recent polls show the public is particularly prone to distrust business. A September 1998 poll found more than half of the people conclude a company is guilty of something if it is being investigated by a government agency and more than half believed companies are probably guilty when a lawsuit is filed against them.[5]

James Cox, executive vice president and head of the Edelman firm's litigation unit, said that companies are foolhardy when they follow legal advice to dodge the media. "Public relations should be used early in a lawsuit to win the hearts and minds of prospective judges and jurors and to bring expert witnesses to argue a client's case in print before it goes to trial." He added that during a time of increased exposure a company's reputation and brand equity must be protected. Margo Slade, assistant national editor of *The New York Times* urged companies not to duck the press or treat reporters as if they were "armed and dangerous."[6]

If anyone has a question about saying "no comment" to a reporter, just ask the management at Corning Inc. In 1997, when Courtney Kelly-Roe of the *Corning (N.Y.) Leader* was told "no comment," the reporter concluded that Corning was in a "state of emergency." *Bloomberg Business News* and the Associated Press picked up the story, and in one single day on the New York Stock Exchange the company's stock dropped in value more than $1 billion. After the damage had been done, Corning did respond, calling the story "filled with inaccuracies." Then later, still in a reactive, damage-control stage, it admitted it had overestimated the growth of its fiber optic business. The company cut its third-quarter sales and earnings projections from 30 percent to 20 percent. Corning's stock, which had been trading in the mid-$60 range, dropped to a low of $24 during 1997 before it began to recover in the $30 range.[7]

NBC's Judy Smith was deputy White House press secretary in

the Bush administration and says Marlin Fitzwater taught her that you don't have to explain what you don't say. Also an attorney and for two years special counsel to the U.S. Attorney for the District of Columbia, she says to avoid babble. "If a question is asked and you don't know the answer, or if you are confronted with a rumor, be honest and be brief," she says. Here is one way she suggests to reply: "I don't have that answer yet, but I will get it for you." And when badgered she suggests you take a deep breath, be straightforward and say, "I don't know the answer but I'll find out."[8]

Hooray for Hollywood?

There is probably no greater paranoia in dealing with the media than in the entertainment industry. Rules and protocol are never followed. Often rumors are planted by Hollywood publicists. The *New York Post*'s Steve Dunleavy quotes Cathie Saxton as saying "I once worked for astronaut Neil Armstrong and he told me that publicity is a double-edged sword: If you live by it, you can die by it." Even while referring to Bernie Bennet as "another super flack," he quotes him as saying "I only know one rule in this business, and we all learned it from our parents: Honesty is the best policy."[9]

The late Meg Greenfield, in her *Newsweek* column about how various political and presidential administrations contribute to their own misery even more than the press could ever hope to do, wrote that the framework for the drama is created first by a "series of dodges and feints and denials and plain falsehoods that set them up for exposure. They continue to let the truth out only under pressure and in dribs and drabs, each time having to admit a little more and also explain a lot more about their previous, now discredited assertions." She notes that this only creates an ever-increasing and more attentive audience for the story.[10]

"Don't restrict access. It's like waving a red flag. It signals hiding something," says Tim Wheeler, environmental writer of *The Baltimore Sun*. "Reporters want to have access to people who know the issues. Attorneys are the worst. You must go over the lawyer's head to the top person. Attorneys want to control and even refuse to talk about documents that are public."[11]

In his book, *My American Journey*, Colin Powell points out how he believes crisis incidents should be handled. He noted the loss of KAL Flight 007 (a Korean Air Lines 747 flight that killed 269 passengers) and that it is best to get the facts out as soon as possible, even when new facts contradict the old. He wrote that "untidy truth is better than smooth lies that unravel in the end anyway." He noted that five years later the U.S.S. Vincennes shot down an Iranian airliner killing 290 passengers and crew. "It was a tragic blunder. We said so and released the facts publicly as fast as possible," said Powell.[12]

During the Persian Gulf Desert Storm operation, Powell had an argument with General Norman Schwarzkopf regarding television comments that four Scud missile sites had been taken out when in fact air reconnaissance photos showed that the targets were fuel trucks. A CNN camera crew shot film of the destroyed trucks and contradicted Schwarzkopf. Powell told his general to "protect your credibility—it's a precious asset." Powell's rule is that it is better to admit a mistake than be caught in one.[13]

Lawyers Are Often the Problem

Anyone practicing crisis communications has heard someone say, "If you lose in the court of public opinion, it doesn't matter what happens in the court of law." In a crisis, the ultimate objective should be to win in both the court of public opinion and the court of law.

Attorneys are responsible for protecting the company's legal position while the public relations counselor is responsible for protecting the company's image and reputation. And there will be conflicts. Developer Douglas Durst was besieged by bad press for weeks after scaffolding collapsed at his Times Square Condé Nast construction site. He said from the beginning there was tension between his public relations counsel, who advocated immediate assistance to the thousands of displaced workers and residents, and the lawyers, who advised caution. The lawyers won. Durst lost.[14]

One attorney who supports the right of publicists to remain silent is Ron Levy, president of North American Precis Syndicate. He suggests that public relations professionals not only have the right but the duty not to answer a reporter's question in the following circumstances:

1. You don't know the answer.

2. An "I don't know but I'll find out" answer will sound like an admission of guilt.

3. Management may prefer that the answer come from someone more expert than you.

4. You have reason to believe your answer will be twisted.

5. Management has told you not to answer until you clear it with the lawyers.

6. Answering would be unlawful.

7. The inquiry is not for business information but for personal secrets.[15]

For a strategic communications plan to work in the crisis mode, the attorney must understand the communications goals and help the public relations adviser understand the legal goals. This author disagrees with how attorney Levy suggests handling the media and recommends the following seven ways a person should respond:

1. "I don't know, but I will find out and get back to you."

2. The inflection and tone of how the response is made will not be an admission of guilt.

3. "I am not the person you should be asking that question of . . . you need to talk with (and give name)."

4. Emphasize and re-emphasize the point to be made, in a brief, concise sound bite so there is no way it can be twisted. If the person is fearful of an answer being distorted, the person needs media training.

5. "Before I can go into more details with you on that I have to talk with our attorneys. There may be some legal implica-

tions and please bear with us. We will get back to you as quickly as possible."

6. "By law I am prohibited from discussing that matter. I hope you will understand. If you need further clarification I will get you in contact with our attorneys."

7. "Your question is really outside the scope of the incident and touches on matters confidential to our company. I am sure you understand and I regret I cannot go into that in detail at this time."

All the reporter wants is some kind of response. The reporter is doing his or her job and has to explain to the assignment editor why there is no quote or there is a blank tape with someone being silent or saying "no comment." To respond even in ambiguity is better than no response at all. The most important consideration is to be honest and sincere and assure the reporter that you are telling the truth.

In an April 30, 1998, press conference, President William Clinton came up with creative ways to avoid saying "no comment" to 15 of 29 questions he was asked. Here are some examples: "I don't have anything to say about that." "I cannot comment on these matters because they are under seal." "I have nothing to add to my former answer." "I have been advised, and I think it's good advice under the circumstances, but I just don't have anything else to add about that."[16]

Harold Suckenik, a lawyer who has long been active in public relations, says lawyers should never head the public relations department of a company or organization. "Lawyers normally operate in an adversarial milieu and are used to addressing small audiences, such as a judge or 12 jurors, as compared to audiences that may number in the millions," he says. "Lawyers are also used to working very slowly. They believe that the longer things take, the better—people forget things, move, die, give up, etc. Media, however, travel at blinding speed."[17]

Law schools don't prepare their graduates to enter the legal world knowledgeable about media relations, crisis management or even public relations. Even a one-day seminar for graduating seniors would be better than no exposure at all. This creates serious problems during crisis situations when an attorney will want to stonewall the media and all public disclosure while the public relations and crisis communications professional will want immediate and full disclosure. One must wonder if a course isn't given for attorneys to be suspicious of journalists. Attorneys are almost unanimous in their belief an apology is completely out of the question because it could open the door for lawsuits.

Crisis communications may be getting help if U.S. District Judge Stanley Sporkin in Washington, D.C. gets his way. He believes it is time for a university to create an institute of crisis management to teach business people how to handle corporate emergencies. Judge Sporkin has lectured on this subject for a decade and told *The Washington Post* that a "vast majority of crises are avoidable." He discussed developing an academic program with Paul Brest, dean of Stanford University Law School, which already has merged crisis management training into its executive education programs and in-house counsel seminars.[18]

An attorney was the recipient of the first Muzzle Award given by Intel's chairman and CEO, Andrew Grove. The award, a leather dog muzzle mounted on a wooden plaque, is given after a company official makes a foolish remark in print. The first Muzzle was given in the early 1980s after General Counsel Roger Borovoy was quoted as saying, "Negotiating with the Japanese is like negotiating with the Devil."[19] In this case, perhaps silence would have been golden.

Sometimes one has to wonder whether or not *The Madwoman of Chaillot* by Jean Giraudoux was required or optional reading in law school. The author wrote: "You're an attorney. It's your duty to lie, conceal and distort everything . . . ."[20]

An Outspoken Opinion About Attorneys

Sir Henri Deterding, the co-founder and chairman of Royal Dutch Shell, has some strong opinions regarding attorneys. Here are excerpts from a letter he sent from his London headquarters in 1916 to an executive in his New York office who wanted to retain an attorney:

> You gave me rather a start with your letter, because I gather from it that you employ solicitors much oftener than we would ever dream of doing. Although we have an enormous business here, we very rarely consult lawyers. We only do so when there is really a legal difference or legal difficulty, whilst it seems to me that you employ them practically in every instance.
>
> Lawyers are not business people, however large a lawyer's experience may be, in the conduct of business he is absolutely useless. A lawyer placed at the head of a concern, would soon bring the business to rack and ruin. He is not a creative genius, he is able to give his opinion, if a case is laid before him, but to ask a lawyer to draw up a contract for you is a most foolish thing to do, and this is bound to lead to trouble. Our custom here is to draw up a contract before having seen the lawyer and then to ask him to put it in a more legal shape. Such a contract is more likely to embody the spirit of what has been agreed upon than one drawn up by the lawyer; to ask his opinion as to what you should do or not do is the worst possible way of conducting business, which should be kept as far as possible from the lawyers.
>
> . . . A lawyer is absolutely unfit as a businessman, he is to give advice if trouble arises and if you employ him, say six times a year, this can be considered the average maximum. . . . I hate to see a lawyer in our office, if I want him I go to his office and limit the conversation to the shortest possible period. Allowing a lawyer to be practically in daily touch with me, would certainly take 90 percent of my time which ought to be devoted to money making and not to discussing legal squabbles or legal phraseologies.[21]

Lawyers Should Practice Law . . . Not Public Relations

The worst mistake a good attorney can make is to step over the line, go beyond his professional training and experience, and become involved in strategy involving another professional discipline. Lawyers should practice law. Period. Lawyers should become no more involved in public relations or crisis communications than a public relations professional should tell attorneys what and what not to do. Few attorneys have ever taken a course or been trained in public relations, crisis communictions or public affairs. The most significant point is whether or not what is being done is legal.

"When it comes to separating legal advice from other kinds of business advice, attorneys need to be more careful than they have in the past," says James Lukaszewski. "In the legal arena, attorneys are held accountable for their legal advice. Public relations practitioners have to help attorneys understand where the line is between legal advice and business advice and remind the attorneys that when they cross that line there are potential liabilities for them and their organization."[22]

Don't Always Blame Lawyers

The final decision for what course of action is to be followed rests with the CEO, so total blame cannot be placed on attorneys for crisis situations. More often than not the communications professional and the lawyer will disagree on how aggressive to be, how much can be told to the media and the public, and when it can be told.

A lot depends on the culture of the institution. Nonprofit organizations tend to be more conservative because of a volunteer, outside board of directors. Most cannot respond quickly when a consensus of the board is needed in a crisis situation. The board's chairperson will probably have the final decision be that of the attorney rather than the public relations communicator.

In the military, rank may have its privilege, but it creates problems in crisis situations. A lieutenant or captain may be very reluctant to tell a general what should be done, and then the senior executive is not getting the best advice. Also flag officers may be overly cautious in taking advice from a junior officer, even if the flag officer has had professional training in the communications field.

The same is true at all levels of government. Attorneys are more likely to be more adamant in their demands about what can and cannot be said and will always opt for silence. Senior executives in government are more likely to heed the advice of their legal counsel than their public relations practitioner. However, the farther one travels from the "D.C. beltway," the greater the influence of the communicator. Governors and mayors, in a crisis situation, are more apt to take advice from their public relations counsel, press officer or pollster than their lawyer.

Keeping Communications Privileged

Lukaszewski cautions attorneys and public relations practitioners to be aware that the attorney-client privilege protects certain confidential communication between lawyer and client from discovery in civil, criminal or administrative proceedings. He says the work product doctrine protects from discovery (although not absolutely) materials prepared or collected by an attorney in preparation for or in anticipation of litigation.

"Under the Work Product Doctrine, public relations work that, in an attorney's opinion, should be protected from discovery must be 'prepared, developed, or collected at the direction of an attorney in preparation for or in anticipation of possible litigation,'" he continues. "The doctrine includes materials prepared by investigators, consultants, accountants, engineers, etc., who are 'acting under an attorney's direction.'" He notes that obviously you must consult an attorney for specific guidance and warns that waiver of the work product doctrine can occur easily. "Virtually any unauthorized disclosure of information to parties without specific direction or authorization by counsel waives protection," Lukaszewski says.[23]

A Collaborative Effort

Relationships between the legal and public relations counselors need to be more collaborative believes Kathy R. Fitzpatrick, associate professor at Southern Methodist University. "Both serve the institution and it can't be an oil-and-water team," she says.[24]

Fitzpatrick, who is an attorney with a bachelor's degree in journalism, sees a trend in public relations associated with litigation to force defendants to settle before going to court. "In a court of law you are concerned with a closed universe—the judge and jury; the rules of procedure and law, and a legal vocabulary," she says. "In the court of public opinion you have to deal with the general public and target audiences and constituents. Litigation public relations is not an attempt to interfere with due process, may be an attempt to influence resolution of conflict and should be a proactive effort to maintain the positive reputation of the client company."[25]

The plaintiff's typical strategy is to be aggressive with the following objectives: to counteract defendant's advantage (David v. Goliath) and gain public sympathy, to bring public attention to an issue, to force a favorable settlement, to invite class action participation, to embarrass and discredit the defendant and to pre-empt impending suits by another party.

Fitzpatrick says a defendant can have three typical strategies: defensive, with a "no comment" approach; responsive and end up scrambling; or proactive by defining the situation and managing the issues and process. She outlines the following as objectives for defendants: to preserve the client company's credibility; to counteract negative publicity resulting from public charges; to make the company's viewpoint heard; to ensure balanced media coverage; to diffuse a hostile environment; to aid public understanding of the charges and judicial process; and to take advantage of increased media attention and enhance the organization's visibility and reputation among important constituents.[26]

Spinning the Story

Richard Edelman, CEO of Edelman Public Relations Worldwide, was criticized by many in his public relations profession when he was quoted in *Esquire* saying: "In this era of exploding media technologies, there is no truth except the truth you create for yourself."[27]

"My professional objective has been and continues to be a bringing together, a reconciliation, of my client's interest with the public interest," says Harold Burson, chairman and founder of Burson-Marsteller. Robert Irvine, head of the Institute for Crisis Management, said Edelman's quote "doesn't fit into any crisis situation. If you don't have the facts or are not planning to reveal them, then you shouldn't be talking to the public. Edelman's quote is the kind of thing that can kill a PR person in a crisis situation."[28]

The final decision on what to do has to rest with an organization's CEO. The question the CEO should ask of his or her public relations counselor is "How will this impact the image, reputation, sales and future of our company?" Then the attorney should be asked "Is there anything illegal in what the public relations counselor is recommending?" The attorney's advice should only be in the area of whether or not what is being done is legal or not.

Many professionals say the more CEOs listen to their attorneys than their public relations counselors, the greater the chance an incident has of becoming a crisis. Vickee Jordan Adams, senior vice president of Ketchum Public Relations, says one of the most damaging aspects of Texaco's response to a discrimination suit was using outside attorneys as spokespersons. "A lawyer delivering company policy sounds likes a hired gun," she says. "Where was the diversity committee? Where were senior minority staffers? Where was the corporate communications statement about company policy?," she asks.[29]

Lawyers prompted *The Dallas Morning News* to sue Texas A&M University. The newspaper claimed the university's attorneys were not forthright in producing requested public documents, misled and possibly even lied to investigative reporters, and did everything possible to circumvent the Texas Open Records Act.[30] The newspaper agreed to dismiss its lawsuit when Texas A&M adopted new procedures for all open-records requests. The agreed-to order replaced the general counsel as the recipient of all open-records requests by naming the executive director of university relations, A&M's top public relations officer, as the new responsible party.

Boards of Directors Also Can Be Problems

A well-intentioned board of directors that wants to micromanage can also create a crisis. Just ask Anthony DeCristofaro and Sunshine Janda Overkamp who were at the United Way of America when the board vetoed a pre-emptive media approach. Both wanted to go public regarding the scandal that enveloped William Aramony, the organization's leader for more than 20 years. Over-kamp, then United Way's senior vice president and now vice president for membership, marketing and communications at the Council on Foundations in Washington, D.C., said the board and management knew of Aramony's improprieties months before the media. DeCristofaro, vice president of corporate communications, wanted to be open with the media. He said that when the public relations department became closed off to the media, reporters looked to others within the organization for details. "The building became a sieve of information," he said. "The result was an experience you can't buy and probably don't want to."[31]

Sometimes Even the News Media Won't Comment

Reporters, producers, publishers and others in the news media don't always set a good example for people they want to interview. Alan Hirsch, president of G+A Communications, New York, collects articles when the news media say "no comment" or avoid comment. Here are several from his collections:[32]

"*New York Post* editor Ken Chandler and *Post* publisher Martin Singerman didn't return repeated calls. Sports editor Greg Gallo said through a secretary that he was unavailable,"

—*Newsday*, December 13, 1996

"Both father (Arthur O. Sulzberger) and son (Arthur Sulzberger Jr.) couldn't be reached for comment."   —*The Wall Street Journal*

"An ABC spokeswoman, Eileen Murphy, said it was network policy not to say how many phone calls had been received. . . . She also said Mr. Brinkley could not be reached for comment yesterday because he was on the road."   —*The New York Times*

"A spokeswoman for Channel 2 said Carey (general manager) could not be reached for comment."   —*Newsday*

Yet sometimes media companies will suppress stories that might hurt them. Richard Bressler, Time Warner's chief financial officer, asked journalist Steven Brill to kill a profile of William Baer, a Federal Trade Commission official, scheduled to appear in a Brill newsletter. Brill was the founder of *Court TV*, *The American Lawyer* and several smaller legal and business publications owned by Time Warner. Peter Haje, Time Warner's general counsel, asked Brill to kill a story in *The American Lawyer* about the Scientology litigation because it criticized reporting in *Time* magazine. Another company attorney asked him not to cover a case on *Court TV* involving a Warner music company.[33]

His Honor the Mayor . . .

New York City Mayor Rudolph Giuliani loves to be in the public eye. He regularly appears on the television talk shows, including David Letterman. But the glitter is wearing off with the media because the Giuliani administration is making it difficult for reporters and civic groups to get information about the city. Newspapers and civic groups have filed suits and Freedom of Information Act requests. Several groups compared the difficulty and hard work for every document to what lawyers go through in the legal discovery process.[34]

The *New York Daily News* won a major victory when the New York State Supreme Court ruled that the Giuliani administration improperly refused requests from the newspaper for reports on wrongdoing by city officials. The state's highest court said that the law "provides for maximum access, not maximum withholding."[35] Now City Hall is giving *The Daily News* the silent treatment for writing about close lawyer friends of Giuliani who get lucrative lobbying contracts.[36]

Incidents included not giving *New York One TV* a copy of the mayor's daily schedule, or for two months not returning calls to Wayne Barrett of the *Village Voice* after he had written a story Giuliani and his aides considered negative. City Hall staffers proffered the excuse that they wouldn't have time to do their jobs if they spent time answering reporters' questions all day. Elizabeth Kolbert, columnist for *The New York Times*, says there is no need for the mayor to stonewall since "crime is down, the economy is good and Giuliani appears to be a shoo-in for re-election."[37]

No Response = Implied Consent

A "no comment" is better than lying to a reporter according to Frank Swoboda of *The Washington Post*. "Lie once and you are a liar forever," he says.[38] Former White House press secretary Mike McCurry said he got into trouble because he made a conscious choice not to ask President Clinton about his relationship with Monica Lewinsky. "I didn't seek the truth about Monica," he says. Yet he maintained his personal integrity by sticking to one important standard, "I cannot compound or further any lie."[39]

Never miss an opportunity to tell the public a positive story. However the attack may come—a newspaper editorial, a comment on a talk-radio show, an erroneous remark made by a television reporter or even a letter to the editor—look at the negative as being an opportunity not only to correct an error or misunderstanding but to say even more.

Texas A&M University missed a terrific opportunity to let the public know its positive side by not responding to an editorial of June 26, 1994, in *The Houston Post*. The editorial dominated the Sunday editorial column and included the Aggie logo in a two-inch square block in the middle of the text. Here is the editorial:

STAINS ON AGGIELAND
A&M must solve problems or suffer consequences

Several years of upsetting incidents and outside investigations show the Texas A&M University System—particularly its flagship institution at College Station—is in a lot of image-tarnishing trouble.

A&M regents had better give the College Station Campus and system administrations a thorough shakedown before long-term damage is done to the Aggies' reputation—and before faculty-recruiting is harmed.

Problems besieging A&M include:

• The National Collegiate Athletic Association had the university on probation last year for a basketball infraction. Then in January, the

NCAA put A&M's football program on probation for five years and barred it from bowls and television next year because of charges some players took a school booster's money without working for it.

• The proud Corps of Cadets was accused of harassing, abusing and assaulting female members—charges for which an investigating panel found evidence.

• The hiring of the outgoing national archivist as director of the George Bush President Library, to be located at A&M, became controversial.

• The board of regents upset A&M faculty members and may have harmed the university's potential for recruiting top-flight faculty by almost voting this year to stop granting faculty tenure, which means job security.

• The university was embarrassed when a chemistry professor took a $200,000 donation from a person subsequently convicted of securities fraud for a questionable research project: turning mercury into gold. New controls over donations were ordered.

In the past year, actions of the regents, A&M administrators and employees at various levels have been under constant investigation by the Texas Rangers, the Brazos County district attorney and grand jury, A&M internal auditors, the University Police Department and the state auditor.

The investigations started because of an anonymous letter to regents complaining about actions of regents Chairman Ross D. Margraves Jr. and alleged irregularities by others.

Since then, the A&M System has had two chancellors, the university itself has had three presidents, Chairman Margraves has resigned from the board of regents and the powerful university vice president of finance and operations, Robert Smith, has been demoted to a less-important job and subsequently he retired.

The probes have produced a series of startling news stories, including:

• Reports of freewheeling spending by and on the board of regents. In some cases on their families.

The Dallas Morning News reported the regents spent more than $1.6 million in mostly public funds in three years. That was more than was spent by regents at the University of Houston, Texas Tech University and the University of North Texas combined during the same period.

More than a third of the A&M regents' spending was for flying them, and sometimes their spouses and children, throughout Texas on university aircraft, *The News* said. The regents' expenditures hadn't been audited in about 10 years.

• Allegations that Margraves used his position for personal benefit, which he has vehemently denied, and took numerous trips paid for by a company under contract to operate the university bookstore.

• The indictment of two board of regents secretaries for falsifying government records to show alcohol purchases with public funds as food and soft-drink purchases.

• The March 31 firing of the system's chief legislative lobbyist after which he was charged with official misconduct for misuse of state funds. He pleaded no contest and was fined and ordered to make restitution of $1,486. Then he reported to investigators several allegedly illegal acts by other A&M employees.

• Within a week after A&M administrators adopted a new policy requiring employees to report suspected theft or fraud to internal auditors and the university police, four were charged with criminal misconduct.

A woman was accused of forging a doctor's note endorsing her application for 30 days' paid sick leave. Another woman was charged with using state equipment to make business cards and fliers for private business. A third was charged with misappropriating $2,336. And a man was accused of taking a university computer.

With all these charges of wrongdoing, one wonders how many others may turn up as the audits and investigations continue. And there are six other campuses in the A&M System that so far haven't been touched by the investigations.

The regents, system administrators, state auditors and the Legislature should see that all wrongdoing is rooted out as quickly as possible. They should check for similar improprieties at the other campuses too.

For the sake of protecting and enhancing A&M's growing prominence among American universities and preserving Texans' long-felt pride in their institution at College Station, the Aggies must get their act together.[40]

The author, then head of public relations at the university, prepared a response for the president and it was discussed at the Monday morning meeting of the president's executive cabinet. The new president, an Aggie, had only been in place several weeks. The only person at the table experienced in media relations, other than the author, recommended it be sent immediately. The others were too afraid to commit and preferred to be passive.

The author said a quick response was needed so the letter could be published in the newspaper the following Sunday. The vice president and editor of *The Houston Post*, Gerald Garcia, was a graduate and friend of Texas A&M. After more than 30 minutes of discussion, the president said more time was needed to review the response and asked the five members of his executive cabinet to review it as a committee and then respond.

The response incorporated the university's mission statement and goals and objectives. Statements made were part of the university relations strategic plan with key words based on market research done two years before. Here is the proposed response letter:

Letter-to-the-Editor response
to The Houston Post *June 26 editorial*

THE POSITIVE SIDE OF TEXAS A&M UNIVERSITY

Generally speaking, bad news is good news for the media. This was reaffirmed recently by CNN which noted that its ratings had dropped. Anyone who read your editorial Sunday could have come away with a terribly wrong perception of Texas A&M University.

It is true that the university has and still is going through some difficult times. I don't offer any excuses for what has happened, but this is not unlike what has happened at so many other great universities in this country. The incidents you reported have been embarrassing to all Aggies, but have not impacted or hurt the university in three areas so very important to us—teaching, research and public service.

Please let your readers have these facts:

1. More and more high school graduates want to come to Texas A&M University. This year we had more than 15,000 applicants for 6,100 freshman slots. We are now the third largest university in this country.

2. An increasing number of minority students want to be part of the Aggie tradition. This fall our admission of freshman African-Americans is up 14 percent and Hispanics 5 percent.

3. We continue to attract the brightest honor students as well. We expect a record number of National Merit Scholars to enroll at Texas A&M this fall. Two years ago we passed Yale and Princeton and last year we passed Stanford, to rank fourth in the U.S. in this category.

4. Among all public colleges and universities, Texas A&M has the highest retention rate and graduation rate in the state not only for all students, but minority students as well.

5. Both the private sector and federal government continue to look to our outstanding capabilities in research. Last year the National Science Foundation ranked us eighth in the country in research expenditures. With $322 million this year, we may be listed higher in the next rankings.

6. The negative incidents have not hurt the generosity of Aggies, friends and corporate America. Nearly three years ago we launched the largest capital campaign undertaken by a public university with a goal of $500 million. This month we expect to pass the $375 million mark, eight months ahead of schedule. Our endowment places us sixth among colleges and universities in the country.

7. Women athletes at Texas A&M receive larger scholarships on an average than their male counterparts, an average of $4,193 compared to $4,069 for men. The university now supports more women's teams than men's. We have achieved gender equity in our intercollegiate athletic program.

8. During the past four years, there has been a 23 percent increase in the number of student-athletes who received degrees within the six-year period stipulated by the NCAA. A five-fold increase was attained for Aggie African-American student athletes. The university has led the country the last three years in graduating former student athletes who take more than six years to graduate. Many of these are professional athletes. If these figures were included in the NCAA figures, A&M's graduation rate would increase to 70 percent for all student athletes.

9. Participation in our Corps of Cadets continues to increase and this year we expect the largest number of cadets in several years.

10. We lead all state colleges and universities with more than 500 of our students participating in study abroad programs.

11. In partnership with other universities, we operate six University Outreach Centers throughout the state and 80 percent of the students who participated in the first program for at risk students are now attending a college or university.

Texas A&M University truly is a world class institution. As soon as we can put these negatives behind us, we will be even stronger.

While I have been president now for less than a month, I can assure you that we Aggies already are getting our act together.

Ray M. Bowen—President, Texas A&M University

It was mid-August, nearly two months later, when the president's top advisers finally agreed on the response. By then it was old news and too late to ask the paper for space for a response. This was a decision made by a new CEO, not an attorney. The CEO listened to his overly cautious, reactive advisers, none of whom had training or experience in public relations, much less crisis communications. By not taking the advice of the communications counselor, Texas A&M gave "implied consent" to what was written in the editorial and missed a tremendous opportunity to tell a very positive story at a time it was very much needed.

Don't let your opportunities pass you by. Continue to educate the CEO and senior management on crisis management. The two previous presidents at Texas A&M required senior management to take annual training in crisis management and media relations. With various management changes, a majority of the president's executive cabinet, including the president, had not received any training in this area. However, ignorance is never an excuse when working to avoid a crisis.

Endnotes

1. William Shakespeare, *Henry VI*, part II, act IV, scene II.

2. Bergen Evans, *Dictionary of Quotations*, Delacourte Press, New York, N.Y., 1968, pg. 631.5.

3. James E. Lukaszewski with Douglas A. Cooper, "You're Courting Disaster . . . Without A Litigation Communications Strategy," *Executive Action*, The Lukaszewski Group, White Plains, New York, April/May/June 1992.

4. *Jack O'Dwyer's Newsletter*, November 13, 1995, pg. 7.

5. *PR Reporter*, January 4, 1999, pg. 6.

6. *Jack O'Dwyer's Newsletter*, November 13, 1995, pg. 7.

7. "Corning Makes List of Worst PR Gaffes," *Jack O'Dwyer's Newsletter*, January 15, 1998, pg. 2.

8. Judy A. Smith, "Learning from Crisis: In the Heat of the Battle," *The Public Relations Strategist*, pg. 33.

9. Steve Dunleavy, "Kathie Lee Should Try Locking Lips, To," *The New York Post*, May 16, 1997.

10. *Newsweek*, "The Last Word" by Meg Greenfield, December 2, 1996, pg. 100.

11. Tim Wheeler, environmental writer, *The Baltimore Sun*, during meeting of environmental communicators, Baltimore, Maryland, June 12, 1997.

12. Colin Powell, *My American Dream*, pg. 285.

13. Ibid.

14. "After The Fall, *Public Relations Tactics*, October 1998, pg. 1.

15. *Jack O'Dwyer's Newsletter*, January 24, 1996, pg. 3.

16. Stephen C. Rafe, APR, "How to Say 'No Comment,'" *Public Relations Tactics*, October 1998.

17. *Jack O'Dwyer's Newsletter*, June 18, 1997, pg. 8.

18. *Jack O'Dwyer's Newsletter*, September 11, 1996, pg. 7.

19. *Public Relations Tactics*, Public Relations Society of America, September 1977, pg. 6.

20. *The International Thesaurus of Quotations*, compiled by Rhoda Thomas Tripp, Thomas Y. Crowell Company, New York, 1970, pg. 525.34.

21. Letter from Sir Henri Deterding, co-founder and chairman, Royal Dutch/Shell, to Mr. Luykx in New York, September 13, 1916.

22. Letter of September 4, 1997 to the author from James E. Lukaszewski, The Lukaszewski Group Inc., White Plains, New York.

23. James E. Lukaszewski, "The Public Relations Practitioner and Privileged Communication—the Work Product Doctrine," *Executive Action*, The Lukaszewski Group, White Plains, New York, January/February/March 1998.

24. Kathy R. Fitzpatrick, "The Newest PR Discipline: Managing Legally Driven Issues," annual conference of the Public Relations Society of America, Nashville, Tennessee, November 11, 1997.

25. Ibid.

26. Ibid.

27. John Taylor, "Spin, You Sinners—The shame of shamelessness," *Esquire*, December 1996, pg. 74, and "PR Execs Concerned Over Esquire Article," *Jack O'Dywer's Newsletter*, December 4, 1996, pg. 1.

28. "PR Execs Concerned Over Esquire Article," *Jack O'Dywer's Newsletter*, December 4, 1996, pg. 1.

29. *Jack O'Dwyer's Newsletter*, April 2, 1997, pg. 7.

30. *Dallas Morning News v. Texas A&M University, et al*, Cause No. 93-04440, 345th District Court, Travis County, Texas, September 10, 1993.

31. *PR News*

32. *Jack O'Dwyer's Newsletter*, January 1, 1997, pg. 3.

33. Jonathan Alter, "The Dog That Barked," *Newsweek*, July 21, 1997, pg. 53.

34. *Jack O'Dwyer's Newsletter*, May 21, 1997, p. 7.

35. *Jack O'Dwyer's Newsletter*, May 28, 1997, pg. 1.

36. *Jack O'Dwyer's Newsletter*, June 18, 1997, pg. 8.

37. Ibid.

38. "Honesty Is Best Policy in a Crisis," *Jack O'Dwyer's Newsletter*, June 30, 1999, pg. 2.

39. "McCurry on McCurry," *Ragan's Media Relations Report*, June 1, 1999, pg. 3.

40. *The Houston Post*, June 26, 1994, editorial page.

CHAPTER FIVE

YOU CAN FIGHT BACK AND WIN

If you are wrongfully attacked, fight back. If your image or reputation has been unfairly damaged, you need to correct the story. Even worse, if sales and revenues have been impacted, a quick turn-around is critical. Sometimes you can be guilty by association and need to separate your institution from others. Be sure you pick your battles carefully and have planned the campaign.

When a lawsuit is filed against the media, it generally is for libel. Libel law places a heavy burden of proof on the plaintiff—the company that believes it has been wronged—which makes it difficult for the prosecutor. Also many jury awards are reduced or thrown out on appeal.

The Associated Press defines libel as "injury to reputation." Words, pictures or cartoons that expose a person to public hatred, shame, disgrace or ridicule, or induce an ill opinion of a person are libelous.[1] The state of California has a more detailed definition: "Libel is a false and unprivileged publication by writing, printing, picture, effigy, or other fixed representation to the eye, which exposes any person to hatred, contempt, ridicule, or obloquy, or which causes him to be shunned or avoided, or which has a tendency to injure him in his occupation."[2]

Black's Law Dictionary defines libel in its most general sense as "any publication that is injurious to the reputation of another." This can include defamation expressed by print, writing, pictures or signs. A number of cases are cited further elaborating on the definition of libel. States can define defamation of a private person so long as they do not impose liability without fault.[3]

The case of *N.Y. Times v. Sullivan* is cited because under the First Amendment, there can be no presumption of malice or bad faith consistent with freedom of the press if the plaintiff is a public figure. Malice must prove that the defendant published material either knowing it to be false or recklessly without regard as to whether it is true or false. Prior to this decision in 1964, which went to the U.S. Supreme Court, media comment on the conduct of public officials or public figures was free from liability for libel only in certain limited circumstances, usually difficult to prove during a trial. Facts had to be substantially true. This shifted the responsibility to the plaintiff to prove actual malice and that the material was false.[4]

Ethics and Libel

The first line in the Code of Ethics of the Society of Professional Journalists is: "The Society of Professional Journalists believes the duty of journalists is to serve the truth." Section III, Ethics, says: "Journalists must be free of obligation to any interest other than the public's right to know the truth." And under Section IV, Accuracy and Objectivity, paragraph 1 is: "Truth is our ultimate goal," and paragraph 3, "There is no excuse for inaccuracies or lack of thoroughness."

Pointing out that libel is injury to reputation, the Associated Press in Chapter 2 of its Libel Manual writes, "There is only one complete and unconditional defense to a civil action for libel: that the facts stated are PROVABLY TRUE. (Note well that word, PROVABLY.) Quoting someone correctly is not enough. The important thing is to be able to satisfy a jury that the libelous statement is substantially correct."[5]

When a reporter considers that the information in hand is *probably* true and not *provably* true, there is a problem. This is what leads to litigation. A 52-page report by the Libel Defense Resource Center found that between July 1994 and June 1996, on-appeal defendants were successful in reversing the verdicts in nearly half of the cases and also succeeded in having the awards reduced. The study showed that 12 of 25 appeals were reversed outright. It also confirmed that libel defendants were far more successful when appealing cases involving public plaintiffs than in appeals involving private plaintiffs. This compared to 43 percent, or 64 of 149 cases, where liability was reversed from plaintiffs' verdicts between 1984 and 1986.[6]

However, companies and individuals have sued the media and won. While the size of punitive damage awards is increasing, the number of media cases going to trial is low. There were fewer trials in 1996 than the average per year in the 1980s.[7] General Motors took on NBC because it felt that the network's *Dateline NBC* news magazine program used misinformation and rigged tests to show that a line of its pickup trucks were unsafe. In its filmed "tests," NBC used explosives to dramatize the supposed unsafety of GM trucks.[8]

Supermarket chain Food Lion was awarded $5.5 million from Capital Cities-ABC when a jury found the methods *PrimeTime Live* used to gather the story were the same as fraud, trespassing and breach of loyalty.[9] The amount was subsequently reduced to $315,000.[10]

A small Houston firm that sold mortgage-backed securities, MMAR Group Inc., went out of business shortly after *The Wall Street Journal* depicted it as a freewheeling operation that overpriced its product and deceived the Louisiana pension fund, its top customer.[11] A seven-person federal jury found that the October 21, 1993, story by reporter Laura Jereski libeled the firm and awarded a record $222.7 million in damages, nearly four times the next biggest libel award.[12] Of this amount, $200.02 million was for punitive damages.[13]

Nearly four years later, Houston federal Judge Ewing Werlein Jr. eliminated $200 million in punitive damages but let stand actual damages of $22.7 million against Dow Jones and $20,000 in punitive damages personally against writer Jereski. If affirmed by the courts, this would be the largest ever allowed to stand. Floyd

Abrams, an attorney who has represented major news organizations in First Amendment legal battles, said he was not surprised that the court reduced the amount. "Had this judgment remained in effect, it would have chilled all reporting by all newspapers," he said.[14]

Former U.S. Senator Alan K. Simpson (R-Wyo.), who prides himself on having a reputation of being a fierce media critic, says: "America's media elite have become lazy, complacent, sloppy, self-serving, self-aggrandizing, cynical and arrogant beyond measure. We live in a society in which journalistic ethics—commitment to fairness, respect for privacy, even simple human compassion—all seem to take a seat way in the back of the bus."[15]

Simpson said in high school journalism he was taught about the five Ws—who, what, where, when and why. He says today "maybe we need to use the five Cs because the professional today is more interested in conflict, controversy and cleverness than it is in clarity." He writes that the fifth C is for coiffure and how television newspeople must always have their hair carefully coiffed.

Sometimes an apology from the media with some financial settlement will be a victory for a company. Philip Morris sued ABC News for $10 million. It was settled with an apology and payment of $15 million for legal work. In its letter of apology, ABC continued to maintain that the "principal focus of the reports was whether cigarette companies use the reconstituted tobacco process to control the levels of nicotine in cigarettes in order to keep people smoking." The ABC statement also noted that Philip Morris "categorically denies it does so."[16]

Jane Kirtley, head of the Reporters Committee for Freedom of the Press, told *USA Today* that the settlement "sends the message that corporate America can use a libel suit to discourage investigative reporting." In contrast, Richard Funess, president of Manning, Selvage & Lee/Americas, said, "The networks must look long and hard at this incident . . . tabloid journalism has crept into TV . . . the networks must be more careful in their quest for ratings."[17]

A family-owned California dairy, after being talked out of suing *The Los Angeles Times*, took on a county and state bureaucracy by mounting an aggressive, proactive marketing communications campaign and ended up getting media support and winning back its customers.

Food Lion—Not Libel But Investigative Methods

The issue between Food Lion and ABC was not over libel, but over the way *PrimeTime Live* obtained the story that it aired November 5, 1992. The accuracy of the story was not an issue in the litigation. The report, narrated by Diane Sawyer, accused the supermarket chain of selling rat-gnawed cheese, expired meat and old ham and fish washed in bleach to stop the smell. Food Lion asked for $52.5 million to $1.9 billion in punitive damages. The jury deliberated six days before agreeing on $5.5 million to the company and $47,750 to its employees. The jury foreman said, "The media has a right to bring the news, but they have to watch what they do."[18]

PrimeTime Live producers Lynn Dale and Susan Barnett were hired as food handlers and infiltrated several stores to expose alleged wrongdoings by using tiny cameras and microphones hidden in their clothes and wigs. The show interviewed seven current and former Food Lion employees who talked about unsanitary handling practices. The company said the story was deceptive and the broadcast was staged and misleadingly edited.[19]

The court reduced the award to $315,000 and refused Food Lion's request that ABC pays its legal fees. ABC attorney Nat Lewin said large penalties should not be imposed on the media for being deceptive to get a story unless it results in bodily harm. "Making false representations in order to get into position to see, report or photograph what has been concealed has been an integral part of investigative journalism for centuries," Lewin said.[20] Attorneys for the supermarket chain argued that what ABC wanted was "tantamount to a license to cheat, lie and trespass with blanket protection of the U.S. Constitution."[21]

First Amendment attorneys, professional associations representing media interests and television executives expressed concern over the decision. Roone Arledge, president of ABC News, noted that the punitive damages were 4,000 times the amount of compensatory damages. "If large corporations were allowed to stop hard-hitting investigative journalism, the American people would be the losers," he said.[22] Andrew Heyward, president of CBS News, said, "There is a public disenchantment to a degree with exploitative journalism and some of the backlash has spilled onto legitimate investigative reports."[23]

Speaking to a group at the National Press Club in Washington, D.C., ABC's Sam Donaldson said he was still using hidden cameras for a story. He added that ABC lost the case because the jury found the network trespassed when its employees lied to get Food Lion jobs.[24]

Sometimes You Should Not Fight Back

Donald Trump wanted the New Jersey Casino Reinvestment Development Authority to condemn several mom-and-pop properties across the street from Trump Plaza Hotel & Casino in Atlantic City. After three and a half years of eminent-domain proceedings against Sabatini's Restaurant, a pasta parlor run since 1968 by 64-year-old Clare Sabatini and her husband, a neighboring cash-for-gold store owned by Josef Banin and a three-story former boarding house owned by elderly widow Vera Coking, "The Donald" expanded his Trump Plaza by building around the three properties.[25]

When "Doonesbury" cartoonist Garry Trudeau heard of the situation, he made it a national story by drawing a week's worth of comic strips in February 1997 lampooning Trump. Not amused, Trump called Trudeau "a third-rate talent," which prompted more negative publicity. James Kennedy, executive director of the state development agency, did not appreciate the unfavorable publicity and backed off from plans to seize the properties.[26]

Big Mac vs. British Veggies

McDonald's should have thought twice before spending $16.4 million to win $98,198 in damages against two British vegetarian activists in the longest running court battle in the United Kingdom.[27] The 314-day trial in 1994 had 28 pretrial hearings, 130 witnesses,

40,000 pages of documents and an 800-page ruling from Justice Roger Bell. Former mailman Dave Morris and bar worker Helen Steel had called McDonald's "a multinational corporate menace that abused animals, workers and the environment, and promoted an unhealthy diet." The activists claimed victory because they brought to public and media attention the company's business practices. Justice Bell said McDonald's was ""culpably responsible for animal cruelty and ran ad campaigns that exploit impressionable children."[28]

Morris and Steel distributed pamphlets in the late 1980s entitled "What's wrong with McDonald's? Everything they don't want you to know." Paul Preston, McDonald's top executive in the United Kingdom, said he was "broadly satisfied," but puzzled by the judge's comments on animal cruelty. "My responsibility is to protect our reputation and that's exactly what we've done."[29] The court found that some of the charges, such as "mistreatment of chickens," were true, but that the company does not destroy rain forests, poison its customers or discriminate against employees.[30]

In an editorial, *The Washington Post* wrote, "If slanging McDonald's in print were grounds for an action of libel in this country, we can think of whole academic disciplines that would be forced to shut up shop, not to mention nutritionists and those folks who keep describing all your favorite foods as containing 'the equivalent of six Big Macs' in calories or fat." The editorial noted a great difference between American free-speech guarantees and the kind of constraints inherent in British libel law, in which corporations can sue individuals for defamation. Believing a statement to be true is no defense against libel if a judge rules it was false.[31]

The New York Times wrote, "McLibel a nadir in McDonald's PR history" and a "Pyrrhic victory."[32] "The PR equivalent of food poisoning," was what *USA Today* wrote.[33] "The family-friendly multinational that squashes free speech," was how *Newsweek* described the results.[34]

McDonald's was particularly castigated by the media in the United Kingdom. The *Financial Times* accused the company of failing to understand British culture. "McDonald's is guilty of completely misunderstanding one time-honoured British tradition—an acceptance of harmless eccentrics. Steel and Morris, with their oddball ideas, are much more a part of Britain than McDonald's. Their successors will still be ranting and raving on Britain's high streets long after the last McDonald's Golden Arch has been dismantled."[35]

Following the trial, the activists immediately began mass distribution of the same leaflets but in even greater numbers. While thousands of publications are being distributed around Britain, the information also has been placed on the Internet.[36]

Texas Cattlemen Have a Beef With Oprah

Should the Texas cattlemen have sued the most popular woman on television to recoup losses of more than $12 million plus unspecified damages? Not only was there no win in the court of law, there was a big loss in the court of public opinion. Everything negative about beef was talked about again and again during the trial, which became an international event for Amarillo, a city of 150,000 in the northwest Texas Panhandle.

The trial was the first test of the "food disparagement" or so-called veggie libel laws that have been enacted in 13 states. The laws, which grew out of the 1989 scare involving the use of the chemical Alar in apple orchards, make it possible for farmers and ranchers to win damages from consumer groups, health advocates, journalists or anyone who spreads false information about the safety of a good product. Critics predict the U.S. Supreme Court will rule the laws unconstitutional violations of free speech.[37]

David J. Bederman, a law professor at Emory University in Atlanta, notes that had these laws been on the books years ago, they could have been used to punish the people who first warned about the dangers of DDT and tobacco.[38] One has to ask if growers could have sued George Bush, when he was president, for his comments about broccoli.

What created all of the controversy was the *Oprah* show that aired on April 16, 1996. This was shortly after British officials announced that mad cow disease had been linked to the deaths of 20 people in Britain who ate infected beef. Appearing on the show was Howard Lyman, a Montana cattle rancher turned vegetarian activist who said that feeding animal parts to cattle was a common practice that could spread mad cow disease, or bovine spongiform encephalopathy (BSE), to humans in the United States. Mad cow disease, which destroys the brain, and forced the slaughter of 1.5 million cows in Britain.[39]

Winfrey also had as a show guest Gary Weber, an animal expert from the National Cattlemen's Beef Association. Lyman compared the disease to AIDS. After Lyman supplied more details, Winfrey said: "Now doesn't that concern you all a little bit right here, hearing that?" The studio audience responded with cheers. "It has stopped me cold from eating another hamburger," she continued. "I'm stopped."[40]

After the broadcast aired, cattle prices, which had already been falling, dropped to near 10-year lows. Ninety minutes after the show went on the air in Chicago, cattle prices had fallen $1.50 a pound, testified Tim Brennan, a futures trader and member of the Chicago Mercantile Exchange. Brennan said a colleague tipped him to the show's topic moments after it went on the air and he hastily placed a "sell" order. Winfrey's attorney suggested it was the traders themselves who caused the biggest cattle market plunge in a decade and not his client.[41]

Hollywood descended on Amarillo as Winfrey moved the production of her show there during the trial. Patrick Swayze, Clint Black and his wife, Lisa Hartman, all Texans, were among her first guests. Bumper stickers expressed the emotion of the townspeople: "Amarillo Loves Oprah" and "The Only Mad Cow in America Is Oprah." As popular as her show is, only 7 of 58 people in the jury pool had ever seen it.[42]

A Rat in a Happy Meal?

Sellers of food and beverage products are particularly vulnerable to accidents as well as fraud. By its quick response, Pepsi refuted claims by people who said they found syringes in their Pepsi can. So when Michael Zanakis, a 43-year-old neurophysiologist from New Jersey, demanded $5 million from McDonald's to keep quiet about supposedly finding a fried rat's tail in his son's Happy Meal, the company went to the FBI. The FBI discovered that Coca-Cola wrote a $4,600 check to Zanakis in 1993 when he said he had swallowed "greasy particles" from a can of Coke. Zanakis could face 145 years in jail.[43]

Many food companies have risk managers who investigate each incident to determine the legitimacy of the complaint. But all too often businesses settle with an accuser rather than fight the charges even if they know they are right. They are concerned about the threat of negative publicity rather than prepared to take advantage of the incident to tell the positive things the company is doing to prevent such incidents from happening in the first place.

StarKist and Environmentalists, Charlie and Flipper

For years environmentalists targeted the tuna industry and especially StarKist, the world's largest and only major U.S. tuna canner, for fishing practices that caused the accidental death of dolphins. Demonstrations were staged for the media against fishermen in communities where the company had plants. As the industry leader, StarKist was a natural and convenient target.

While consumers showed concern over dolphins, it was unclear how they would react to possible price increases with a change in policy to protect dolphins while fishing for tuna. The company, a subsidiary of H.J. Heinz, was concerned about opposition from fishermen. It discussed the pros and cons with its public relations counsel, Edelman Public Relations Worldwide, and decided, rather than fight, to take the lead and be the first in the industry to announce a "dolphin safe" policy. Executives from Heinz and StarKist met with environmental and government leaders to gain their support prior to a Washington, D.C., press conference. StarKist employees were told the news prior to the press conference. The internal message was tailored to the sensitivities of employees at plant locations most affected by a policy change.

Media and public reaction was positive. It was the lead story on the ABC network evening news and reported in *Time*, *Newsweek* and *U.S. News & World Report*. As sales increased, the campaign continued to leverage StarKist's leadership with environmental programs for children including an in-school program and the "StarKist StarKids" environmental award.[44]

StarKist anticipated problems and consumer reaction. It took its position knowing it might be unpopular with fisherman and in communities where its packing and processing plants were located. This proactive approach prevented a future crisis that threatened its reputation. The concept of having Charlie the Tuna and Flipper swim together in an ad campaign led to improved business and overwhelming consumer support. The campaign was honored with a Silver Anvil by the Public Relations Society of America.

Public Figures Are Especially Vulnerable

A March 2, 1976, story in the *National Enquirer* brought action from Carol Burnett. The publication wrote: "In a Washington restaurant, a boisterous Carol Burnett had a loud argument with another diner, Henry Kissinger. Then she traipsed around the place offering everyone a bite of her dessert. But Carol really raised eyebrows when she accidentally knocked a glass of wine over one diner and starting giggling instead of apologizing. The guy wasn't amused and 'accidentally' spilled a glass of water over Carol's dress."[45]

Burnett's attorneys demanded a correction or retraction. On April 6, the newspaper published this: "An item in this column on March 2 erroneously reported that Carol Burnett had an argument with Henry Kissinger at a Washington restaurant and became boisterous, disturbing other guests. We understand these events did not occur and we are sorry for any embarrassment our report may have caused Miss Burnett."[46]

On April 8 she filed suit and what came out in the trial was that Burnett, her television producer husband, Joe Hamilton, and three friends were dining in Washington where she was invited to perform at the White House. During dinner she had two or three glasses of wine but was not inebriated. She talked with a young couple at a table next to hers. When curiosity was expressed about her dessert, apparently a chocolate souffle, she gave the couple small amounts of it on plates they had passed to her table. A family behind her table offered to exchange some of their baked Alaska for a portion of the souffle, and they as well were accommodated. As she and her party were leaving the restaurant, a friend introduced her to Henry Kissinger. After a brief conversation, they left the restaurant. There was no "row" or argument. The conversation was not loud or boisterous. Burnett never "traipsed around the place offering everyone a bite of her dessert," nor was any wine or water spilled and no "giggling instead of apologizing."[47]

In 1981 a jury awarded Burnett $1.6 million with $300,000 in compensatory damages and $1.3 million in punitive damages. The judge reduced the judgment to $50,000 compensatory and $750,000 punitive for a total of $800,000. Following appeal by the *National Enquirer,* an appeals court reduced the punitive damages to $150,000 for a total settlement of $200,000. The court held that the $750,000 award was not justified since it constituted approximately 35 percent of the defendant's net worth and nearly 50 percent of her net income for the period under consideration. With regard to compensatory damages, the court held that the item at issue was libelous on its face, concluding its message carried the implication that Miss Burnett's actions were the result of some objectionable state of inebriation. As a result she was required to show the court only those general damages arising from her loss of reputation, shame, mortification and injured feelings.[48]

Some People Just Don't Get Any Respect

Rodney Dangerfield took his case all the way to the U.S. Supreme Court, which let stand a lower court decision that left him with a $45,000 libel judgment from the *Star*. In 1995 a federal court ruled that the tabloid newspaper's 1990 piece branding Dangerfield a pot-toking, coke-sniffing drunkard was false, but limited the award, saying that there was no evidence the story had caused him any emotional distress or damaged his reputation. The trial judge refused to impose punitive damages because the owners of the *Star* were losing money and its parent company was not found liable for the libel.[49]

A well-publicized and historic case was when General William C. Westmoreland, commander of U.S. forces in Vietnam from 1964 to 1968, sued CBS, alleging inaccuracies in a CBS News Special Report about Vietnam. The reputation and integrity of CBS News were in jeopardy. In May 1982, CBS was looking forward to telling good news to executives from its 200 affiliated stations who gathered for a three-day gala in San Francisco. CBS had just regained its No. 1 place in entertainment ratings and the *Evening News* also was in first place. Then on May 24, *TV Guide* crashed the party with a cover story headlined: ANATOMY OF A SMEAR: HOW CBS BROKE THE RULES AND 'GOT' GEN. WESTMORELAND. The cover had photographs of Mike Wallace and the general along with George Crile, the *CBS Reports* producer who was responsible for the broadcast of *The Uncounted Enemy*. The story was written by two of the magazine's best reporters on the television beat, Sally Bedell Smith and Don Kowet. [50]

TV Guide alleged all manner of journalistic crimes and misdemeanors in Crile's production of the documentary that featured Wallace. CBS made the case that while in Vietnam, Westmoreland had bowed to political pressure to show progress in the war and that he had led a conspiracy to misrepresent the size and strength of enemy forces to Congress, President Lyndon B. Johnson and the American people. Several days after the broadcast, the general and supporters held a press conference claiming CBS had taken an entirely appropriate discussion in the American intelligence community and blown it into an "exposé" of military deception. [51]

CBS president Gordon Van Sauter named Burton "Bud" Benjamin, a CBS producer and executive, to head up the unprecedented inquiry. Unlike a review by attorneys geared to a possible legal defense of the show, Benjamin's mandate was to investigate the broadcast with an independent, objective eye. In July he issued his 59-page "white paper" noting 11 major flaws, including Crile's "coddling sympathetic witnesses," choosing to interview mostly people who supported the program's overall conclusions and the broadcast's failure to prove there had been a conspiracy. He also noted that eight supporters of the producer's premise were interviewed by only one supporter of Westmoreland and he for only 21 seconds. The report, which found CBS News' standards had been violated, was not for public release. Instead, Van Sauter said "CBS News stands by this broadcast." He also added that the broadcast would have been better if Crile had sought out more people to interview who disagreed with the broadcast's premise.[52]

In September, Westmoreland filed a $120 million libel suit against CBS. When Judge Pierre Leval ruled that CBS had to give the Benjamin report to the general, the flaws of the broadcast got a new round of treatment in the media.[53] After 18 weeks in court, Westmoreland and CBS reached an agreement: no money and virtually the same statement from the network that the general could have had a year earlier. For nearly three years the credibility and integrity of CBS was attacked. While CBS celebrated the settlement as a victory, it risked the loss in public confidence.[54] There are some people who believe Westmoreland was vindicated and he had been wronged by the network. Both Westmoreland and CBS were right to take their cases to the public and fight back.

To Pasteurize or Not to Pasteurize

In the late 1970s, Alta-Dena Dairy, a family-owned company, was the country's largest producer of raw certified milk and raw certified milk products. Raw certified milk is bottled under the strictest sanitary conditions because it is not pasteurized. Harold J. J. Stueve, managing director of the dairy, believed strongly that people should have the most healthful and nutritious milk possible–the way it comes from the cow without any processing or preservatives.[55]

The dairy's milking herd and production facilities were located in the City of Industry in Los Angeles County. The cows were strictly supervised by a veterinarian and fed a diet that included vitamins and raw carrots. Before the cows were milked twice a day, they were showered from above and below and their udders hosed off and wiped with a towel used only once. The cows were the epitome of bovine hygiene.

Regardless what the Stueve family did, they could not please the bureaucrats at the Los Angeles County Health Department who believed all milk should be pasteurized. It became a crisis whenever the health department ordered a recall of raw certified milk because of suspected salmonella. Salmonella is a bacteria that can cause vomiting, upset stomach and sickness, especially in children and senior citizens. The same bacteria can be present in poultry and eggs and can be spread by food handlers using the same knives and cutting boards for poultry and salads.

When Alta-Dena sent random product samples to the health department's laboratory for testing, it also sent duplicate samples to an independent laboratory contracted by the dairy. Any time a case of food poisoning in Los Angeles County was reported, the health department immediately suspected Alta-Dena's raw certified milk. In a number of cases the salmonella was traced back to improper food handling.

After several milk recalls in two months, the dairy decided it had to fight back. Sales of all products were dropping—even its pasteurized milk, cottage cheese, ice cream, yoghurt, butter and cheese. Home deliveries were being canceled. Major chains were no longer selling Alta-Dena products. And the health department was pressing for mandatory pasteurization of all milk.

Harold Stueve hired ICPR for public relations help. At first he wanted to sue *The Los Angeles Times* for libel because of the stories it had published about the recalls. Instead, he took the advice of his new public relations counsel and his attorney and decided to fight back with an aggressive, proactive marketing public relations campaign.

Starting From Scratch

The dairy never had professional help with marketing communications and had produced most brochures, pamphlets and other materials in-house. An excellent relationship had been established with health food stores not only throughout Southern California, but throughout the state and even the United States where many of its products were shipped and sold.

After an immersion course in raw certified milk, the dairy industry, the conflict with the health department and the history of the dairy itself, the agency's account team began its work:

1. Harold Stueve became the spokesperson for the dairy. Media calls were referred to him with ICPR and the attorney involved. He was quickly given media training that continued as "on-the-job training" with a critique after every interview.

2. With no crisis plan in place, the agency began analyzing every possible way to counter the problem, contain it and reposition the dairy. This was a continuous effort, looking to solve immediate problems and determine what needed to be done for the long term.

3. Newspaper clipping and broadcast monitoring services were retained. There was an immediate response with a letter to the editor anytime a story was published that was not 100 percent factually correct.

4. A number of fact sheets were prepared that included the history of the dairy, the Stueve family, raw certified milk, other products, health and sanitation standards and production comparisons between raw certified and pasteurized milk, reference-documented medical studies on the health benefits of raw certified milk, and information on salmonella and its sources.

5. A commercial photographer was hired to take stock photographs of the dairy, its cows, its production process and the principals.

6. The information kits and other background information were sent to media throughout Southern California. For the first time, assignment editors, city editors, business editors, reporters, medical writers, food editors and columnists had source information on everything they needed to know about Alta-Dena Dairy and its products.

7. Television assignment editors and newspaper reporters were

notified of the agency's new assignment and encouraged to call with any requests. A trust had to be established to convince the media that information from the dairy was credible and truthful. The media were told Harold Stueve would be available at any time. Reporters were encouraged to come to the dairy for personally guided tours by him and see first hand its spotless, sanitary conditions.

8. Talk show hosts were contacted to have Stueve as a guest. The agency encouraged each show to also give equal time to the health department, who would not provide a spokesperson.

9. Sports was selected as the medium to give the dairy the most impact in the shortest possible time. A radio and television package was purchased for both the Los Angeles Lakers professional basketball team and the Los Angeles Kings professional ice hockey team. Special promotional nights were part of the package. The advertising copy line was "The Dairy That Cares About Your Health." The public was told that raw certified milk was a nutritious food with all of its original vitamins and proteins, without any preservatives or additives.

10. The agency's creative team developed a number of different story lines for news releases. An educational effort was made to let the public know about the various sources of salmonella and how easily the bacteria could be spread at home and at foodservice establishments, and how important it was to thoroughly wash one's hands after handling poultry. Pitch letters were sent to appropriate media and followed up with personal calls.

11. Arrangements were made with the Century City Shopping Center, the largest complex of its kind in the Los Angeles area, for Alta-Dena to construct a special promotional display. The theme was "A Year in the Life of a Cow." Throughout the public mall area display stations featured

how much hay a cow would consume, how many cartons of milk a cow would produce, a "petting zoo pen," free sample stations with frozen yoghurt and selected other products, and hourly cow-milking contests. Literature was produced and distributed and the story of raw certified milk told to the thousands of people who passed through the exhibit during the week.

Media Trust Established

As the agency encouraged reporters to visit the dairy and see for themselves, the health department issued more product recalls. The county health department would issue its news release at 5 P.M. on a Friday or the eve of a holiday, especially if a recall was involved. The releases did not have home telephone numbers so the bureaucrats did not have to respond to media questions. In spite of business and social commitments, Stueve, the dairy and the agency did everything possible to accommodate the media.

The run-and-hide policy of the health department worked to the advantage of the dairy. A critical turning point in relationships with the media came when not one just broadcast journalist, but reporters from several stations, began giving the agency a heads-up: "We just got word from the health department that they will be issuing a news release at 5 P.M. today." ICPR alerted its client and called the media back to let them know when and where they could reach Stueve for comment. The media knew the dairy had absolutely nothing to hide and began to question the veracity of the health department.

The Continuing Effort

A close working relationship was established between the agency and Alta-Dena's outside legal counsel, William Dannemeyer, who later represented Orange County in the U.S. House of Representatives. On Dannemeyer's recommendation, the dairy began sending product samples to a second independent testing laboratory and one that did work for the state health department. In time, the county health department issued a recall. At that time both laboratories testing for the dairy were contacted. There was no trace of salmonella in samples at either lab. This was strong ammunition for the dairy to use in suggesting that the health department had contaminated its own samples, had erred in its findings or had a bias against Alta-Dena, because two independent labs, one doing work for the state, found otherwise. It was a tremendous victory for the dairy.

A few weeks later the chairman of the California Legislature's Agriculture Committee publicly apologized to the Stueve family and Alta-Dena Dairy for the way it had been "maligned" by "well-meaning but overzealous bureaucrats" who had acted beyond their responsibility. The chairman also asked the Los Angeles County Health Department to apologize. It did not.

The marketing communications effort was expanded, including building public traffic at the dairy with scheduled tours for school and groups as well as individuals. The sports promotions with the Lakers and Kings were among the 10 most successful ever done at The Forum. Within a year the dairy had re-established its market position and then it began to grow. In less than 10 years the dairy's sales had quintupled.

Media Question Being Held Accountable

The media is under scrutiny. There are a number of organizations that follow the various types of stories written for publication and taped for broadcast. One such group is The National News Council, which was established in 1973 as a place where the public could turn when it felt a news story was inaccurate or unfair and to hold the press accountable and responsible. While Mike Wallace of 60 Minutes says journalists must understand the consequences of the lack of accountability, his executive producer, Don Hewitt, disagreed. Speaking at the 19th annual Frank E. Gannett Lecture in New York, on December 4, 1996, Wallace said that news organizations should face "the insensitivity and volume of criticism that's coming from within the press itself" and that a news council "could strike a blow for a better public understanding in a time of skepticism about us of who we are and what it is we do." Hewitt says such new organizations are vulnerable to manipulation by special-interest groups. "While legitimate news organizations may make mistakes, and we all do, we do not have axes to grind." He cited as examples groups including Accuracy in Media, right-to-life and pro-choice organizations, Mothers Against Drunk Driving, Gay and Lesbian Coalition and the Tobacco Institute.[56]

In one of the most litigious societies in the world, such watchdogs or councils, supported by both the media and consumers, could be a refreshing alternative to the courtroom.

Endnotes

1. *The Associated Press Stylebook and Libel Manual*, Norm Goldstein, editor, Addison-Wesley Publishing Company, Reading, Mass., 1994, pg. 269.
2. Civil Code, State of California, § 45.
3. *Black's Law Dictionary*, sixth edition, West Publishing Co., St. Paul, Minn., 1990, pg. 915.
4. Ibid. *New York Times v. Sullivan*, 376 U.S. 254, 84 S.Ct. 710, 11 L.Ed.2d 686 (1964).
5. *The Associated Press Stylebook and Libel Manual, op cit.*, pg. 283.
6. Libel Defense Resource Center, news release, August 21, 1996, New York.
7. Libel Defense Resource Center, *op cit.*
8. *Jack O'Dwyer's Newsletter*, August 30, 1995, pg. 1.
9. Associated Press by Estes Thompson in *The Philadelphia Inquirer*, January 23, 1997, pg. 2.
10. Associated Press, "ABC: Award slashed in Food Lion case," *The Philadelphia Inquirer*, August 30, 1997, pg. A3.
11. *Time*, "More Bad News for Dow Jones," March 31, 1997, pg. 64.
12. *Newsweek*, "One Heck of a Whupping," by Larry Reibstein, March 31, 1997, pg. 54.
13. Libel Defense Resource Center, *op cit.*
14. Rick Gladstone, Associated Press, "Judge overrules $200 million punitive award in libel case," *The Philadelphia Inquirer*, May 24, 1997, pg. 6.
15. Alan K. Simpson, *Right in the Old Gazoo*, William Morrow and Company, Inc., New York, 1997, pgs. 6-8.
16. *Jack O'Dwyer's Newsletter*, August 30, 1995, pg. 7.
17. Ibid.
18. Associated Press story by Estes Thompson, *op cit.*
19. *Time*, Ginia Bellafante, "Hide and Go Sue," January 13, 1997, pg.

20. Associated Press, "ABC: Award slashes in Food Lion case," *The Philadelphia Inquirer*, August 30, 1997, pg. A3.

21. Ibid.

22. Associated Press by Estes Thompson, *op cit.*

23. *Time*, Ginia Bellafante, *op cit.*

24. "ABC-TV Still Using Hidden Cameras," *Jack O'Dwyer's Newsletter*, May 21, 1997, pg. 1.

25. John Curran, Associated Press, "Panel won't seize land for Trump," *The Philadelphia Inquirer*, January 24, 1998, pg. B1.

26. Ibid.

27. "McLibel," *U.S. News & World Report*, June 30, 1997, pg. 48.

28. Dirk Beveridge, Associated Press, "McDonald's purees British vegetarians in a libel case, but is vilified," *The Philadelphia Inquirer*, June 20, 1997, pg. A11.

29. Ibid.

30. "McDonald's Wins Suit; Leaflets Continue," *Jack O'Dwyer's Newsletter*, June 25, 1997, pg. 7.

31. "Libel and the Big Burger," editorial, *The Washington Post*, June 23, 1997, pg. A18.

32. *The New York Times*, editorial page, June 20, 1997.

33. *USA Today*, June 20, 1997.

34. "Pyrrhic McVictory," *Newsweek*, June 30, 1997.

35. *Jack O'Dwyer's Newsletter*, July 9, 1997, pg. 7.

36. Dirk Beveridge, Associated Press, *op cit.*

37. Curt Anderson, Associated Press, "Top court may slice and dice 'veggie libel' law," *Philadelphia Daily News*, January 21, 1998; Aaron Epstein, "It's no joke: Defame food, risk wrath," *The Philadelphia Inquirer*, December 29, 1997, pgs. A1, A5; and Sue Anne Pressley, "Testing a New Brand of Libel Law," *The Washington Post,* January 17, 1998, pg. A1.

38. Ibid.

39. Sue Anne Pressley, *op cit.*; Bob Janis, Reuters, "Cattlemen trembling as Oprah trial nears," *The Palm Beach (Florida) Post*, January 18, 1998, pgs. 1F, 3F; Martin Babineck, "Lawyer says Winfrey incited her audience against beef," *The Philadelphia Inquirer*, January 22, 1998, pg. A2; Shaheena Ahmad and Marissa Melton, "Oprah takes the bull by the horns," *U.S. News & World Report*, January 26, 1998, pg. 15; and Chip Brown, Associated Press, "Winfrey says she sought balance," *The Philadelphia Inquirer*, February 5, 1998, pg. A9.

40. Ibid.

41. Mark Babineck, Associated Press, "Oprah's lawyer goes after the livestock trader," *Philadelphia Tribune*, February 13, 1998, pg. 5A.

45. Mark Babineck, Associated Press, "Lawyer says Winfrey incited her audience against beef," *The Philadelphia Inquirer*, January 22, 1998, pg. 2; Babineck, "In Texas, full house for Oprah," *The Philadelphia Inquirer*, January 24, 1998, pg. 1A; and Kerry Curry, Reuters, "In Texas, Oprah Winfrey greets fans during jury selection," *The Philadelphia Inquirer*, January 21, 1998, pg. A12.

43. Brendan I. Koerner, "Another tale of a rat," *U.S. News & World Report*, April 14, 1997, pg. 14.

44. Edelman Public Relations Worldwide crisis home page, *www.edelman.com:80/clc-star.html*, December 31, 1997.

45. *California Appellate Reports*, 3rd series, 144, 1983, Appendix California Supplement, Bancroft-Whitney Co., San Francisco, pg. 991.

46. Ibid.

47. Ibid.

48. Ibid.

49. W. Speers, "Dangerfield a loser again—just $45,000 richer," *The Philadelphia Inquirer*, April 29, 1997, pg. F2.

50. Peter J. Boyer, *Who Killed CBS?*, Random House, New York, 1988, pgs. 182-186.

51. Ibid.

52. Ibid.

53. Ibid.

54. Peter J. Boyer, *op cit.*, pg. 192.

55. Rene A. Henry, the author, was a partner in the marketing public relations firm of ICPR, Los Angeles, responsible for the Alta-Dena Dairy account and information in this chapter related to the dairy.

56. *Jack O'Dwyer's Newsletter*, January 1, 1997, pg. 3.

CHAPTER SIX

EVEN THE GOVERNMENT MAKES MISTAKES

"Sloppy work by the FBI has come to typify what we now expect of the U.S. government. No one seems to be in charge."
—Douglas H. Schewe, Madison, Wisconsin[1]

"Working for the government means never having to say you're sorry."   —*The Cosby Show*, CBS, August 10, 1998

Add this to a 1996 survey commissioned by Porter/Novelli that showed that 8 percent of the people believed the government to be a believable source of information. That means 92 percent of the American public do not believe what they hear from the government. Only the tobacco industry, with 6 percent, and political parties, with 2 percent, were considered less believable.[2] In a "Whom do you trust?" national survey of 1,003 adults by the Pew Research Center for People and Press, only 6 percent trusted the federal government. City-county and state governments rated slightly better at 14 percent and 9 percent, respectively.[3] A *Time*/CNN poll found that 80 percent of Americans believe the government is hiding the truth about the existence of intelligent life on other planets.[4]

A book by scholars at Harvard's Kennedy School of Government reports a 30-year decline in public trust in government. The authors cite four contributing trends: changing values; fear of economic change; the expanding gap between political elites and most

Americans; and the role of the mass media. Negative political ads on television and a more critical and intrusive media further the public's cynicism and distrust.[5]

Government agencies and the military are already at a disadvantage in a crisis because of a lack of credibility with the public that must be convinced it is being told the truth. Because of this, crisis communicators in government need to place a priority on strategic communications planning. Unfortunately, this all too often is not possible because of the institutional culture. The typical public affairs office in a federal department or agency is headed by a political appointee, often with limited public relations experience. Few are experienced in long-term strategic planning and issues management. Many only know a political campaign approach. This makes it difficult to win public support in a crisis when the opposition uses the most sophisticated, state-of-the-art communications techniques and retains the best available public relations professionals.

Secrecy Builds Distrust

Senator Daniel Patrick Moynihan (D-N.Y.) believes that too much secrecy is one reason the public distrusts government. "There's a massive overclassification of information in government today—not because of national security concerns—but because the U.S. does not want to release information that may embarrass it," says Moynihan. He told an audience at the National Press Club on June 13, 1997, that there is very rarely any real risk to current national security from publishing facts related to transactions in the past and even fairly recent past.

With more than 3,200 political firms and more "spin doctors" in Washington than lobbyists, it is no wonder there is so little trust. Or as Mortimer B. Zuckerman, editor-in-chief of *U.S. News & World Report*, wrote about Bill Clinton's former political consultant, Dick Morris: "He knows nothing. He thinks he knows everything. That clearly points to a career as a political consultant."[6]

At one time the only crises inside the beltway were those such as former House Ways & Means Chair Wilbur Mills (D-Ark.) frolicking in the tidal basin pool with the "Argentine firecracker," Fanne Fox, or former presidential hopeful and Senator Gary Hart (D-Colo.) photographed with Donna Rice after challenging the media to try and catch him in an extramarital affair.

Senator Howell Heflin (R-Ala.) sneezed when meeting with some reporters, reached into his pocket for a handkerchief and pulled out a pair of women's panties. Once the story was all over Capitol Hill, his office distributed the following news release:

Statement of Sen. Howell Heflin—Handkerchief: "I mistakenly picked up a pair of my wife's white panties and put them in my pocket while I was rushing out the door to go to work. Rather than take a chance on being embarrassed again, I'm going to start buying colored handkerchiefs."[7]

Unfortunately not all government crises can be handled as easily as Senator Heflin's. There was Watergate. The Clinton impeachment. Irangate. Tailhook. Whitewater. Abscam. Starr being Starr. Monicagate. Payoff scandals at the U.S. Department of Housing and Urban Development. Various incidents involving the FBI and CIA.

The public trust factor in the government further disintegrates when agencies charged with intelligence and security, including the CIA and National Security Agency, arrest former employees as spies for selling secret documents to foreign governments. Then the FBI, considered the premier law enforcement agency, carelessly mishandled laboratory tests. Where are "agents" Fox Mulder and Dana Scully when they are needed? Unfortunately the real world doesn't mirror television's X-Files.

Then there are scores of crises involving state and local governments. The Los Angeles City Police Department. The Los Angeles District Attorney. Take any given case. And Marion Barry, whose terms as mayor of Washington, D.C., were interrupted by a period of time in prison. Hollywood responds to negative situations, which are written into scripts for dramatic shows, sitcoms and movies.

Lack of Management Continuity

In the federal governmrent there is little management or policy continuity. The White House appoints the officials who run the government at the various departments and agencies. These political appointees establish and manage administration policy. Career employees execute the policy. Many cabinet secretaries, assistant secretaries and agency administrators and directors leave before the end of the entire four-year term of the president. Few are in the same position for two terms. This means a constant change at the top. Few Fortune 500 companies could survive such disruption. For example, a successful program is in place and working, a change in policy may eliminate it, alter its focus or priority, or replace it with a new program.

Making the IRS User Friendly

How can the public like an organization that is designated to take their tax dollars? The Internal Revenue Service has an image problem from the very beginning. It is easy to find horror stories but few positive stories about happy customers.

Jeffrey Birnbaum, of *Fortune*, wrote that if the public knew how the IRS spent $3 billion to update its computers, what remains of its reputation would be completely lost. Between 1988 and 1995, systems crashed, 1040s came flying off conveyer belts and one evening news program told of workers who had shoved unprocessed returns, some even with checks attached, into wastebaskets and ceiling ducts.[8] New commissioner Charles Rossotti comes to the IRS with a background in computer technology as opposed to being a tax lawyer. One of his priorities is to redo the last 10 years of computer "improvements."[9]

Trust in government was further shattered when the Senate Finance Committee held hearings about IRS abuses. One woman testified that the IRS had dogged her for 17 years to pay a tax bill that the agency admitted had already been paid by her former husband. When she offered to pay anyway, she never received a bill, but the IRS placed liens on her new husband's house, salary and re-tirement fund. In order to shield their assets, the couple had to file for divorce and bankruptcy. Many IRS employees testified anony-mously behind partitions with their voices distorted by electronic synthesizers. They said the agency had become increasingly au-thoritarian, secretive and loath to admit mistakes.[10]

The hearings produced as many questions as answers. Why can't the IRS give citizens straight answers? Is it because Congress writes confusing tax laws? In 1997, Congress added 800 new pages of regulations to a tax code already more than 9,000 pages long.[11]

IRS was challenged to change its culture and mind-set so tax-payers could expect efficient service.[12] The IRS had been viewing every taxpayer as a potential cheat and now will be customer-oriented so the taxpayer is innocent until proven guilty. The IRS had Saturday open houses at regional offices in 33 major U.S. cities.[13] Some 6,300 taxpayers who attended were welcomed by smiling agents wearing buttons proclaiming "We Work for You." They helped their "customers" with tax problems. This gesture gen-erated what many believe to be the first positive press the IRS re-ceived in years. The *Denver Post* told the story of Wanda MacColl whose back-tax dispute was not immediately resolved, but an IRS agent waived $1,800 in penalties and agreed to personally handle her case. At a Baltimore open house, some taxpayers even met new Commissioner Rossotti and Treasury Secretary Robert Rubin.[14] The agency undertook one of the most aggressive customer service campaigns of any government agency. Using its Internet site, www.irs.ustreas.gov, people can download forms and publi-cations and get answers to hundreds of tax questions.[15]

The Nineties—A Decade of Sex and the Military

A letter to the editors of *Time* best summed up the American pub-lic's attitude: "If everyone in the armed forces who committed adultery and lied about it was discharged, the U.S. would be totally unprotected."[16] The tabloid-style stories of Army sex from Aberdeen Proving Ground to the so-called double standard applied to 1st Lt. Kelly Flinn and Gen. Joseph Ralston were only part of the story.

One would have thought that the military would have learned from the scandalous and rowdy Tailhook incident in Las Vegas. There were isolated incidents until the Army had a crisis at Aberdeen Proving Ground, Maryland. Female recruits, usually in their late teens and early 20s, now account for about 20 percent of the Army. Drill sergeants passed around a list of female recruits who were willing to have sex. At Aberdeen it was called "The Game." Other female recruits, who were willing partners, used sex to get ahead.[17] The Aberdeen crisis touched not only drill sergeants but the commanding general of the post.

"Stress created by physical or verbal abuse is nonproductive and prohibited," says a current Army training manual. Being nice is "in" and discouraging words are "out" for drill sergeants. But no one told them about sexual harassment.[18] Obstacle courses are now renamed confidence courses. The new standards call for trainees to wear gym shorts, T-shirts and sneakers and to run on their own instead of in formation. Navy recruits are given blue cards to hand to a trainer when they are feeling blue. At Quantico, Marine recruits had the help from a footstool placed in front of an eight-foot wall they had to pass.[19]

In order to keep the Army at its current level of 495,000 soldiers, its 5,000 recruiters must bring in 90,000 new recruits each year. Many of the Army's problems start before the female recruits begin basic training.[20] One recruiter estimates that up to 15 percent of male recruiters commit offenses including buying alcohol for prospective recruits and inviting them to "socialize and drink" at their apartments.[21]

"The Army is a safer place for women than any other organization in America," says Col. Ann Drach, who is in charge of the 1st Combat Support Command in Kitzingen, Germany.[22] A 1995 Defense Department survey showed 8 percent of Army women said they had been subjected to a rape or attempted rape. By comparison, studies of universities that have found between 10 percent and 28 percent of college women said they have been victims of rape. Many female recruits say harassment was worse in high school than in the military.[23]

Flinn and Ralston—A Double Standard?

Few incidents receive the public notoriety as did the cases of 1st Lt. Kelly Flinn, the Air Force's first female B-52 pilot, and four-star Gen. Joseph Ralston, in line to become chairman of the Joint Chiefs of Staff. Because of the way the Pentagon and *The Washington Post*, *60 Minutes* and the media positioned the story, the American public may never forgive the Air Force or Sheila Widnall, its first woman secretary, for the treatment of Flinn. Attorneys can take credit for this. The public relations staff of the Air Force could not take any proactive approach because the lawyers were concerned about an individual's right to due process and privacy.

The Flinn and Ralston stories are quite different. According to the Pentagon, Flinn had sex with a civilian man married to an enlisted woman, lied about it and disobeyed orders to end the affair. When his name surfaced as a candidate to head the Joint Chiefs, Ralston, who flew 147 missions over Vietnam and Laos and was highly decorated, admitted he had an affair 13 years earlier when he was separated from his wife and divorce proceedings were under way. Ralston's career crash-landed.[24]

In a poll conducted by *USA Today*, the American public believes that a double standard for adultery exists in the military that favors men and high-ranking officers. The poll revealed that at least half of all married men and women have had an affair and know a close friend or relative who has had one.[25] Those surveyed distinguished between the two cases—75 percent believed Ralston's affair 13 years earlier should not have disqualified him from being considered to chair the Joint Chiefs of Staff, while 50 percent compared to 46 percent believed Flinn should have been forced to resign over U.S. Military Code charges, including adultery.[26]

Pentagon statistics refute the double standard. In 1996, only nine women of 174 military personnel were prosecuted for sexual misconduct, including adultery. Seven of the women, however, were in the Air Force, according to Maj. Monica Aloisio, a spokes-person for the U.S. Department of Defense.[27]

Public Holds Professors and Preachers to Higher Standards

In the workplace, the American public held academicians and clergy far more responsible and accountable. The USA Today poll revealed that 73 percent believed a college professor should be dismissed for having an affair with a student or a member of the clergy for having an affair. This dropped to 55 percent for a military officer having an affair with a person of lower rank or a boss having an affair with an employee. Sixty-one percent said a military officer who had an affair with someone not in the military should not be dismissed.[28]

The incidents became the topic of late night host monologues. "Let me get this straight. If you commit adultery, you can't Chair the Joint Chiefs of Staff but you can be Commander-in-Chief," said David Letterman.[29]

Support for Flinn was driven by Duffey Communications, an Atlanta public relations firm. The strategy positioned Flinn as a victim of an obsolete, biased and unjust system. Initially, there was little media interest beyond the North Dakota base where she was stationed. When The Washington Post began investigating the story, she limited television to 60 Minutes. When the story was picked up by wire services, media calls poured in. Duffy sent the first news release out May 6 to build public support for Flinn before the May 19 hearing.[30] During the crisis, only Newsweek and The Los Angeles Times reported Flinn hired a public relations firm.[31]

The media were told Flinn would have limited availability after May 16 because of the need to concentrate on the trial. During this time, the Duffey firm was in touch almost daily with The New York Times, USA Today, The Los Angeles Times, Associated Press and the television networks. Support also was built on the Internet through the Duffey firm's home page. The family rallied public support with a letter-writing campaign to Congress and the Pentagon.[32]

After Widnall accepted Flinn's resignation and granted her a general discharge, Flinn's love letters to Marc Zigo were released. The lawyers didn't allow Air Force public relations to do this until Friday afternoon of Memorial Day weekend when there was little media interest and after Flinn resigned. "A survey by Maricopa Research found 65 percent of American adults think the Air Force should accept Flinn's offer to resign and grant her an honorable discharge, while only 24 percent opposed that solution," wrote the *Atlanta Journal Constitution* on May 22.[33]

The Air Force communicators were handicapped by their attorneys because of the military justice system. However, this did not restrict Flinn's public relations firm from taking a very aggressive approach.

Rating the Media in Volts and Amps

Secretary of Energy Hazel O'Leary, a former industry communications specialist, spent $46,500 to hire a firm to rank reporters on how favorably or unfavorably they wrote about the U.S. Department of Energy. Of course, the analysis became Page One news in *The New York Times, The Washington Post* and *The Wall Street Journal.* During a budget battle and during a year when Congress closed down the government by laying off thousands of "non-essential" employees, this was a flagrant example of government waste. As O'Leary and her staff questioned its image problem, some in public relations were adamant that she had "every right to monitor journalistic performance."

The secretary and her department "weren't just paranoid, they were nuts," according to Joseph T. Nolan, former vice president, public relations, for Chase Manhattan Bank and Monsanto Co. "It is nonsensical for business and government executives to blame the media for what ails them. Proper performance is the real key," says Nolan. He notes that more and more government officials and business executives, worried about their image, have become obsessively suspicious of reporters." He suggests that the best image-enhancement strategy is to do the right thing—and get caught doing it.[34]

Boycott the Olympics—The Soviets Will Leave Afghanistan

In 1980, White House lawyer Lloyd Cutler urged President Jimmy Carter to use the U.S. Olympic Team as a bargaining chip to force the Soviets to leave Afghanistan by threatening to boycott the Games in Moscow. It didn't work because Cutler and his staff had not done their homework. The decision and Carter's response were based on impulse and emotion and were carried out in a less-than-professional fashion.

Cutler's recommendation and Carter's actions nearly destroyed the modern Olympic movement. Some compared the action to that of Roman Emperor Theodosius in A.D. 393 when he ended the Games after 1,200 years. The athletes, coaches and administrators wanted to go to Moscow. The White House brought tremendous pressure to bear on the sponsors not to fulfill their commitments and even threatened the tax-exempt status of the U.S. Olympic Committee.

The result—the Soviets were still in Afghanistan four years later when it and its Soviet Bloc nations retaliated and boycotted the 1984 Olympic Games in Los Angeles.

The ignorance of the president's key advisers regarding the Olympic movement and protocol in international sports was exemplified two years earlier. In Athens in May 1978, the International Olympic Committee awarded Los Angeles the 1984 Games. To show the world that the nation was supporting Los Angeles, a signing ceremony was arranged at the White House so President Carter could host Lord Killanin of Ireland, president of the International Olympic Committee, and show his personal support for Los Angeles.

Also present for the October 12, 1978, event were the IOC's executive director, Monique Berlioux; Los Angeles Mayor Tom Bradley; John Argue, president of the Southern California Committee for the Olympic Games and one of the driving forces in bringing the Games to the city of the Angeles; John Ferraro, president of the City Council; Deputy Mayor Anton Calleia; Robert Kane, president, and Colonel F. Don Miller, executive director, of the USOC.

Calleia noted that the signing of the agreement between the city's organizing committee and the IOC ended months of intense negotiations in which Los Angeles had been perceived by the IOC as challenging its right "to own and run" the Olympics. For the first time, the agreement was not executed by the host city. The USOC provided the guarantee and became a partner with the non-profit organizing committee. The U.S. government was not a signatory to the document.

"Our hope was that being in the White House and with the president of the United States, would build upon good will created in recent negotiations in Mexico City and serve to promote an air of mutual respect and cooperation," said Calleia. "We extracted some unprecedented concessions from the IOC. It was time for us to be gracious."

"When we arrived at the White House we were led into the Roosevelt Room, almost adjacent to the Oval Office," said Argue. "In every other country in the world, when the head of the IOC arrives, the red carpet is rolled out. The president of the country is there to welcome him. Lord Killanin did not expect that kind of reception, but he did expect to meet Carter.

"Jack Watkins, a White House staffer, coordinated the activities. After a delay, Jody Powell came in and said: 'The president has no time to see you.' Carter, who was next door, was a no-show. The fact that our guests from Europe were stood up by the president without an adequate explanation or apology was a slap in the face of Lord Killanin and his Democrat colleague, Tom Bradley. It was an almost impossible protocol faux pas to explain to our guests. It was truly an amateur performance. The president could have stuck his head in and told everyone that an emergency had arisen, then apologized for not being able to spend more time and left. What should have been a positive event turned out to be a disaster," said Argue.[35]

Calleia believes that Powell could have been more diplomatic. "Powell could have told us 'The president has become tied up on a matter of national security and apologizes' which would have been accepted by everyone," said Calleia. He further recalls that day marking the start of Israeli-Egyptian negotiations on a peace treaty based on Camp David accords in which Carter had had "hands-on" involvement. "After the contract signing a former Bradley staffer then working for the president, Michael Pohl, took us on a tour of the White House," said Calleia. "In the basement we ran into Israeli Foreign Minister Moshe Dayan. It was rumored that U.S. Secretary of State Cyrus Vance and the Egyptian Foreign Minister Muhammad Ibrahim Kamal also were on hand. It is possible the president was personally involved in these negotiations. Whether or not he could have taken a time out to greet Lord Killanin and the delegations from the U.S. and International Olympic Committees and Los Angeles is a matter of conjecture. But the fact remains that we were disappointed that he didn't do a brief drop-in or send an apology. Lord Killanin handled the situation with poise and dignity."

In spite of the embarrassing and frustrating treatment at the White House and the subsequent boycott by the Soviets, the Los Angeles committee went on to stage the most successful and profitable of all Olympic Games. Years later when Argue visited the Carter Presidential Museum and Library he noted with interest that the boycott is nowhere in evidence. "Apparently the Carter curators are not proud of it," he said.

Spin Turns to Backspin for the Spin Doctor

In November 1996 the Joint Legislative Audit and Review Commission of the Virginia Legislature issued a report critical of Governor George Allen's administration with regard to the environment. The report accused the Virginia Department of Environmental Quality of "coddling industrial polluters and neglecting to enforce water-quality laws. It noted that under Allen, water-pollution fines collected by the state declined from $327,000 in 1992 to $4,000 last year [1995]."[36]

During October, November and December, the Allen administration and the Department of Environmental Quality were very much in the news for not seeking enough fines against Smithfield Foods Inc., the largest pork producer on the East Coast and one of

Virginia's biggest polluters. Smithfield, with a gift of $125,000, was Allen's largest contributor in an effort to elect Republican legislators and had been cited repeatedly by the U.S. Environmental Protection Agency for dumping hog waste into a Chesapeake Bay tributary.[37]

A "Dirty Tricks" Memo

On December 20, 1996, Michael McKenna, spokesman and policy director for the Department of Environmental Quality, drafted a memo to Thomas L. Hopkins, director of the department, Deputy Director T. March Bell and Julie Overy, a spokeswoman for the governor. Following are excerpts from McKenna's memo, loaded with football jargon to please the governor, whose father was the legendary NFL coach of the same name. Here is what he wrote:[38]

> I think we need to have a strategy to play for the next 30 days to get us out from under the JLARC [the joint legislative committee] report. Let me propose the following:
>
> Starting on the 27th, and every three or four days thereafter, we should issue a release questioning a new aspect of the report. My preference would be to arrange the release in the following order:
>
> • "DEQ claims JLARC distorted fines"
>
> • "DEQ alleges JLARC lied to General Assembly (on case examples)"
>
> • "DEQ asserts pattern of inaccuracy in JLARC report (general)"
>
> • "JLARC report flawed; fails to note accomplishments"
>
> Shortly, like in the next week, get the Governor to sign a letter (draft attached) which we can send to the *Post* [Washington], NYT [*New York Times*] and other papers.
>
> Immediately engage in some play action to freeze the linebackers. Three possibilities [Ed. note: his memo actually contains four] come to mind:
>
> • First, file a FOIA [Freedom of Information Act] with JLARC for correspondence with the press; make the FOIA under our names so they know we're the ones coming after them.
>
> • Second, file a FOIA with EPA [U.S. Environmental Protection

Agency] asking for correspondence between EPA and all our friends (including JLARC) with the intent of comparing whether JLARC in (sic.) the loop.

• Third, have one of us write a letter to JP asking for his opinion as to whether we have a cause of action for libel against JLARC; leak it to the press.

• Fourth, get someone in Congress to send a letter to EPA asking them to provide documentation backing up JLARC's analysis, as well as EPA's own assessment of the validity of JLARC analysis using EPA numbers; leak this to the press and have a Congressional oversight guy talk (off the record) about a potential oversight hearing.

Media Support EPA

McKenna went on to detail additional strategies in his memo. The same day he was drafting his memo, editorials appeared in both *The Washington Post* and *The New York Times* applauding EPA for its actions in Virginia. "Whatever else Virginia Gov. Allen may point to with pride when he leaves office, he had best not mention the waters of the Commonwealth, where his administration has had a certifiably poor record in enforcing environmental laws," wrote editors of *The Washington Post*. "Only after . . . scathing reports did his administration win a court order to force compliance by one of Virginia's biggest polluters."[39]

In writing about EPA's actions against Smithfield Foods, an editorial in *The New York Times* said: ". . . the fine . . . is not excessive for a company whose revenues are nearing $4 billion or inappropriate given the violations it is charged with, which include dumping a toxic brew of fecal coliform, ammonia, cyanide, oil and grease into the Pagan River. Though the action was directed at the company, it was also a stinging rebuke to the Virginia state government. . . ."[40]

Getting Caught

On January 10, McKenna's letter was reported by *The Washington Post*. It led off: "An internal memo from an official in Gov. George Allen's Department of Environmental Quality proposed several ways to try to discredit a legislative report that savaged the governor's environmental record, such as threatening a libel suit or a congressional inquiry."[41]

As aides to the governor and officials at the state's environmental department tried to distance themselves from McKenna's paper, Allen's deputy press secretary, Julie Overy, dismissed the memo.[42] The next day McKenna resigned.[43] Department Deputy Director Bell told reporters he wanted to find out who leaked the memo to the press and was having new locks installed on some offices. He denied knowing anything about handwritten changes on the memo in question, but newspaper reports said the letter had handwritten changes of an editor.[44]

Tell the Truth and Do It Quickly

In a story two weeks later, Rex Springston, of the *Richmond Times-Dispatch,* interviewed experts who said "The Allen administration's continuing headache over a dirty-tricks memo is a classic public relations disaster. The administration made a bad situation worse by not telling the whole truth right away."[45] "The original action was bad enough but they just keep compounding the problem by obfuscating and not dealing with what happened forthrightly," said Dr. Mark J. Rozell, a professor and political analyst at American University in Washington, D.C. "It's pretty elementary in the field of public relations that when you have a mistake, go public (and) get it over with. Make it a two-day story and take your hit. These guys obviously don't know that. They keep digging themselves deeper and deeper."[46] "[They] committed a classic mistake by not releasing all information immediately," said Larry J. Sabato, a professor of political science at the University of Virginia.[47]

At first Allen officials said they knew of only three people who got the memo. Then director Hopkins said the memo was discussed January 5 at a high-level meeting of seven people including Becky Norton Dunlop, Allen's secretary of natural resources.[48]

April Fool!

The crisis should have been over by Super Bowl Sunday, but it wasn't. If there was anything significant about April Fools' Day, that was when *The Washington Post* reported that McKenna was hired by the Washington law firm of Baise & Miller shortly after his resignation. The firm represents FMC Corp., a company that Virginia is suing for up to $100 million to recover its share of cleanup costs at the Avtex Fibers plant in Front Royal. Hopkins called the 440-acre Avtex site "among the worst contaminated toxic waste sites in the U.S. as well as the Commonwealth of Virginia."[49] Baise & Miller hired McKenna to "find out the facts" from his former agency bosses and help the law firm prepare a defense against the state's suit.[50]

Both Republicans and Democrats attacked the relationship. Virginia Attorney General James S. Gilmore III, then campaigning to succeed Allen as governor (which he did), and DEQ's Bell, said it was legal. Then Allen wrote to Hopkins barring any dealing with McKenna, saying only Gilmore, who was handling the lawsuit for the state, should deal with him.[51] Virginia's "revolving door" lobbying law bars McKenna from lobbying the Legislature or governor's office for a year, but it doesn't bar him from dealing with his former agency.[52]

When Is the Fat Lady Going to Sing?

End of story? Not yet. One might wish for Bugs Bunny to pop out and say, "That's All Folks!" but there was more to come.

On May 20 the *Richmond-Times Dispatch* reported that after McKenna resigned, he received $7,800 for compensatory time. State delegate Kenneth R. Plum (D-Fairfax) questioned the propriety of the payment to McKenna because the agency "reeks of cronyism and partisanship." Plum sought an independent investigation by the state auditor of public accounts about the circumstances and justification for the use of taxpayer dollars.[53] In mid-June, Hopkins asked Bell to resign. When a state auditor accused the new deputy director of the agency, James L. McDaniel, of aiding the misconduct that forced his predecessor to resign, Hopkins responded "we screwed up," and blamed Bell. Allen's office had no comment.[54]

Where Was the Department's Leadership?

During all of the controversy Dunlop was noticeably absent. Critics pointed to her past behavior as an administrator in the U.S. Interior Department in the Reagan administration until being forced to resign under pressure from Congress after angering both Democrats and Republicans. "Her fingerprints are all over this," said Virginia Delegate W. Tayloe Murphy Jr. (D-Warsaw). "This is coming entirely from her. She's the one who makes the decisions over there."[55]

Dunlop got headlines on July 16, after a third straight day of high ozone levels, when she called the White House demanding that President Clinton shut down the federal government to improve the air quality around the District of Columbia. Her actions were ignored and condemned as political grandstanding by Democrats and environmentalists.[56]

Dumb, Dumb, Stupid

When the U.S. Park Police in Washington illegally dumped 50 cases of beer into the Potomac River, it held a press conference to show the world how it had unknowingly violated the Clean Water Act. While many government agencies were celebrating the act's 25th anniversary, Maj. J. J. McLaughlin professed ignorance of the law as the runoff flowed from a compactor. Television and newspaper coverage of the media event prompted calls from even the FBI.[57]

The Park Police confiscated the beer from visitors to the annual Fourth of July festivities at the Mall. Other visitors, realizing they were in violation of the law, just abandoned their alcohol. During the ensuing months until the October 30 press event, various groups offered to take away the trash containers filled with beer cans and bottles. One was the Beer Institute, a trade association that represents brewers and suppliers to the industry. "The institute viewed the continuing media stories about the disposal as negative and the accompanying photographs as a public relations disaster," said the institute's Jeff Becker. "This was not a good thing from our perspective." Becker said he plans to contact Mc-Laughlin and make the same offer for the 1998 Independence Day celebration.[58]

A Blueprint for Successful Community Relations

The U.S. Army Corps of Engineers is perhaps one of the most misunderstood of federal agencies. Yet its response to a cleanup of chemical munitions in a residential neighborhood is a blueprint for risk management and successful crisis community relations.

On January 5, 1993, construction workers were installing a utility line to a new home in the tony Spring Valley neighborhood of northwest Washington, D.C. Everything was routine until workers unearthed World War I chemical munitions that launched one of the most unique and challenging environmental restoration projects in the country. Within hours, the normally quiet, affluent neighborhood was overtaken with bomb disposal units.

The Corps of Engineers searched historical records and determined that more than 600 acres would require investigation for possible additional buried munitions. American University is located on the site today that once was used by the War Department in 1917-1918 as a research center to develop and test chemical weapons and the effectiveness of toxic chemicals and substances. It became the first research center of the Chemical Warfare Service.[59]

The site was closed in December 1918, one month after the war ended. Approximately 100,000 troops had trained at adjacent Camp Leach in temporary buildings and trenches also on the site. Restoration began by burning all temporary buildings that were dangerous because of gas saturation and by filling in trenches, pits, dugouts and other similar work areas.

During the January 1993 emergency removal operation, the recovery team safely removed 141 munitions and assorted debris from the site. On February 2, 1993, Phase II began and the responsibility was transferred to the Corps' Baltimore District. Using historical photographs, documents and aerial photography, the Corps matched them to current topography maps of the area and identified some 30 areas for specific investigation. Most were surface features that included ground scarring, ammunition storage pads and the sites of former buildings.

Community Relations a Priority

Cleaning up a formerly used defense site in an established residential community presented the Corps with several challenges, including developing and implementing new Army policies and procedures on issues involving community safety, real estate, reimbursement and public affairs to evacuating and supporting the residents of the Spring Valley community.

Once rights-of-entry were obtained from property owners in the nine different work zones, workers surveyed 490 properties using ground-conductivity meters and magnetometers to find buried metal objects. Workers found 73 suspect objects which required further investigation and some even excavation.[60]

The first of nine excavations began on October 13, 1993, and the last was completed in February 1995. All roads in the neighborhood were closed to the public. The largest operation required the evacuation of 240 homes built over a ring of former World War I trenches. An on-site Corps office was established adjacent to Sibly Hospital and near the community. As a safety precaution, nearby residents were asked to leave their homes by 8:30 A.M. during the daytime removal operations and to not return until after 6 P.M.

Involve the Community

To encourage community participation, the Corps asked volunteers to serve as zone captains and represent their zones at weekly meetings. The zone captains quickly established themselves as working liaisons between the residents and the Corps. At the beginning of the project, nightly public meetings were held in a local church to detail the operation's status. Residents were told they were eligible for reimbursement of their expenses directly related to the evacuations. They also could use services provided by a support center established at a local church. Throughout Phase II the Corps worked continuously to minimize the impact on the community.

With intense media interest, a specific time was established to film, video and interview on the first day of each excavation operation. The Corps' public affairs office also provided additional access when requested.

Had community relations and communications not been a Corps priority, the entire operation could have been a disaster. The successful effort of nightly town meetings involving community residents and providing access to the media helped eliminate rumors, panic, demonstrations and litigation. With the support of the Spring Valley community, the Corps not only succeeded in accomplishing its mission, but created a blueprint for future projects.

LAPD Blues

Few police departments have come under fire for as long a period of time as has the Los Angeles Police Department. The riots in Watts and some of its cases have been the most widely reported in the country. Except for the riots that followed, the Rodney King incident in 1992 may never have received such widespread media exposure.

During the O. J. Simpson trial, the department's image was something out of one of Hollywood filmmaker Mack Sennett's "Keystone Cops," until Detective Mark Fuhrman gave the public another perspective. Once considered one of the country's very best police departments, it now is identified with widespread ineptitude, brutality, racism and sexism.

Surrounded by the entertainment capital of the world, the police may have offended producers, directors and writers because of remarks and story lines made from time to time in television dramas and sitcoms and feature films. The very positive images of Sgt. Joe Friday and *Dragnet* or *Adam 12* end up more like *Car 54 Where Are You?*

LAPD seems to be continuously embroiled in controversy and crises. Police Chief Willie Williams, brought in from Philadelphia following the King incident, did not have his contract renewed by the Police Commission. A 22-page statement from the commission said that Williams "has proven unable or unwilling to consistently translate his words into actions."[61]

Another Scandal

While the City of Los Angeles waited for the appointment of a new police chief, the department again was rocked by scandal. Legal papers filed in a lawsuit stemming from the fatal shooting of a police officer's estranged wife revealed a departmental code of silence protecting rogue cops from criminal prosecution. The alleged corruption is more than accusations of spousal abuse and includes rape, stalking, off-duty shootings and assault. Added to that, a report scheduled to be made public will confirm that the "Men Against Women" club that Fuhrman called a "joke," was an institutionalized form of harassment against female officers.[62]

Glenn Sagon, principal of Sagon-Phior Group, Los Angeles, volunteered to help rebuild LAPD's image. He used the knowledge gained in promoting television series such as *Law & Order* and *Cops*. Some $500,000 was raised for advertising support and a billboard campaign launched in the summer of 1996. The billboards showed a uniformed officer with a child and the headline, "Ending Fear . . . Together we can make it happen. LAPD."[63]

Another Los Angeles PR professional, Kathleen Buczko of NMC Partners, says actions speak louder than words. She believes the LAPD has been successful in small areas but failed in two important ways. "They haven't effectively merchandised their success stories and they haven't admitted when mistakes have occurred," she says. "They tend to be much more reactive than proactive." She said the police have attempted to communicate using basic, rudimentary techniques such as press releases, speeches and increased community involvement Buczko believes it is crucial for LAPD to re-educate the community so credibility can be rebuilt.[64]

Tim McBride, a 33-year veteran of the force, heads community affairs and has a staff of 26 uniformed officers to oversee public relations efforts. "When we have the opportunity with the press, we take a much stronger approach in supporting our officers instead of getting involved in minor issues that become media squabbles," he says. "We put out the human side of our organization." This approach involves profiling success stories and officers who have contributed to reforms LAPD is trying to implement.[65]

Federal Bureau of What?

The FBI was once the most prestigious of all federal agencies. Its reputation was pre-eminent worldwide, except perhaps in the United Kingdom where Scotland Yard got the No. 1 ranking. The Bureau chased anarchists and Bolsheviks in the '20s, gangsters and bootleggers in the '30s, fascists in the '40s, communists in the '50s and civil-right leaders and antiwar protesters in the '60s. Democrats and Republicans alike have consistently supported the FBI with budget increases to fight crime.[66]

The scandals of the FBI's laboratory, called "The gang that couldn't examine straight," overshadowed successes such as the imprisonment in 1992 of Mob boss John Gotti, the conviction of the World Trade Center bombers, the capture of the alleged Unabomber and the peaceful end, in June 1996, to the 81-day Montana Freemen standoff. The laboratory does as many as 600,000 examinations a year and its credibility has been undermined by 10 workers faulted in a study by the Justice Department. The agency expects to get hundreds, if not thousands, of motions that are going to encompass every part of the lab, from fingerprint comparisons to tire-tread analysis.[67] The lab was blamed for flawed scientific work and inaccurate testimony in major cases, including the Oklahoma City bombing.[68] Added to this was the botched arrest of Richard Jewell as a suspect in the Atlanta Olympic bombing and the 1992 standoff at Ruby Ridge where Randy Weaver collected $3 million in the wrongful deaths of his wife, Vicky, and teenage son.

In its most recent embarrassment, the FBI was accused at a Senate hearing in May 1999 of using heavy-handed and often bumbling tactics to try to prove terrorists had shot down TWA Flight 800 over Long Island in July 1996. Six months after the crash, the Bureau of Alcohol, Tobacco and Firearms concluded in a 24-page report that mechanical failure had caused the tragedy.

The FBI dismissed the report as unprofessional and reprehensible and tried to get the Treasury Department to suppress its release.[69]

During the hearings, Senator Charles Grassley (R-Iowa) said, "In my view, the FBI risked public safety." The agency was accused of ignoring evidence that did not point to the idea that a bomb or missile brought down the plane. It wasn't until November 1997 that the FBI publicly acknowledged that a mechanical flaw had ignited the Boeing 747's central fuel tank which put pressure on the airlines to begin correcting the problem.[70]

FBI Director Louis Freeh has been trying to change the agency's culture, but critics charge he is obsessively secret, bullheaded and micromanages. "We do many, many good things every day. Children are saved, explosive devices are defused, pedophiles are arrested, gangs are taken off the streets," he says. "I'm not saying we shouldn't be criticized for mistakes, but I know that the successes of the men and women of the FBI take place every day."[71]

Perhaps Freeh and his public affairs office can look to minisuccesses of the Los Angeles Police Department as a model to adopt. A turnaround image is just not going to happen by itself. An aggressive, proactive strategic communications plan must be created and implemented, complete with balanced media and public outreach efforts. Success stories need to be marketed to Congress, the executive branch, the media and the American public.

The Inspector General and the FAA

Seldom have there been internal disagreements stronger than the one between the U.S. Department of Transportation's Inspector General, Mary Schiavo, and the Federal Aviation Administration. She was independent of the Secretary of Transportation and her job was to investigate problems at the department and see that they were fixed. She was an attorney, a former prosecutor, had a passion for aviation and was licensed as a pilot when she was 18 years old.

In *Newsweek*, Schiavo wrote that her office found serious deficiencies in airline inspections, parts and training, and in the air traffic-control system. "Rather than checking every aircraft, many inspectors simply examine whatever plane happens by when they are on duty," she wrote. "I go out of my way to stay off commuter airlines. I have skipped conferences because I would not fly on marginal airlines. In recent years, small commuter planes have been more than twice as likely to be involved in an accident as the major carriers, and until this year the FAA allowed them to operate under significantly less stringent safety standards."[72]

Schiavo's recommendations and reports were largely refuted or ignored by the FAA and the department until the May 11, 1996, ValuJet crash in the Florida Everglades. The night following the crash, she went public with Ted Koppel on ABC's *Nightline* contradicting FAA administrator David Hinson who insisted the airline was "safe to fly." Schiavo disclosed FAA statistics that Valu-Jet's safety record was 14 times as poor as that of other discount airlines and added, "I would not fly ValuJet."[73]

No one "inside the beltway" could recall when an Inspector General went as public with information so critical of the department. Government officials made television appearances to reassure the public that discount airlines were safe to fly. The spin doctors were turned loose.

Crisis Mode at DOT

Top officials at the Department of Transportation shifted quickly into a crisis mode. Secretary Frederico Peña reassured the public on national television: "I have flown ValuJet. ValuJet is a safe airline, as is our entire aviation system." He insisted: "If ValuJet was unsafe, we would have grounded it."[74]

In her book, *Flying Blind, Flying Safe*, Schiavo writes that Peña "protected an airline just the way government officials had for decades." According to her, had it not been for an anonymous phone call, "FAA officials very likely would have continued with their charade." The field staff in Atlanta recommended in February that ValuJet be grounded. "They put it in writing. Someone quashed the memo."[75] As FAA officials stonewalled Schiavo and the media and said they knew nothing about it, she found the critical memo written in official FAA jargon. "The memo, written three months before the crash, proved highly embarrassing to the

FAA and helped force the agency to re-evaluate its self-assured contention that ValuJet was a 'safe airline,'" she wrote. Following public outrage the FAA grounded ValuJet on June 17.[76]

Reverse Thrust, Reverse Spin

The FAA backed off its spin. One day there were even charges that Schiavo was "politically motivated" since she served as assistant secretary of labor in the Reagan administration and was appointed to Transportation by President George Bush. But her documented evidence was so strong that no one bought it. The media and Congress listened. The public wanted to know more about what she found. In 1992 she found trouble in seven of the 10 FAA regions, that 43 percent of the parts airlines purchased from suppliers were bogus, that engines were inspected only 52 percent of the time, and security was lacking at major airports when 40 percent of the time her staff passed inspections carrying fake bombs, guns and knives.

According to Schiavo, Secretary Peña and FAA Administrator Hinson delayed releasing her report critical of security until after the 1996 Atlanta Olympic Games. She claims it was sent to the White House and even the National Security Adviser with a request that the document be classified. Peña and Hinson did everything possible to distance themselves from Schiavo. She resigned on July 3, 1996.[77]

In a report on the crash, the National Transportation Safety Board criticized the FAA for not requiring fire-suppression systems and for inadequately overseeing the rapid growth of the low-budget airline. Nine years earlier, because of a 1988 fire, federal safety experts called for smoke detectors to be in cargo holds. However, the FAA bowed to industry pressure and rejected the recommendation.[78] "Had the recommendation been implemented, it's only questionable whether the ValuJet accident would have happened at all," said Jim Hall, chairman of the safety board on *Meet the Press*. He noted that more than a year after the ValuJet crash and nine years after the measure was first recommended, not one plane with a sealed cargo hold has been fitted with a fire detector and extinguisher.[79]

The FAA increased security at airports by requiring everyone to have a government-issued photo ID and be asked questions such as "Did you pack your own luggage?" and "Has your luggage been in your possession at all times?" The agency has yet to implement a 1990 congressional mandate with a three-year deadline to develop and install scanners that could screen for plastic explosives. There is a machine that can do the job called the CTX5000 SP made by InVision Technologies, but the cost is $1 million. "The airlines don't want to do it and the FAA won't force them," says an InVision spokesperson.[80]

On September 24, 1997, ValuJet Airlines changed its name to AirTran Airlines.[81]

A Cloud Can Have a Silver Lining

Some good does result from a crisis. Sometimes it takes an incident blown into a full-scale crisis before necessary action is taken. This certainly was the case with Mary Schiavo and the U.S. Department of Transportation. Now the National Transportation Safety Board and all parties involved are listening to the public's demands for greater air safety.

Endnotes

1. *Time*, "Letters," May 19, 1997.
2. *Jack O'Dwyer's Newsletter*, August 7, 1996, pg. 2.
3. "Whom do you trust?," *The Washington Post*, May 4, 1997.
4. "Public Still Alienated," *Government Executive*, August 1997, pg. 8.
5. Joseph S. Nye, Jr., Philip D. Zelikow and David C. King, *Why People Don't Trust Government*, Harvard University Press, Cambridge, Mass., 1998, and "Why Government Fell From Grace," *Government Executive*, January 1988, pg. 8.
6. Mortimer B. Zuckerman, Editorial, "Famous Lost Words," *U.S. News & World Report*, January 13, 1997, pg. 68.
7. Press Release, Office of Senator Howell Heflin, Alabama, July 19, 1994.
8. Jeffrey Birndaum, "Does Not Compute," *The Washingtonian*, December 1997, pgs. 53-56.
9. Ibid.
10. Paul Glastris, "Lien on Congress," *U.S. News & World Report*, October 6, 1997, pg. 32.
11. Ibid.

12. R. A. Zaldivar, "Reformers want IRS to be user-friendly," *The Philadelphia Inquirer*, October 26, 1997, pg. E3.

13. Ibid.

14. Keith Elliot Greenberg, "A Taxing Challenge," *Public Relations Tactics*, February 1998, pg. 27.

15. Ibid.

16. *Time*, June 23, 1997, "Letters" from Florence L. Egan, Newington, Connecticut.

17. Evan Thomas and Gregory L. Vistica, "A Question of Consent," *Newsweek*, April 28, 1997, pg. 41.

18. John Leo, "A kinder, gentler Army," *U.S. News & World Report*, August 11, 1997, pg. 14.

19. Ibid.

20. Mark Thompson, "Offensive Maneuvers," *Time*, May 5, 1997, pg. 40-42.

21. Ibid.

22. Richard J. Newman, "Army Sex Ed 101," *U.S. News & World Report*, August 11, 1997, pg. 50.

23. Ibid.

24. William R. Macklin, *The Philadelphia Inquirer*, *op cit.*, and Nancy Gibbs, "Wings of Desire," *Time*, June 2, 1997, pg. 26-40.

25. Mimi Hall, "Poll: Double standard exists in military," *USA Today*, June 12, 1997, pgs. 1A, 4A.

26. Ibid.

27. William R. Macklin, "Equal treatment," *The Philadelphia Inquirer*, June 11, 1977, pgs. D1, D10.

28. Ibid.

29. "Verbatim," Notebook, *Time*, June 23, 1997, pg. 19.

30. "Bombs Away—Piloting Kelly Flinn's PR Campaign," *Public Relations Tactics*, Public Relations Society of America, August 1997, pg. 1, and "PR Firm Takes Credit in Lt. Flinn Case," *Jack O'Dwyer's Newsletter*, June 18, 1997, pg. 2.

31. "In Like Flinn," Verbatim, *Air Force Magazine*, September 1997, pg. 66.

32. *Public Relations Tactics*, *op cit.*, pg. 24.

33. Ibid.

34. Joseph T. Nolan, "Track Performance, Not Reporters," *The Public Relations Strategist*, 1996, pgs. 14-17.

35. John Argue and Anton Calleia, correspondence and telephone calls during October 1997 with Rene A. Henry.

36. Ellen Nakashima, "Memo Offers Dirty Tricks To Aid Allen," *The Washington Post*, January 10, 1997, pg. B1.

37. Ellen Nakashima, *op cit.*, pg. B4, and *The Washington Post*, Editorial, "Wishy-Washy on Water Pollution," December 20, 1996, pg. A26.

38. Memorandum from Michael McKenna to Tom Hopkins, March Bell and Julie Overy, December 20, 1996.

39. *The Washington Post*, Editorial, "Wishy-Washy on Water Pollution," December 20, 1996, pg. A26.

40. *The New York Times*, Editorial, "Environmental Defiance," December 20, 1996, pg. A38.

41. Ellen Nakashima, "Virginia Official Resigns Over Memo," *The Washington Post*, January 11, 1997, pg. C1.

42. Ibid.

43. Ibid.

44. Ibid.

45. Rex Springston, "Missteps worsen flap over memo," *Richmond Times-Dispatch*, Richmond, Va., January 27, 1997.

46. Ibid.

47. Ibid.

48. Ibid.

49. Spencer S. Hsu, "Former Va. Environmental Official Hired by Major Polluter's Law Firm," *The Washington Post*, April 2, 1997, pgs. B1, B6.

50. Ibid.

51. Rex Springston, "Governor tells DEQ officials to stay mum," *Richmond Times-Dispatch*, April 3, 1997, pg. B1, B5.

52. Ibid.

53. Michael Hardy, "Probe of DEQ payment sought . . . Memo writer received $7,500 for owed time," *Richmond Times-Dispatch*, May 20, 1997.

54. Spencer S. Hsu, "Environmental Aide Linked to Va. Payment Controversy," *The Washington Post*, July 6, 1997, pg. B3.

55. Scott Harper, *op cit.*

56. Ellen Nakashima, "Va. Call to Shut Washington Is Ridiculed and Ignored," *The Washington Post*, July 17, 1997, pg. D3.

57. Linda Wheeler, "Beer Flowed on Wrong Side of the Law," *The Washington Post*, November 20, 1997, pg. C3.

58. Ibid.

59. "Formerly Used Defense Site Restoration Project, Spring Valley, Washington, D.C.," brochure, *U.S. Army Corps of Engineers*, Baltimore District, Baltimore, Maryland, 1995 and script to video production, "Operation Safe Removal," *U.S. Army Corps of Engineers*, Baltimore District, Baltimore, Maryland, April 7, 1995.

60. Ibid.

61. Alison Stateman, "LAPD Blues," *Public Relations Tactics*, April 1997, pg. 1.

62. "LAPD Blues," *Newsweek*, May 12, 1997, pg. 6.

63. Allison Stateman, *op cit.*, pg. 27.

64. Ibid.

65. Ibid.

66. Nancy Gibbs, "Under The Microscope," *Time*, April 28, 1997, pgs. 28-34.

67. Ibid.

68. Michael J. Sniffen, Associated Press, "New FBI lab chief lacks experience," *The Philadelphia Inquirer*, October 18, 1997, pg. A4.

69. Michael Grunwald, "Hearing on FBI role in Flight 800 probe," *The Washington Post*, May 10, 1999; Shannon McCaffrey, Associated Press, "FBI accused of forcing terrorist theory," *The Philadelphia Inquirer*, May 11, 1999.

71. Ibid.

72. *Newsweek*, National Affairs, "I Don't Like to Fly," May 20, 1996, pg. 32.

73. *Time*, "Flying Into Trouble," March 31, 1997, pg. 53.

74. Mary Schiavo, *Flying Blind, Flying Safe,* copyright 1997 Mary Schiavo, with Sabra Chartrand, Avon Books, *Time,* March 31, 1997, pg. 56-57.

75. Ibid., pg. 57.

76. Ibid.

77. Ibid.

78. Stephen J. Hedges, "Did FAA cause a jet crash?," *U.S. News & World Report,* September 1, 1997, pg. 36.

79. Randolph E. Schmid, Associated Press, "Planes still lack anti-fire devices for cargo holds," *The Philadelphia Inquirer,* August 18, 1997, pg. A2.

80. Cristopher Hitchens, "Airport Insecurity," *Vanity Fair,* June 1997, pgs. 58, 60, 62.

81. "ValuJet changing name and business strategy," *The Press Democrat,* Santa Rosa, California, September 24, 1997, pg. E1.

CHAPTER SEVEN

THE AGGIE PIGS
AND PRESIDENT BUSH

STINK AT PIG FARM AND BUSH LIBRARY

COLLEGE STATION, Texas—Residents of a rural area near Texas A&M University are raising a fuss over the relocation of a pig farm being displaced by construction of the George Bush Presidential Library.

School officials plan to move the Texas A&M Swine Center from a corner of the 90-acre (36-hectares) library site a few miles west to a place known as Brushy Community.

"The bottom line is, Brushy Community residents don't want the pigs out there," said Tam Garland, an A&M veterinarian whose home would be about 300 yards from the pig center. "Whether it's five pigs or 500 pigs, we don't want them. You can't keep a pig from stinking."

—*International Herald Tribune*, Paris, France,
September 21, 1994[1]

With that breaking news story a crisis that Texas A&M University could have avoided went international.

The next day the story was on television throughout the world. CNN International broadcast a feature that showed former President and Mrs. Bush breaking ground for his presidential library. The story cut to pigs wallowing in a pig pen and finished with a strong quote from Rev. Cedric Rouse, minister of the African-American Clayton Baptist Church and president of the residents' association. Rouse called the university's actions "environmental racism." Until this time, the story was reported only occasionally by the local media, the student newspaper and sporadically by the Dallas and Houston newspapers.

The story began in 1993 when the university announced plans to build a new Animal Science, Teaching, Research and Extension Complex on a 582-acre site 8.5 miles from the center of the campus. The new facility was to have a beef cattle center, a sheep and goat, animal euthenics, and nutrition and physiology centers. The land was purchased in 1989 and a beef cattle center opened in 1993.

Expensive homes and ranches, owned predominantly by members of the A&M faculty and administration, were on one side of the center. Across the highway was an established community of Black families, the Brushy Community. This was founded by a group of Black pioneers who moved from Clayton, North Carolina after the Civil War. The Clayton Baptist Church was named for the pioneers' former hometown southeast of Raleigh. Most of the Blacks were hourly-wage employees working for the university in foodservice, maintenance, grounds keeping and other similar jobs.

A Reputation as a Good Member of the Community

For decades Texas A&M and the community had good relations. Few people challenged A&M because of its dominant position. There really was no serious controversy between the community and the university until the decision to have pigs at the new animal center. When George Bush decided to locate his presidential library at A&M, the swine center was in the middle of the 90-acre site. Something had to give.

The first signs of any conflict came when the university was closed for 1993 Christmas holidays. Required announcements were published in the local paper on Christmas Eve and Christmas Day.

In early spring 1994, Dr. Charles Lee, then deputy vice chancellor of agriculture and life sciences, asked the author, then executive director of university relations at Texas A&M, for help. He wanted to contain the situation, was looking for advice how to handle the problem and wanted to head off a crisis. The position of the administration was made clear by Dr. E. Dean Gage, who was the university's interim president: "We are going to do the right thing. We are not going to force a pig farm on the community. The people that live there are not just community residents, they are employees and members of the Texas A&M family. If we have to find another location we will. Let's get closure on this as quickly as possible."[2]

A 180-Degree Turn

Before the dispute could be resolved, the board of regents named Ray Bowen the new president. He was a 1958 graduate of A&M who had been acting president at Oklahoma State. Bowen took over as president in June 1994 and named Dr. Jerry Gaston, a sociology professor, as interim vice president of finance and administration. Working in tandem, the two took a hard line against the people in the community. This violated all principles of both community relations and employee relations. An incident rapidly escalated into a full-blown crisis.

Tension increased at the meetings between the community and A&M. Faculty members joined with the Black community to form a coalition. The university held all meetings on campus during business hours. This meant that the African-Americans from the Brushy Community had to take off from work without pay. The more the community leaders pushed for fairness, the harder the line the university took. Bowen and Gaston clearly drew a line in the sand. Anticipating a major international crisis about to explode, on December 12, 1994, the author prepared a detailed situation analysis for A&M's leadership.

SITUATION AND ISSUES ANALYSIS

Subject: Animal Science Teaching Research Education Center/ Swine Center

Background: During the spring of 1994 the primary issue was to reduce the number of pigs on the site to alleviate any problems related to air and water pollution. This was done by locating half of the animals to a new site in McGregor.

The issue today is that the community does not want any pigs at all near its community and wants a new location for the Swine Center.

Key Issues

- There is a community of nearly 200 families surrounding the proposed center. Half of the families are poor African-Americans. All are against the relocation of any pigs to the new Animal Science Center.

- The accusation of "environmental racism" against Texas A&M.

- Adversaries could use the George Bush Presidential Library Center as the primary media focus with the Texas A&M University administration accountable and responsible.

Specific Issues

Planning

UNIVERSITY—Extensive planning and study over a number of years with impact statements.

- Downsized plan at an additional cost of $600,000.

COMMUNITY—"Planners talked to only four families, none of whom were Black."

- 60 percent of prevailing winds will affect 100 Black families and four churches (two of which are African-American and one Asian-American).

"The research, impact analysis and site selection were not properly or professionally done."

- The community has proposed alternative sites.

"The university has circumvented the law by downsizing and using a loophole to avoid reporting to the state natural resources authority."

"With less than 1,000 pigs there is no authority for air and water quality. A&M is free to do whatever it wants with no controls."

"This violates the basic principles of good urban planning—placing livestock in a residential area."

"This is nothing more than environmental racism."

"The architectural firm should be held liable for doing an improper impact study and analysis."

[Author note: Quotes are comments made by members of the Brushy Community affected by the new center.]

Technology

UNIVERSITY—State-of-the-art technology.

- Facilities are designed for twice the number of pigs and capacity of waste.

- Odor and pollution of air and water will be controlled.

- Center will be an environmental showplace for everyone to see.

- University will guarantee the technology that there will be no odors or pollution.

- All odors will be monitored. The swine industry now spends $25–30 million each year on technology.

COMMUNITY—"Any lagoon will leak. Data from Iowa points out Texas A&M has not done its research."

"The system proposed is primitive. The technology is inferior and would not be allowed by EPA."

"Livestock animal waste is the No. 1 ground polluter in the U.S."

"During heavy rains, lagoons can overflow and contaminate ground water and the Brazos River."

"Current water table is at 70' in sand with a high hydraulic absorption capacity."

"Spreading lagoon waste as fertilizer will only take the pig smell from a small, confined area and spread it over a larger, broad area."

"Regardless of what is done, pigs still will smell."

Community Relations

UNIVERSITY — The university wants to be a good citizen. It is listening to what people in the community want.

COMMUNITY — "There is constant conflict between 'town and gown.' The university has terrible community relations. Texas A&M is very arrogant, especially its attorneys." Faculty cited examples of where they had worked where there were excellent 'town and gown' relationships (i.e., Illinois). "A&M needs to respond to community needs."

"We cannot trust the university to keep its word. A new administration may reverse what had been promised by a previous administration. The recent indictments and convictions prove that 'Aggies do lie, cheat and steal.' You can no longer trust anyone at Texas A&M."

"When the university allowed the Ku Klux Klan to have a campus rally, it turned off a lot of Blacks in the Bryan-College Station community."

Construction

UNIVERSITY — State-of-the-art construction technology will be used.

COMMUNITY — "Every building the university builds is flawed and needs immediate attention. Major items are excluded or overlooked." Community leaders cited several buildings (medical school, new vet medicine building and architecture) that have been recently opened as having major construction flaws.

Maintenance

UNIVERSITY —Any problems will be immediately corrected.

COMMUNITY — "Maintenance is a low priority at Texas A&M." Professors from the community cited classrooms where 20 percent of the seats are broken and students have to sit in aisles or on the floor, with complaints having been made for as long as three years.

"University employees and faculty know that maintenance is an inherent problem at A&M."

Real Estate Values

UNIVERSITY —The university undertook a study and found that there had been no appreciable loss of real estate property values.

COMMUNITY — "Location of any pigs near a residential community will destroy property values."

"People are taking losses already with the knowledge that pigs will be located near the community."

"People cannot afford to move and live anywhere else."

Emotional Impact

UNIVERSITY —Decisions have to be made with students as a priority.

The facility is important to the livestock industry in Texas.

The university has spent an additional $600,000 to accommodate the needs of the community.

COMMUNITY — "The Black families do not have air-conditioning. Unlike rich White folks, we cannot shut our windows and turn on air conditioning to shut out the pig smell."

"If the smell is no problem, then why not leave the facility where it is. If it is a problem, why is the smell OK for 100 Black families and not the Bushes?"

"The social activities of the Black community take place outdoors both at the churches and individual homes. This would not be possible with odors from the pigs."

"Most Black families cannot afford dryers and hang clothes to dry on clotheslines. Are these people expected to go to work with their clothes smelling with the stench of pigs?"

"Who is more important? The 100 Black families and the Brushy Community or A&M students?"

"You can't 'spring clean' with hog smell coming through a house."

"We want Texas A&M to be the best university in the country—providing the best education and teaching possible for the students and our children who will be future students. We support A&M, but A&M needs to support us."

"A&M has handled this wrong from the very beginning. I am tired of bad press. This will only create more bad press and it is my university. The university is behaving wrong. Listen to the folks."

"We are too poor to try to fight A&M and its staff of attorneys."

"We want an answer soon so we know if we have to start fund raisers and benefits to get money to pay our attorneys."

"If you are concerned and listening, do what we ask."

"The worry of having a pig farm is our neighborhood is killing us—blood pressure, nerves and worry about those of us with asthma and respiratory diseases."

Executive Summary

UNIVERSITY—The university has studied this problem for a number of years and believes it has made a valid decision regarding the location of the new Animal Science Center and, in particular, the Swine Center. It believes this is in the best interests of everyone involved. In recent months when serious concerns have been raised by the community, the university has listened to the community. It first downsized the facility at considerable expense and found a site in McGregor to accommodate half of the swine. Now, the university is listening to complaints from the community that it does not want any pigs located on the site of the proposed Swine Center. The university wants to be a good citizen and neighbor and is considering its options.

COMMUNITY—The community believes that the university is making it the victim because the pigs have to be moved from their present location to make room for the new Bush Presidential Library Center. The families are concerned about air and ground water pollution, the impact on their environment and lifestyle and how this could destroy the value of their homes and property. State-of-the-art technology and the additional cost to the university are not considerations.

Media Relations Evaluation

For public and media reaction, the community will focus on the Bush Library and the Bush family as much as it will on the university for creating this problem. The controversy will become a significant race issue.

If this happens, the controversy becomes a media crisis and the story will be one of national and even international magnitude. A possible story line could be about "the lives of 100 Black families being destroyed because of the Bush Library."

During the Saturday (December 10) meeting, the community indicated it would wait for a response from the university before taking further action. If the issue escalates the media interest will do so accordingly. The issues involved with this controversy are exactly what *60 Minutes, Hard Copy, 20/20, Eye-to-Eye* and other television news magazines are looking for, as well as all national newspapers and magazines.

With a quick response, this controversy could be contained without embarrassment to President Bush and his family and any further embarrassment or tarnish on the image of Texas A&M.

Recommendation

1. The university should issue a press release and statement this week that would:

   • thank the community for making known its concerns;

   • assure the community that all concerns are being reviewed and considered;

   • announce that all work on the new center and the Bush Library is being temporarily suspended; and,

   • put construction on hold until the university has plans for an alternate site that is acceptable to the Brushy Community as well as the neighbors in the new community.

2. President Bowen should meet with the community Tuesday evening, December 20, and assure them that he is personally involved and outline the process that will be taking place.

3. If a decision is made to still locate a downsized Swine Center on the proposed site, then a *What if?* analysis must be prepared and discussed.

Rene A. Henry
December 12, 1994

This was not what the Aggie administration wanted to hear. President Bowen no longer wanted the author's advice regarding this crisis. The author warned about timing since the university was going to close for the Christmas holiday season which would have been a perfect time for the opposition to mount a campaign. Most university officials would not be available to defend their position.

The administration did compromise by holding a meeting on December 20 with the community residents in the Animal Science Center in the community. The morning of the meeting, the story was statewide. The headline in the *Houston Chronicle* was "Rural residents turn up noses at A&M pig farm . . . Bush library forcing swine center to move."[3] The headline in *The Houston Post* was "Community wants no 'stinking' pigs."[4] "Disgruntled over swine . . . Some residents are angry with A&M's plans to move pig farm because of new Bush library" was the headline in *The Dallas Morning News*.[5] All ran an Associated Press story that led with: "COLLEGE STATION, Texas—Residents of a rural area near Texas A&M University are raising a stink over the relocation of a pig farm being displaced by construction of the George Bush Presidential Library."[6] The next day the story was all over the world. Then things quieted while the community and the college tried to find a solution.[7]

University Revises Original Plans

During this time, the university modified the design of the complex to relocate the Swine and Dairy Products Centers, established a water quality management plan with the Texas State Soil and Water Conservation Board and established other practices to as-sure surface- and ground-water protection and air quality.[8] When asked about residents' complaints about the stench of manure, Dr. John Beverly, deputy vice chancellor and associate dean, insisted, "There's not going to be a problem."[9] The university proposed to keep 50 to 75 pigs at the center for teaching and research purposes. However, according to Dr. Albert Schaffer, a professor emeritus of sociology and community resident, if the pigs were allowed to breed there could be 700 to 800 pigs there at any one time.[10]

The conflict involved more than just the swine. Apart from the smells and flies, residents were concerned about contaminated ground water, contaminated aquifers and illness that could be caused by the high level of nitrates, phosphates, other chemicals, and viruses and other micro-organisms. "We are very concerned over losing control of our lives and very existence and having to cope with an obnoxious environment," said Albert Schaffer. "If these matters come to pass, investments in our homes are virtually worthless."[11]

In June 1995, the university moved ahead with construction.

The residents established Residents Opposed to Pigs and Livestock and filed a lawsuit in federal court in Houston in August. Dr. Ruth Schaffer, the wife of Albert and also a professor emeriti of sociology at A&M, expressed her concern over the safety of drinking water. "No one with a well less than 100 feet deep should be drinking out of it at this time," she said.[12] This was amplified by Jim Mazzullo, a geology professor at A&M and also a community resident, who said studies done by a firm contracted by the university revealed the site is "unstable." Mazzullo said: "The report speaks for itself. [The site] is underlaid by unstable clay and has a very shallow water table that makes it incredibly susceptible to contamination by animal waste . . . and the problem is exacerbated because so many people depend on wells in the area."[13]

The geology professor believed one of the proposed university safety measures was essentially flawed. He said that underground plastic liner to contain wastes and other materials with potential health hazards "will not remain impermeable and will leak water quickly" because "the type of clay is expansive and will swell and shrink with the weather. . . . There's just no way to engineer around the clay."[14]

Possible Critters in the Water

According to the U.S. Environmental Protection Agency, nationwide livestock waste impairs river waters to a greater extent than storm sewers and runoff, combined sewer outflows or industrial sources. About 150 diseases can be contracted from drinking water contaminated by animal wastes.

Health safety concerned the fear that cryptosporidia, a parasite organism that is passed in animal feces, will filter into the water system. Catherine Wade, a technician in Texas A&M's College of Veterinary Medicine pathobiology department said that cryptosporidia is a parasite, only smaller than a human red blood cell. The parasite usually causes diarrhea for about two weeks when humans and animals are infected. The body, unable to develop resistance to the parasite, continually loses fluid and minerals.[15]

Problems with pigs anywhere near residential communities has been well-documented by the media. CBS-TV featured problems with pigs in North Carolina where there are more pigs than people. The state's pig population of 8.5 million exceeds the state's 7.2 million people. Television cameras showed farms located in predominantly Black communities and how some 30 percent of the ground water wells near hog farms had become contaminated. Morley Safer of *60 Minutes* said, "A good neighbor never stinks up his community with feces and urine." But this is exactly what happened in 1995 when a rain-swollen lagoon adjacent to one of the farms spilled 22 million gallons of hog feces and urine over the countryside.[16]

Pig Problems Not Isolated in College Station

With increased consumption of pork, which is now a $30 billion industry in the United States, livestock farms are creating controversy wherever they are located. Colorado farmer Galen Travis says it is not just the smell of reeking hog manure that concerns him, but that deep lagoons where hog waste is stored could seep through the dry soil and pollute the Oglalla Aquifier, the underground lake that provides drinking and irrigation water to much of the western Great Plains. Voters in North Carolina, Kansas, Nebraska and Oklahoma are opposing new hog farms and restricting those now in operation.[17]

In January 1996, in the face of pending litigation, Texas A&M began construction on the $5.5 million complex. Even the local newspaper suggested the university delay construction until a court decision was handed down. Here are excerpts from the editorial board's opinion piece:

Our View
A&M SHOULD WAIT A BIT

"Despite court-ordered mediation with unhappy residents of the Brushy Community, Texas A&M University officials have vowed to continue construction of the early phases of an animal science complex that will house sheep and goats and, for periods of three or four months at a time, swine.

"What's the rush? U.S. District Judge Ewing Werlein, Jr. has asked lawyers . . . to come up with a compromise by the end of the month. By continuing its construction . . . A&M officials are saying there can be only one solution: their's.

". . . If the judge rules against A&M, that work—and expense—will be for naught. The prudent and neighborly thing would be to wait for the judge's ruling, whatever it might be.

"The big fear is that government projects take on lives of their own. Once started, they are hard to stop. . . . A delay of a few weeks will push the completion of the animal center back, but so would an adverse ruling from Judge Werlein."[18]

Residents Call on Governor Bush for Help

In January 1996, Judge Werlein did not grant an injunction requested by the residents, but warned the university not to build facilities for animals. He then ordered the two parties into mediation scheduled for March. In February the Schaffers called on Texas Governor George W. Bush for help, since he appoints the regents who approve of such projects. "Unless the governor takes some kind of action," said Al Schaffer, "his father's presidential library will be tarnished with the image of environmental racism." He added that his organization has been patiently working with the A&M administration for nearly two years. "They talk about being good community citizens, but their actions contradict their press releases. The university has been trying to bully this center through its final stages. They have not backed off once from their original plans. Their arrogant attitude has been 'what is good for Aggies is good for the world'."[19]

Governor Bush referred to matter to Mary Nan West, a South Texas rancher and chairman of A&M's board of regents, and Fred McClure, a Dallas businessman and member of the board of regents.

Chairman/rancher West, a strong advocate for the animal center, said that she and her regents did not plan to discuss the issue with the governor. "I don't see why it should be discussed between the governor and the board of regents," she said. "It's not up to the governor or the legislature to tell any university what to build where. I don't know what the big hullabaloo is. I certainly believe the adminsitrators (at A&M), and they tell me they have complied with all the environmental rules and regulations."[20]

"The whole question of moving the complex has been under discussion since the early 1980s," McClure said. "It is not something that was just decided when the president decided to place his library here."[21] The land for the center was purchased in 1989.[22] The decision to build the Bush Presidential Library complex on the site of the existing pig farm was May 3, 1991.[23]

If It Walks Like a Duck, Talks Like a Duck ...

The university's spokesperson, Jim Ashlock, responded by calling Schaffer's comments a misrepresentation of the issue to the governor. "They say we are building a 'pig and livestock farm.' It is not a pig and livestock farm. It is not a farm. It is an educational center."[24]

Public sentiment had turned against the university. In an editorial in the student newspaper, Elaine Mejia, a senior political science major wrote, "Texas A&M world class university with world class problems. . . . Despite the fact that legal action and mediation are pending, administration officials have proceeded with their plans to violate the most basic of land use principles—when possible, it is best to avoid using the same area of land for two competing functions. When land is being used to sustain the lives of American citizens no corporation, government, person or university should be allowed to contaminate it, particularly when there are other options available." After citing many of the statements made by both sides, the Aggie student described cases of environmental racism and environmental justice. She then wrote, "A&M's choosing to locate the center in the Brushy Creek area is nothing unique. Rather, A&M is added to a national list of suspect organizations that may have chosen locations based on the characteristics of their residents—in this case, low-income and African-American. . . . Historically, there has been a disparity in enforcement of environmental regulations as well."[25]

Community Leaders Have Their Say

Community leaders began to speak out. In a letter to the editor of the local newspaper, *The Eagle*, Cora Rogers wrote: "It saddens me and it hurts to know that A&M would want to treat human beings like animals. They think more of their animals than they do about humans. . . . Our lives and health are at stake. . . . A&M can find another place that is not in a residential community . . . that will not pollute the air and water and keep A&M's name out of lawsuits and media. A&M officials have built a reputation of not keeping their word. . . . We have put our roots here. . . . Some people here have worked 20-25 years and have finally retired to what? The hollering of animals at night when we try to sleep, the smell and the flies, bad water or contaminated water, diseases and more health problems to add to what we already have, fires, stress to deal with all of this, and death. Thank you A&M. If hell is anything like this, then I welcome hell."[26]

Another resident, Ruby Ellis, said "We've worked all our lives for what we have. I'm thankful for A&M. It gave us work. But now it looks like they're trying to take our lives." Etta Ruth Williams, whose grandfather was one of the Black pioneers who first settled the community, added, "We won't be able to go outside. We were here before A&M was here, and now it looks like they want to take over our homes. Like most of her neighbors, Williams spent most of her working life at the university in menial jobs. Her mother worked in the campus laundry."[27]

En Fin . . . An Agreement?

When court-ordered mediation March 2 and 3, 1996, and 23 hours of negotiation failed to resolve the dispute, a hearing date was set for March 29 in U.S. district court in Houston. Only minutes before the hearing was to begin, with principals to the litigation and witnesses in the courtroom, the two sides had a preliminary verbal agreement in Judge Werlein's chambers. Two years after the incident-now-turned-crisis began, when the two sides first met on March 29, 1994, the university and community agreed:

- A&M would post a $5 million performance bond to pay for any damage to its neighbors.

- A&M would pay the community $600,000 for legal and other expenses.

- The center will have an average of 1,000 and no more than 1,300 animals of all types would be housed on the site at one time. This is a reduction from 1,687 A&M planned before the agreement.

- No more than 10 pigs would live at the facility full time and 10 sows and their piglets would be there no more than 70 days at a time.

- Some of the manure produced by animals will be removed to another site for composting.

- The residents will have a council to monitor operation of the center to make sure it does not harm the surrounding area.

- A&M agreed not to try and buy more land around the center for agriculture purposes but could for something such as a library.[28]

In May, the general outlines of the settlement was approved by the university's board of regents but the two sides still had a few details to work out.[29] Things got no better during the torrid and humid Brazos summer. By August the organization representing the community, Residents Opposed to Pigs and Livestock, accused the university of trying to renege on the agreement. Rev. Cedric Rouse said A&M reneged on some areas and refused to accept other sections written by A&M attorneys and agriculture specialists.[30]

A Breakdown. Agreement? No!

Negotiations continued until September when Delmar Cain, the school's new general counsel, asked the Residents Opposed to Pigs and Livestock to indemnify the university against all future law-suits from the residents and all people living within two miles of the center. At this time the differences between the residents' at-torney, Bob Hager of Dallas, Texas, and the university had nar-rowed and were close to being resolved. Hager said that it would be impossible if not illegal for indemnification and requested a court date from Judge Werlein.[31]

Rouse said A&M now intends to build a poultry center and a center for exotic animals at the site and to exclude non-university-owned animals from the count. Dr. Al Schaffer said A&M officials now are interested in condemning land near the complex sometime in the future because the agreement had a 15-year moratorium on land purchases in the area. All charges were denied by A&M's as-sistant general counsel, Bill Helwig.

Another major hangup was over providing names of members of the ROPL organization. According to Mrs. Schaffer, Judge Werlein specifically told the university that the community should not provide a list of names until the settlement is signed and then the list would be given not to A&M, but to the Texas Attorney General. She said that A&M was misleading the public by claim-ing it is ready to sign an agreement and blaming the community for not giving it names of members. Lawyer Helwig disagreed saying the judge told the community they would have to submit names be-fore they could expect A&M to finalize the agreement.[32]

Speaking for the community, the Schaffers said many members were afraid of retaliation by the university if their names were on a list provided before any settlement. Both also said pressure had been exerted on some faculty members and they too were con-cerned about vengeful retaliation by the administration.

The situation still is not resolved. Construction on the new Animal Science Center was completed in May 1997. The commu-nity called on the U.S. Environmental Protection Agency for help under both the Clean Water Act and the Civil Rights Act, for envi-ronmental justice, since federal funds were used in a racially dis-criminatory way. The university, now with its third general coun-sel since the dispute began, has committed even more public funds by retaining an outside law firm.

Several times during this conflict A&M had an opportunity to end the crisis. "The university could have had a very favorable settlement at the end of the mediation in March 1996," says Albert Schaffer. "We were worn down. Our attorneys were pressuring us to settle. Then we would have been willing to allow 1,600 animals at the center and take a relatively small sum of money. A&M offered $144,000."[33] The "agreement" reached less than a month later in Judge Werlein's chambers was a maximum of 1,000 animals and A&M would pay the community $600,000.

"We also are concerned about the center's deterioration over time since A&M has a poor record of maintaining facilities, especially agriculture," writes Schaffer. "We also believe that A&M will use eminent domain to expand the facility if we lose the lawsuit. They will build a large swine center for 1,500 or more animals and move the dairy cattle to the area. Moving it from the site opens that area for development."[34]

One publication appropriately summed up the crisis by writing, "Texas A&M University is facing an unusually messy lawsuit—one involving race, George Bush, land use, and animal waste."[35]

A Saga That Continues

On August 12, Roliff H. Purrington Jr., partner in the Austin, Texas, law firm of Mayor, Day, Caldwell & Keeton, wrote attorneys for the plaintiff and cited a number of concessions and expenditures the university had made, including $366,000 to acquire a closed composting system, adding odor and pathogen monitoring systems, and, since the last mediation efforts, spending more than $600,000 on upgrades and environmental controls at the facility.[36]

Noting that "we have no authority to make any settlement offers to ROPL," Purrington added that, "We would, however, recommend something roughly along the following lines to our client: one time cash payments of $2,000 to members of ROPL located north of Highway 60 and along the south side of Highway 60 east of the facility, e.g., those African-American residents whom we believe reside in the 'true' Brushy Community, not those ROPL members along Kemp Road or in the other subdivisions to the east, for instance, where the Schaffers live." Purrington added that the university would expect full releases for any and all claims and dismissal of the current lawsuit with prejudice and in return "TAMU would agree to release ROPL members, particularly Dr. Tam Garland and Drs. Al and Ruth Schaffer from what we believe are, at best, negligent and, at worst, intentional misrepresentations throughout the community and in the press in connection with the nature of the ASTREC facility."[37]

Nearly 18 months after the two sides reached an agreement in his chambers, Judge Werlein, who was appointed to the bench was by George Bush on November 20, 1991,[38] dismissed large portions of the lawsuit. On September 11, less than two months before the Bush Presidential Library was scheduled for formal grand opening events, he cited immunity for Texas A&M under the Eleventh Amendment that generally bars suits against an unconsenting state since a judgment against the university would interfere with the fiscal autonomy of the state.[39]

"After two years in court, to dismiss it was a big shock to us," said Ruth Schaffer. Judge Werlein left intact only the group's claims alleging emotional distress, nuisance and trespassing. Residents Opposed to Pigs and Livestock subsequently filed a similar state district court action in Brazos County that is nearly identical to the federal lawsuit.[40]

Aggie spokesman Ashlock said that the university decided to move the swine facility although other animals, including some farrowing sows, will still be located at the center. The A&M attorneys asked Judge Werlein for a summary judgment in the federal case while state District Judge Carolyn Ruffino instructed both parties to file a status report by December 29, 1997.[41]

The problem, which was nearly resolved only months after it became an incident in the spring of 1994, will have taken nearly four years and cost taxpayers an estimated several million dollars, as well as millions more in embarrassment and loss of reputation for A&M.

According to a the office of the general counsel, at any one time there are about 30 lawsuits involving the university. In addition to the Brushy Community, this included the following:[42]

- A $25 million suit by former freshman and member of the Corps of Cadets, Travis Alton, accusing four top officials of ignoring hazing problems in the now-disbanded Fish Drill Team that led to his being assaulted.

- A dispute with computer scientist Dhiraj Pradhan, who has tenure and holds an endowed chair and is the ninth-highest paid A&M employee with a salary of $181,767, who was suspended in August 1997. The university charges the professor took $100,000 intended for research and Pradhan claims his troubles are caused by his opposition to post-tenure review.

- Doug Donoahue, a former cook in foodservices, claims he was fired because he called attention to food theft and time-card fraud in the department. A&M claims he was a disruptive influence at work. Two former foodservice managers were paid out-of-court settlements in their litigation against the university: Lloyd Smith, former director of the operation, $118,750, and George Nedbalek, business manager, $95,000.

- Matt Carroll, a graduate student in architecture and former commander of the Corps of Cadets, is taking his case to the U.S. Supreme Court. He claims he lost his job as project manager for an A&M project because he refused to sign timesheets that didn't accurately reflect the hours worked by the students employed. He views the episode as a violation of the Aggie Code of Honor, which states: "Aggies do not lie, cheat or steal or tolerate those who do."

Bowen, Gaston and Ashlock responded that the university is an "easy target" for lawsuits. "There's no way an organization as complicated and as people-oriented as this one is not going to have some disputes," said Gaston. "That's the way it's going to be."

Meanwhile, diagonally across the state from College Station, in the Texas Panhandle, hog producers are looking to make the Lone

Star the hog capital of the world. In fact, Amarillo Republican State Senator Teel Bivin said, "I see no reason why this area should not produce 75 percent of the world's pork." The north-ernmost 23 counties of Texas had 52,000 pigs on farms in 1992, some 279,000 by 1996 and an estimated 1.352 million in the year 2000. One magazine wrote: "Banned temporarily from locating in Kentucky and exiled by voter referenda in 18 counties in Kansas, the pork industry is moving whole hog to the Lone Star State. Nippon Meat Packers, with 1996 revenues of $4.9 billion; Murphy Family Farms, the country's largest pork producer; Premium Standard Farms, Va., Inc., a Spanish company; and Seaboard Farms, all now have pork production facilities in Texas and are looking to expand them further to get into the export market to meet demand in Japan, Mexico, Canada and the Pacific Rim."[43]

The A&M crisis damaged both the university's community re-lations and employee relations efforts. One must ask a number of questions in reviewing this case. Why did a crisis like this happen in the first place? If there was a misunderstanding, could it have been resolved with compassion? Several times, Texas A&M had an opportunity to end the conflict, to cut short its financial losses and not lose face. Was it institutional arrogance? Was it ego? Was it a holdover militaristic attitude when A&M was an all-male, all-White military school? Was it a refusal to admit a mistake? Only the leadership at Texas A&M can answer those questions.

Endnotes

1. *International Herald Tribune*, September 21, 1994, Paris, France, pg. 3.
2. Letter from Dr. E. Dean Gage, College Station, Texas, March 26, 1997.
3. *Houston Chronicle*, December 20, 1994, section A, pg. 25.
4. *The Houston Post*, December 20, 1994, pg. A-21.
5. *The Dallas Morning News*, December 20, 1994, pg. 23A.
6. Ibid.
7. Tara Wilkinson, "Brushy Creek residents fight research complex, *The Battalion*, Texas A&M University, College Station, Texas, July 11, 1995, pg. 1.
8. News release, Office of University Relations, Texas A&M University, College Station, Texas, August 16, 1995.
9. Associated Press, "A&M, neighborhood head for court," *The Dallas Morning News*, February 12, 1996, pg. 22A.

10. Chip Lambert and Jim Wyss, "A&M pig center causing controversy," *The Eagle*, Bryan, Texas, pg. 1.

11. Letter from Dr. Albert Schaffer, College Station, Texas, May 22, 1997.

12. Tara Wilkinson, *The Battalion, op cit.*, pg. 6.

13. Chip Lambert and Jim Wyss, *The Eagle, op cit.*, pg. A8.

14. Ibid.

15. Tara Wilkinson, *The Battalion, op cit.*, pg. 6.

16. *60 Minutes*, CBS, December 22, 1996 and July 6, 1997.

17. John Greenwald, "Hogging the Table . . . Corporate pig factories are supplanting traditional farms — and critics are raising a stink about it," *Time*, March 18, 1996, pg. 76.

18. Eagle Editorial Board, "A&M should wait a bit," *The Eagle*, Bryan, Texas, February 4, 1996, pg. A11.

19. Keely Coughlan, "Gov. Bush to Brushy Creek's rescue?," *The Eagle*, Bryan, Texas, pg. A9.

20. Keely Coughlan, "Gov. Bush refers Brushy Creek query to two A&M regents," *The Eagle*, Bryan, Texas, February 21, 1996, pgs. A1, A4.

21. Ibid.

22. Letter from Dr. Albert Schaffer, College Station, Texas, May 22, 1997.

23. Keely Coughlan, "Gov. Bush to Brushy Creek's rescue?" *The Eagle*, Bryan, Texas, February 14, 1996, pg. A9.

24. Ibid.

25. Elaine Mejia, "Brushy Creek reeks of questionable treatment," *The Battalion*, Texas A&M University, College Station, Texas, February 27, 1996.

26. *The Eagle*, Bryan, Texas, February 26, 1996, editorial page.

27. Richard Stewart, "A&M stirs community's ill will with 'arrogant' expansion march," *Houston Chronicle*, February 11, 1996, pg. E1.

28. Associated Press, "A&M, neighbors reach accord," *The Dallas Morning News*, March 30, 1996, pg. 24A.

29. Keely Coughlan, "Regents OK Brushy Creek pact . . . A&M, residents still discussing details of livestock center," *The Eagle*, Bryan, Texas, May 25, 1996, pg. 1.

30. Keely Coughlan, "Brushy dispute smolders . . . A&M denies claims that it reneged on deal," *The Eagle*, August 6, 1996, pg. 1.

31. Letter from Dr. Albert Schaffer, College Station, Texas, May 22, 1997.

32. Keely Coughlan, "Brushy dispute smolders . . . A&M denies claims that it reneged on deal," *The Eagle*, August 6, 1996, pg. A10.

33. Letter from Dr. Albert Schaffer, College Station, Texas, May 22, 1997.

34. Ibid.

35. Rachanee Srisavasdi, "A Community Sues as Texas A&M Tried to Move 1,000 Animals to the Neighborhood," *The Chronicle of Higher Education*, December 6, 1996, pg. A50.

36. Letter of August 12, 1997 from Roliff H. Purrington Jr., Austin, Texas to Robert E. Hager of Nichols, Jackson, Dillard, Hager & Smith, Dallas, Texas.

37. Ibid.

38. Senate Judiciary Committee, February 20, 1998.

39. Residents Opposing Pigs and Livestock, Plaintiffs, v. Texas A&M University, Ray M. Bowen, its President and the Board of Regents of Texas A&M University, Nan West, John H. Lindsey, Michael O'Connor, Robert H. Allen, Allison Brisco, Don Powell, Guadalupe L. Rangel and Royce E.

Wisenbacker Defendants, Civil Action No. H-95-4113, United States District Court for the Southern District of Texas, Houston Division, *Memorandum and Order*, Ewing Werlein, Jr., United States District Judge, September 11, 1997.

40. "Ruling is blow to A&M livestock complex foes," *The Dallas Morning News*, November 13, 1997.

41. Ibid.

42. John Kirsch, "A&M target of lawsuits," *The Eagle*, Bryan, Texas, February 8, 1988, pgs. A1, A5, A8.

43. Robert Bryce, "Making Bacon in the Panhandle," *The Texas Observer*, October 10, 1997, pgs. 8-13.

CHAPTER EIGHT

NATURAL DISASTERS— DON'T ARGUE WITH MOTHER NATURE

During the past 30 years, earthquakes, floods, hurricanes, landslides, tidal waves, tornadoes, tropical cyclones, twisters, typhoons, volcanic eruptions, wildfires and other natural disasters have killed more people than the wars in the Persian Gulf, Iran/Iraq, Afghanistan or Vietnam. The death toll is nearly 3 million and the catastrophes have caused incalculable suffering and personal and property loss.

From 1992 to 1997, 15 U.S. disasters involving deaths from floods, heat waves, hurricanes, blizzards and hail storms caused $70 billion in damages. Damages from the Mississippi River flooding in 1993 ranged from $10 to $20 billion. Almost $4 billion in federal payments went to farmers suffering crop losses during the 1988 drought.[1]

In 1998 alone, natural disasters globally caused 50,000 deaths and economic losses of more than $90 billion compared to 13,000 deaths and $30 billion in losses the previous year, according to Munich Re, a German reinsurance company. The company attributed the catastrophes to a combination of global warming and unusually heavy rain and warned that "even radical environmental protection measures cannot prevent the occurrence of even more and ever costlier natural catastrophes worldwide."[2]

The 1999 World Disasters Report, an annual survey, said the disasters are the worst on record and drove an estimated 25 million people, or 58 percent of the world's refugees, from their homes. It noted that for the first time, "environmental refugees" fleeing droughts, floods, deforestation and degraded land outnumbered those displaced by war. The report also noted that one billion people live in unplanned shanty towns and 40 of the 50 fastest growing cities are in earthquake zones and at least 10 million people live in low-lying coastal areas prone to flooding. As many as 96 percent of the deaths from natural disasters occur in developing countries.[3]

The 1990s were designated by the United Nations as the International Decade for Natural Disaster Reduction. In response, The Annenberg Washington Program in Communications Policy Studies of Northwestern University, Washington, D.C., convened a study group to determine what the latest communications technology can do following sudden disasters.

The importance of communications during and after a natural disaster was emphasized by two officials of the American Red Cross—Robert D. Vessey, director of Disaster Services, and Jose A. Aponte, director of International Services. They cited the experience of a young engineer in 1899 who, after inspecting a dam upriver from Johnstown, Pennsylvania, realized it was about to collapse and raced his horse to the nearest railroad station to telegraph a warning to communities in the valley below. Even though he was using state-of-the-art communications, his message never got through and 2,200 people died in the Johnstown Flood.[4] Johnstown suffered its third disastrous flood in 1977. Although communications technology had significantly improved in 78 years, 58 people died because the message again was not delivered. Vessey and Aponte attributed this to a combination of an overly cautious river forecaster who did not sound an alarm and a Red Cross answering service in Pittsburgh that told the Johnstown chapter to call back the following morning.[5]

Communications can make a vital difference in the first 24 hours, according to David Webster, director of the Annenberg program. Radio is the communications mode of choice for emergency response because it is portable, available and versatile. Battery-powered radios are not susceptible to downed wires, loss of power, damage to switching stations or inundated switchboards. How well the system works depends on how it interlinks. During the Mount St. Helens volcanic eruption, the Washington State Police could not communicate with the National Guard. In foreign disasters, military radio often cannot communicate with civilian short-wave operators.[6]

Since voice radio is not secure and can be monitored by anyone on the same channel, the emergency communications system recommended, whether permanent or mobile, has a radio-teletype or facsimile machine so information can be transmitted in hard copy.[7]

Satellite Video Disaster Assessment

Effective communications can reduce death, suffering and damage following a disaster. LifeNet, a project of the Foundation for Global Broadcasting, was established by award-winning television producer Harold Uplinger. At CBS, Uplinger was responsible for producing such events as the Super Bowl, NFL Championship Games and the Triple Crown in horse racing. During the past two decades he has devoted most of his career to humanitarian causes.[8]

In 1987, Uplinger formed a consortium of international television executives representing 56 percent of the world's television sets. LifeNet was created to provide visual assessment from disaster sites under emergency conditions by coordinating international satellite hookups. The pictures and sounds of the disaster can be transmitted by satellite to allow decision makers on the scene to consult with experts throughout the world. Real-time video transmissions make possible a more objective assessment, saving money, relief efforts and lives.[9]

On May 12, 1987, Uplinger established a two-way video link test between Costa Rica and the Office of Foreign Disaster Assistance of the Agency for International Development in Washington, D.C. LifeNet demonstrated the concept of interactive communications for real-time disaster relief. It was first used in the 1988 Armenian earthquake. While the television news crews focused on the most severely injured children for powerful news reports, LifeNet focused on visual information that helped plan the relief efforts.[10] "The interesting thing about LifeNet is that with today's technology, disaster relief people can be on a site within four hours and transmitting *correct* information back by phone and video," Uplinger adds. "Before, it was days."[11]

Matthew S. Tietze and Lydia A. Kan, consultants with Booz, Allen & Hamilton, believe if LifeNet had been used after the 1989 San Francisco earthquake that better and earlier information about the extent of damage could have improved rescue efforts and helped calm the nation. "Instead, inexact and hysterical coverage of damage in the Bay Area hampered relief efforts and led to a great deal of criticism of broadcasters. The television networks had extensive portable communications equipment and personnel in the Bay Area for the baseball World Series but it was used, with few exceptions, for sensationalist reporting," say Tietze and Kan.[12] "If these resources had been coordinated and personnel trained for this contingency, the media (working with LifeNet) could have arranged a comprehensive video briefing on the quake damage for the President, the Secretary of Transportation and even the Governor of California (who was in Germany at the time), on the evening of the earthquake.

"With this useful information, authorities could have given the public definitive statements on the extent of damage, instructions on how to prepare for aftershocks, and guidance on mobilization to emergency workers. This sort of intervention might have quelled some of the hysteria that swept the country. Because the damage was so poorly characterized in the news, the region's (San Francisco Bay Area) telephone system was jammed by frantic people calling friends and relatives; people at risk were given little guidance about aftershocks; and emergency workers were not well informed," they add.[13]

This Bud's For You!

Pure drinking water is always needed following a natural disaster. From 1992 to 1996, Anheuser-Busch Inc. donated 16 million cans of fresh drinking water to victims. Instead of the familiar Budweiser logo, the cans were white with the Anheuser-Busch Inc.

flying eagle in an A and marked "Drinking Water." In an advertisement with the headline, "Sometimes our most popular product is made without barley, malt, grain, yeast or hops," the company pointed out how it has worked closely with relief organizations since the 1906 San Francisco earthquake.[14]

The Buffalo Creek Dam Disaster

Dams that are mountains of black coal refuse are prevalent throughout Appalachia. These dams hold back slurry that is a thick mix of water, coal waste particles and rock. Each dam is made of unused parts of coal left over after it is washed, creating a simple filtering mechanism for the dirty water. Water is supposed to seep through the dams at a slow rate leaving behind the solids to settle to the bottom. The dams grow larger every day as rock and coal waste are dumped on them from conveyor belts.[15] Today there are 232 coal-waste dams in West Virginia, 155 in Kentucky and 132 in Pennsylvania.

At 8 A.M. on February 26, 1972, after a few days of hard rain, a 30-foot-high dam 550 feet wide at the Pittston Coal Company failed and more than 130 million gallons of black water cascaded more than 15 miles down Buffalo Creek in Logan County. The disaster killed 125 people, injured 1,000, left 4,000 homeless, and demolished 507 houses and 44 mobile homes while damaging nearly a thousand more. In addition, 30 businesses, 1,000 vehicles, 10 bridges, and power, water and telephone lines were destroyed. The country road and rail lines serving the valley's coal mines were severely damaged. It took about three hours to wash out a succession of small southern West Virginia coal towns and reach the confluence of Buffalo Creek and the Guyandotte River at Man, West Virginia.

The coal company's New York public relations office issued a news release that said the flood was "an act of God." The response attempted to absolve Pittston from legal responsibility, but it only reinforced doubts about the ability of government and industry to protect the public. The "act of God" words still sting survivors' hearts.[16]

Congressman Ken Hechler (D-W.Va.) toured Buffalo Creek prior to the flood and warned of the dangers of coal dams. "This was a terrifying shock to both federal and state officials," Hechler said. "They should have been shocked earlier." The dams were supposed to be inspected every two weeks and were not. Pittston employees did not warn authorities that the water behind the dam was rising and only minutes before the disaster had told Logan County officials that everything was under control.[17]

In 1974, lawyers won a $13.5 million settlement for 600 survivors, and four years later another 1,200 survivors won $4.88 million. Less attorneys' fees, the payoff was about $2,700 per person. Pittston's insurance paid most of the settlement.

A citizen's commission report said that company and state officials had been told of problems and that the Buffalo Creek dam had failed before. Governor Arch Moore appointed his own commission which reported: "The dam failure was solely the cause of the Buffalo Creek flood. No evidence of an act of God was found by the commission." Moore settled the state's lawsuit with Pittston for $1 million three days before he left office in 1977, even though the West Virginia Legislature had ordered the Attorney General to sue Pittston. The Army Corps of Engineers billed the state for $3.7 million for repairs to its roads, bridges and other costs. The state ignored the bill until 1982 when interest had ballooned the cost to $9.5 million.[18]

In February 1968, Pearl Woodrum wrote the governor saying the dam was unsafe and, if it failed, would kill all of the people in the valley. She also sent the letter to the heads of the state's Public Service Commission and Department of Natural Resources, the U.S. Geological Survey and the county prosecutor. No one took any action. A permit was required before the dam could be constructed and no permit had been issued.[19]

Indexing Earthquake Risks

A Stanford University civil engineer created an index that ranks major cities by their relative risk of earthquakes. In addition to magnitude and frequency of shakes, Rachel Davidson considered factors including a city's size, number of inhabitants, activities it supports, how physically and economically resistant the area is to damage, and the availability of emergency-response resources.[20] Tokyo was ranked No. 1 with 54 on a scale of 100, followed by Boston (39), Mexico City (38), San Francisco (37) and St. Louis (36). Davidson noted that while San Francisco is more likely to experience an earthquake, should one happen in Boston with its densely packed, older buildings, a mild quake could turn into a major disaster.[21]

Outside of California, few building codes have seismic standards and buildings are more vulnerable. The country's most severe earthquake was December 16, 1811, on the New Madrid Fault that runs under St. Louis. Even a mild trembler in that area would be felt from Chicago to New Orleans and along the East Coast. The other two largest earthquakes in the United States were at Charleston, South Carolina, in 1886 and Anchorage, Alaska, in 1964.[22]

A Potential Disaster That Would Be Inconceivable in American History

People relate earthquakes to California because the state is hit with thousands of shocks every year. About half are strong enough to be felt by many people. In his book, *Earthquake Country,* author Robert Iacopi writes: "Earthquakes are a part of California's heritage and we all must learn to live with them. But the dangers involved are more a result of man's ignorance than of nature's destructive force."[23]

Most major cities along the highly vulnerable Pacific Rim have strict seismic building codes to protect houses, buildings and other structures from damage during an earthquake. These standards have been ignored in other areas of the country. Few state and local governments have crisis plans to deal with an earthquake. Property and casualty insurance companies, however, are concerned, according to James R. Smith, executive director of the Building Seismic Safety Council in Washington, D.C. He believes companies may mandate seismic standards be used for commercial and institutional buildings, hotels and motels and other structures in all parts of the United States in order for the owners to obtain coverage without exorbitantly expensive premiums.[24] Here is how Smith describes what happens in a major shock:

1. Water in rivers, lakes and streams can be thrown completely over the banks and sizeable waves are created.

2. Strong shock waves can uproot trees and snap off the tops of others.

3. Freeways and bridges not built to standards can collapse.

4. Depending on the topography and soil composition, there can be massive landslides.

5. Surface movement ruptures the land causing fissures, breaks, and sinking the land in one area and raising it to a dome in others.

6. Anything in the way of the movement of the primary fault will be ruptured. Visual damage is where roads and fences have been offset horizontally.

7. At great distances the damage is limited generally to high-rise buildings that are swayed by the slow surface waves. Damage also can occur when two buildings set up different motion and pound each other.

What concerns Smith and other seismic experts most is the alluvium and soft soils throughout the Mississippi Valley and along the New Madrid Fault. Earthquake shock waves tend to travel longer distances when they occur in these areas.[25] The New Madrid Fault spreads across the central Mississippi Valley, including southeastern Missouri, northeastern Arkansas and western Kentucky and Tennessee. The United States was sparsely settled in 1811 when the fault let loose. Shock waves were felt in New Orleans, Chicago, Detroit, Washington, Boston and Atlanta. By the end of April 1812, more than 2,000 shocks occurred in this area with five great quakes of 8.0 or larger. The shocks of this period have not been equaled in number, geographic area affected or severity and intensity even by more recent and better-known earth-quakes.[26] The occurrence of such a shock in a region like the Mississippi Valley, on the borders of a great river, is probably un-precedented in the history of earthquakes.[27]

Seismologists measure the size of an earthquake by the Richter Magnitude Scale and express this in numbers and decimals usually between 3 and 8 on a logarithmic scale. An earthquake of 8.3 magnitude is 10 million times as strong as a shock of 4.3. The largest known earthquakes in the world have been at the 8.8 or 8.9 level. The 1906 San Francisco earthquake was 8.3 and the February 9, 1991, San Fernando Valley shock that killed 64 people registered only 6.6.[28]

The Indians of the Mississippi Valley had a tradition that told of a great earthquake that had previously devastated the same region. This also is supported by geological evidence of shocks long before 1811.[29] No feature of the New Madrid area is as conspicuous or striking as the so-called sunk lands, resulting from the settling or warping of alluvial deposits in western Tennessee, southeastern Missouri and northeastern Arkansas. Large trees of walnut, white oak and mulberry that once grew on high land are now dead and submerged 10' to 20' below water while cypress trees, once in swamp land, are on elevated land. Domes of uplifted land 7 to 10 miles in diameter are found in the region.[30]

Scientists and seismologists know much more about predicting earthquakes today. Instruments are used to measure earth move-ment, and some believe there is a release of pressures on a 50-year cycle and others on a 100-year cycle.[31] The seismic council's Smith says two things are certain: "One, We don't know when, but there will be another earthquake along the New Madrid Fault of equal or even greater intensity, and two, we can be prepared."

Prepared—Learning From Experience

The Northridge Fashion Mall, a major shopping mall in North-ridge, California, an area susceptible to earthquakes, was virtually demolished by the 1994 earthquake that hit Los Angeles. Fortun-ately the mall was closed and empty when it was leveled. When the mall was re-opened 18 months later, its management and the community developed a comprehensive crisis management plan.[32] Objectives of the plan are to minimize financial loss and business interruptions, help make customers feel safe, limit a disaster's severity, train staff how to handle disasters, resume business as soon as possible and maintain a positive image within the community.

To test its plan, the mall joins with city and county fire and emergency-preparedness units for an annual four-hour training drill for its employees. All trainees are evaluated and graded. Because of employee turnover, instruction and regular drills are vital.[33]

Somebody Get Toto!

Elaine Hundrieser had only seconds to act when she looked out her office window at the Danada Square West shopping center in Wheaton, Illinois, and saw a huge, dark mass coming directly at her. She yelled "Take cover!" and grabbed a contractor she was meeting with and got under her desk just as a 70-mile-per-hour tornado swept through the area on Friday, July 18, 1997. Following the center's crisis management plan, she first called the fire department, then paramedics and then the police.[34]

The 350,000-square-foot strip center was battered with shattered windows, glass everywhere and a parking lot filled with damaged vehicles and debris from a nearby construction site. "We had no notice," said Hundrieser. "We knew how to help our customers because every quarter we review the plan which covers tornados, fires and bomb threats."[35] "The plan without the drill isn't worth two cents," says Philip Jan Rothstein, president of his own Brookfield, Connecticut, management consulting firm. "Drills, walkthroughs or discussions are essential. If you don't exercise it, there's almost no point in developing the plan in the first place."

Land Ho!

The Riverwalk Marketplace in New Orleans not only had a plan for a boat collision, but employees had just practiced it 10 days earlier. Security and maintenance workers knew just what to do when a freighter went out of control on the Mississippi River and crashed into the center. The collision, which happened on Saturday afternoon, December 14, 1996, injured 116 people and caused millions of dollars in damage to the mall and the 29-story New Orleans Hilton above it. The mall is built on the Poydras Street Wharf along the river.[36]

Mall workers evacuated 6,000 people who were on the site at the time. A surveillance camera near the mall's riverfront showed a man standing on the wharf looking at the ship only moments before the collision. Someone pulled him to safety just as the camera went out. No lives were lost in the accident. Brian Lade, Riverwalk general manager, believes it is important to include retailers in any plan. "When you have 6,000 people in the shopping center and only 30 mall employees, you can get a lot of help from 500 retailers helping people to safety," he says. Retailers as well should have their own plans.[37]

As a result of the ship accident, Riverwalk organized an emergency alert system that will enable the U.S. Coast Guard to warn mall officials of any out-of-control ship heading its way. Management installed cameras facing the Mississippi so they can immediately determine whether to evacuate; hooked up an emergency evacuation message to the music system; and purchased a Marine Band radio to monitor the emergency channel.

Hurricane Andrew and the University of Miami Hurricanes

How the University of Miami dealt with Hurricane Andrew is a tribute to its president, Edward T. Foote II, who demonstrated how the effect of a crisis can be mitigated, minimized and controlled by strong leadership. On Saturday, August 22, 1992, Hurricane Andrew was 1,000 miles east of Miami and people in Florida began preparing as they had for scores of previous hurricanes.[38] Ironically, a hurricane delayed the opening of the university on September 17, 1926. That devastating storm killed 130 people, left 10,000 homeless and delayed the school's inaugural. Miami's ath-

letic teams were appropriately nicknamed the "Hurricanes" in
November of that year.

In planning for crises, Foote brought together the university
leadership at least once a year to review emergency procedures,
share information and try to anticipate the worst. His team already
had gone through the hurricane emergency drill, reviewed procedures and met to compare notes and make preliminary decisions.
The anticipated arrival of Andrew was going to coincide with the
first day of new-student orientation on Monday. A Sunday evening
reception to welcome parents of new students was canceled along
with other functions. Foote had his team concentrate on securing
residential colleges and apartments, where people could ride out
the storm, as well as all other buildings on the five university
campuses.

The hurricane built in intensity during the evening. At 3:30
A.M., Monday, August 24, winds that peaked in excess of 164
miles an hour slammed into Coral Gables and felled 1,263 trees on
the Miami campus, smashed 800 windows, damaged 50 roofs, gut-
ted many buildings and offices and did $23 million of damage that
included lost medical school revenues. Some 5,000 enrolling fresh-
men, their parents, faculty and staff were stranded in residential
buildings.

"We could not have anticipated the catastrophic magnitude of
Hurricane Andrew, but the procedures we had in place helped
guide our actions, especially during the first days of shock and
devastation," said Foote. "Had we been even better prepared, we
would not have had the problems of communications . . . no working telephones, regular or cellular. Leaders who cannot communicate cannot lead. Our revised procedures now have back-up alternatives that would have served us well in 1992."

After the peak of the storm passed at 6:30 A.M., Foote tried his
cellular phone without success. The transmitting towers had been
damaged. His police radio barely reached public safety headquarters in Coral Gables and the quality of transmission varied greatly
depending on atmospheric conditions and battery strength. By 9
A.M. he contacted the campus police and had the dispatcher send

a police car to take him to the campus since he believed it would otherwise be difficult to get through security checkpoints. He found the devastation unimaginable and most of the campus without electricity and therefore air conditioning, water and telephones. Drinking water was contaminated and fallen power lines created further danger. The university's Health Center did have emergency power.

Delay the Opening of School

In the hours following the hurricane, Foote re-established the normal chain of command and then divided all issues into three categories:[39]

1. Priority was the well-being of the university family—new freshman and their parents, faculty and staff. All 7,000 employees were located by telephone, word of mouth or by university police, who were sent to the most damaged areas. A 40-person volunteer phone bank reached 4,600 employees. Homes of 419 faculty and staff were either destroyed or seriously damaged.

2. Institutional problems were handled, from maintaining security to clearing the 1,263 fallen trees.

3. His team then dealt with communitywide issues.

Foote delayed the opening day of classes two and a half weeks and sent students home, paying their round-trip transportation. "We were running out of food and potable water for an emergency community of several thousand. Marriott, who caters our food-service, was doing an outstanding job, but suppliers could not make deliveries," he said. By the end of the week the population in the residential colleges and apartments had dropped from 5,000 to 350.

The university sent out crews to help faculty and staff board up homes, made emergency loans and rented apartments so those homeless would have a place to sleep. Power was restored to the computer center so paychecks could be issued on time. Without water, toilets would not flush, so 80 portable toilets were acquired and placed around the campus. Water service was not restored until a week after the hurricane. It was days later before there was hot water or telephone service fully restored. Cooking was reduced to sterno with light from a kerosene lamp.

Helicopters were chartered to provide necessary transportation for Foote to visit all six campuses, which would not have been otherwise possible because of impassable roads. He had a professional photographer document the damage for insurance purposes. The campus police were on 12-hour shifts. Security guards were hired and posted at key places around the campus. During the first three weeks crime was limited to two armed robberies and a little pilferage.

On the second day after Andrew, Foote began daily one-hour meetings of the university leaders for sharing information, announcing or making decisions, contingency planning, dealing with emergencies and emotionally supporting each other. The meetings, which included academic and administrative leaders, police and medical officials, continued until September 9 when the university returned to a normal system of communications.[40]

Foote frequently went on radio and television news shows to report on the status, damage done, recovery plans, when people were expected to return to work, how they were to be paid and what emergency assistance was available. Since many students were from the Northeast and Chicago, special efforts were made to schedule him on radio shows in those markets to inform parents and students of Miami's recovery and plans to reopen. The university began publishing a daily report which covered everything from the potability of campus water supplies to emergency instruction. This continued for three weeks.[41]

Community Relations

Nearly 500 Miami employees and students went out in the community to work in the first days following the storm. As state and federal authorities established tent cities and emergency medical care and food and clothing distribution points, clinics were established by the university's Schools of Medicine and Nursing in Homestead and Florida City, the most devastated areas. Faculty members from architecture and engineering volunteered their services. Several worked with colleagues at The Citadel to coordinate a national volunteer engineering initiative to help assess the damage and its causes. Members of the law faculty organized emergency seminars and services on legal and insurance issues arising from the destruction.

Be Prepared to Innovate

Foote notes that the better the preparation and standing emergency procedures, the less need there is to innovate. However, he believes that there is no substitute for creative thinking on the spot, especially in emergencies. He also says it is necessary to prioritize issues and this can easily get lost in a crisis. "For the most part, our standing emergency procedures served us well. The major exception was communications. We assumed that one form of communication or another would remain intact. We were wrong. Our telephones, radios and televisions all failed us. Many of us could not even communicate face-to-face because the roads were impassable," he said.

A Stronger and Better Institution

Foote believes that, in spite of the damage, the university emerged from Hurricane Andrew a better and stronger institution. Insurance, funds from the Federal Emergency Management Agency and emergency state funds covered most of the financial losses. He believes the greatest benefit was the strengthening of the university's collective confidence.[42] Miami's actions that others can follow in a natural disaster include:

1. Anticipate all potential crises and anticipate what to do to avoid them.

2. Develop a crisis management plan for each anticipated problem.

3. Be prepared with a team in place and bring the leadership

together at least once a year to review emergency procedures.

4. As soon as possible after a disaster, re-establish the chain of command and personal communications.

5. Have backup plans and systems for emergency communications. (Be sure the system links with all other local, state and federal emergency response agencies and departments.)

6. Be innovative and flexible and adapt to changing situations.

7. Establish regular meetings of the leadership team as soon as possible.

8. Do what is necessary to take care of the immediate family — students and their parents, faculty, employees and friends.

9. Begin communicating to all stakeholders as quickly as possible. Manage the way you want your story told, not by rumors or by uninformed, unofficial spokespersons.

10. Be a good citizen and provide help where possible to others in the community.

11. The CEO should be out in front displaying leadership.

12. As soon as the crisis is over, review and critique the plan and have an even better one in place the next time.

A Place to Begin

The Federal Emergency Management Agency, popularly called FEMA, helps organizations prepare, respond, prevent and recover from disasters. The federal agency recommends companies and institutions prepare for natural disasters common to their areas and has considerable information available on earthquakes, tornadoes, hurricanes, floods and fires. Its Internet address is www.fema.gov.

Endnotes

1. *Climate Change*, July 1996, Climate Information Manager, U.S. Environmental Protection Agency, Washington, D.C.

2. Reuters, December 31, 1998.

3. Paul Brown, *London Guardian*, June 24, 1999.

4. Robert D. Vessey and Jose A. Aponte, "Needed: The Right Information at the Right Time," *Communication When It's Needed Most*, The Annenberg Washington Program in Communications Policy Studies of Northwestern University, 1989, pg. 8.

5. Ibid.

6. Ibid., pg. 9.

7. Ibid., pg. 16.

8. Rene A. Henry, *Our Changing Earth*, treatment for television miniseries, May 14, 1993.

9. Matthew S. Tietze and Lydia A. Kan, "LifeNet: A Real-Time Disaster Assessment and Assistance Service," *Communication When It's Needed Most*, *op cit.*, pg. 31.

10. Ibid., pg. 32.

11. Harold Uplinger, letter of August 2, 1997 to Rene A. Henry.

12. Ibid.

13. Ibid.

14. Anheuser-Busch, Inc., St. Louis, Missouri, advertisement, 1996.

15. Jack McCarthy, "A man-made disaster," Ken Ward, Jr., "Coal dams still loom over W. Va.," and Robert J. Byers, "Buffalo Creek: Changes lie just below the surface," *Sunday Gazette-Mail*, Gazette Online, Charleston, West Virginia, July 27, 1997.

16. Ibid.

17. Ibid.

18. Ibid.

19. Ibid.

20. Laura Tangley, "Disasters — Shake and Rattle," *U.S. News & World Report*, September 1, 1997, pg. 16.

21. Ibid.

22. Robert Iacopi, *Earthquake Country*, A Sunset Book, Lane Publishing Co., Menlo Park, California, 1981, pg. 4.

23. Ibid.

24. Correspondence and telephone calls with James R. Smith, executive director, Building Seismic Safety Council, Washington, D.C., November and December 1997.

25. Ibid.

26. Myron L. Fuller, *The New Madrid Earthquake*, Department of the Interior, U.S. Geological Survey, Bulletin 494, U.S. Government Printing Office, Washington, D.C., 1912, pgs. 4, 7, 17.

27. N.S. Shaler, "Earthquakes of the western United States," *Atlantic Monthly*, November 1869, pgs. 549-559.

28. Robert Iacopi, *op cit.*, pgs. 5, 30-32.

29. Myron L. Fuller, *op cit.*, pgs. 12, 109.

30. Ibid., pgs. 63, 65, 70.

31. Ibid., pgs. 155-157.

32. Melanie Conty, "Northridge knows the value of a drill," *Shopping Centers Today*, November 1997, pg. 25.

33. Ibid.

34. Melanie Conty, "Training for disaster best way to avoid it, owners, staff learn," *Shopping Centers Today*, November 1997, pgs. 1, 24.

35. Ibid.

36. Ibid.

37. Ibid.

38. Edward T. Foote II, "Memorandum to File Re: Hurricane Andrew, August 24, 1992," October 15, 1992 and "Weathering the Storm: Leadership During Crisis," *Educational Record*, Spring 1996, American Council on Education, Washington, D.C.

39. Ibid.

40. Ibid.

41. Ibid.

42. Ibid.

CHAPTER NINE

DO THE RIGHT THING—
TAKE RESPONSIBILITY
AND WIN PUBLIC SUPPORT

You never want to experience a crisis, especially on a holiday weekend. But this is what happened when Ashland Inc., on New Year's weekend 1988, had its first major oil pollution accident in its 64-year history.

Saturday afternoon, January 2, at its facility 15 miles southeast of Pittsburgh, a storage tank collapsed releasing a 30-foot tidal wave of 4 million gallons of diesel fuel. Approximately 700,000 gallons of fuel spilled into the Monongahela River and threatened the drinking water of communities in Pennsylvania, Ohio and West Virginia.

What followed was a textbook procedure for handling crises. Ashland did the right thing and set an example for other companies. CEO and chairman John R. Hall put concern for the public above legal considerations and won support from the public, the media, employees, stockholders, environmentalists and even regulatory agencies. Before the week ended he sent a $210,000 check to Allegheny County.

SATURDAY, JANUARY 2, 1988 [DAY 1]

5:02 P.M. While being filled, a storage tank collapsed at Ashland's terminal in West Elizabeth, Pennsylvania. Nearly 4 million gallons of fuel burst from the ruptured tank, slammed into another tank releasing 20,000 gallons more of gasoline, surged over

165

containment dikes and onto adjacent properties. The terminal's dike was large enough to hold the entire contents, but ruptured so suddenly it sent a wave of oil over the embankment. It was discovered later that the oil had found its way to a storm drain, located on adjacent property, that emptied into the Monongahela River.[1]

5:21 P.M. Ashland officials notified all emergency response organizations.

5:30 P.M. Pittsburgh Public Safety Director Glenn Cannon began calling out emergency personnel and city Public Works Department employees.

8:30 P.M. A county Special Intervention Team found additional leakage and diesel fuel in storm sewers.

9:00 P.M. Five-inch hoses inflated with air were stretched across the Monongahela downstream from the spill to a lock eight miles downstream.

10:00-11:00 P.M. The Special Intervention Team found damage to another storage tank and to pipes connected to a tank filled with gasoline. Ashland began to empty gasoline from that tank into a barge.[2]

11:00 P.M. Ashland established its command post at the spill site.

MIDNIGHT About 1,200 nearby residents were evacuated as a precaution since diesel fuel was in the river and the sewage system. Water intake valves on the river were closed, and 50,000 people faced potential water shortages. The Coast Guard halted all river traffic from the site to the point in Pittsburgh where the Monongahela meets the Allegheny River to form the Ohio River. Adjacent rail lines and highways were temporarily closed. Darkness and below-freezing winter weather added to the already difficult situation.[3]

SUNDAY, JANUARY 3 [DAY 2]

3:00 A.M. Hazardous materials units 20 miles downstream attempted to contain the spill. Additional teams arrived during the morning and afternoon.

7:45 A.M. Western Pennsylvania Water Co., a utility that serves 750,000 customers, closed one of its two water pumping stations. Officials pleaded with the public to conserve water.[4]

MORNING Hall rushed to his office as soon as he was called. With his president, Charles J. Luellen, he talked with colleagues at the accident site and elsewhere. He then isolated himself from distractions and had subordinates handle all outside queries. Later than day he called Pennsylvania Governor Robert P. Casey and told him Ashland intended to clean up the mess as fast as it could.[5] Dan Lacy, vice president of corporate communications, recommended against a press release. "When a situation is evolving so rapidly, a release isn't good enough."[6]

NOON Some 1,200 residents returned home. Governor Casey put the National Guard on alert to deliver emergency drinking water to hospitals and residents.

AFTERNOON Media descended on the scene. The first of what became twice-a-day press conferences was held. The Coast Guard reported that 700,000 gallons flowed into the river and the rest was contained near the tank. "Our first priority will be the cleanup effort and that will take some time." said Ashland's Lacy.[7]

MONDAY, JANUARY 4 [DAY 3]

6:30 A.M. When Hall arrived at work, he thought everything was under control.[8] By midmorning, he found things were not. Calls from public officials, reporters, local water companies and members of Ashland's own emergency management team revealed discrepancies about the facts. Reporters initially were told the tank was new and the company had a permit to construct it. Hall then learned his people spoke too soon—the tank was reconstructed from 40-year-old steel and a written permit had not been issued. He was further concerned when he learned that the tank had been tested with an alternate rather than the prescribed test. He let his management know he was frustrated and wanted the right information.[9]

EARLY AFTERNOON The oil spill, 6 to 11 inches thick, was now 47 miles downstream headed toward Wheeling, West Virginia.[10] The temperature dropped overnight making cleanup even more difficult, but helped congeal the fuel which was beneficial for fish and wildlife.[11] Governor Casey ordered $2 million in state funds to be used for the cleanup. Ashland was paying for the emergency hazard teams. A series of navigational locks and dams, only three miles from the terminal, churned the oil and water causing it to emulsify and sink below the recovery booms. Officials feared this would contaminate submerged water intake pipes and treatment facilities. Water shortages forced some schools to close.[12]

As company engineers and government regulators began their investigations, questions were asked about why the tank collapsed. The 40-year-old tank was moved from Cleveland, Ohio, to West Elizabeth. The metal was tested and its structural integrity passed all inspections. However, the Allegheny County fire marshal, Martin Jacobs, said his office had not issued a construction permit for the tank to be rebuilt. An Ashland spokesman said a permit was issued in 1986, but Jacobs may not have been notified because of its age.[13]

LATE AFTERNOON The situation worsened from an environmental to a public health and safety problem because of limited available water. Hall wanted to make a public statement, but his lawyers cautioned he should carefully consider admitting any mistakes because of liability. Hall felt he had to be candid and called for a press conference the following day in Pittsburgh.[14]

TUESDAY, JANUARY 5 [DAY 4]

Flying to Pittsburgh, Hall rehearsed for the press conference with his advisers asking anticipated questions: "How long will it take to clean up the spill?" and "How much will it cost?" Hall stopped first at the spill site and commended tired workers for their work.[15]

Dozens of reporters confronted him as he began the media event, thanking everyone who participated in the cleanup activity. He apologized to the people of the Pittsburgh area for the incident. "The company expects to pay the cost of the cleanup and reimburse the government agencies for reasonable expenses," he said.[16]

Hall admitted that the company did not have written building permits and did not follow standard steps to test the tank.[17] "In hindsight I might question the use of 40-year-old steel," he said. "We did not follow our normal refinery procedures in testing the tank after it was completed. I wish our people had pursued the application process [with Fire Marshal Martin Jacobs] more diligently." The company first said the tank was new.[18] Hall believed that the best thing to do was to tell everything he knew. "If we made mistakes, we have to stand up and admit them."[19]

In his remarks, Hall said: "I want to assure you that Ashland is a responsible corporate citizen. We have operated successfully in the oil refining business for 64 years, and maintain high safety standards at all of our operations, including 23 terminals similar to the one at Floreffe. We also have been responsive to community concerns where our operations are located. We intend to maintain that tradition and stick with the job until the cleanup is complete."

Ashland got praise from an attorney for the U.S. Environmental Protection Agency. "[Ashland] is assuming . . . all costs associated with the spill. The company has gone beyond what the EPA could do by providing additional water supplies to towns downriver. Federal regulations prevent EPA from providing alternative water supplies in case of a spill," he said.[20]

WEDNESDAY, JANUARY 6 [DAY 5]

Hall cancelled business trips to stay in Pittsburgh and meet with political leaders and editorial boards of local newspapers, and to telephone governors of Ohio and West Virginia.[21] Ohio Governor Richard Celeste declared a state of emergency for river communities preparing to close water intake pipes. The oil slick was now 17 miles long, 18 feet deep and 67 miles from Pittsburgh.[22]

Water service was partially restored to 23,000 people in the Pittsburgh suburbs of Robinson Township and North Fayette. Conditions were expected to be normal by the weekend.[23]

In USA Today, Gerald Meyers, former chairman of American Motors Corporation and professor of crisis management at Carnegie-Mellon University said: "It looks as if they are dealing professionally with a bad situation. Ashland is following the rule carved in marble in (public relations) offices: Get the bad news out, and get it out fast." Ashland's Lacy said the company was following a crisis management practice that has been used for years. "Our attitude is to be candid and respond rapidly," he said.[24] The company subsequently decided that its previous practice lacked enough detail and developed a master plan based on its oil spill experience.

Ashland's efforts were not enough, however, to stop the first of the lawsuits. Four suburban Pittsburgh residents sued Ashland alleging "corporate maliciousness and negligence" that disrupted water service. They sought up to $10,000 each in compensatory and punitive damages and to make it a class-action suit.[25]

THURSDAY, JANUARY 7 [DAY 6]

Hall stayed in Pittsburgh. People began filling swimming pools with water. The oil slick was now 115 miles from the accident. Pipes were stretched across the river hooking up with communities that draw water from wells. As cities closed water intakes from the Ohio River while the fuel passed, others upstream were able to resume service.[26] Cleanup crews continued to work 24 hours a day operating floating booms in the Ohio and Monongahela rivers.[27] Various observers attributed the collapse of the storage tank to cold weather, bad welds, poor testing and brittle steel. All predicted that the initial crack will be traced to a weld.[28]

FRIDAY, JANUARY 8 [DAY 7]

Allegheny County received a $210,000 check from Ashland. "In my memory, this is the first time payment has ever been made so expeditiously. It's just a new experience for us," said Tom Foerster, chairman of the county Board of Commissioners. "[The payment] demonstrates the good will and good faith of the Ashland Oil Company to do whatever they can possibly to restore all of us to our pre-spill conditions."[29]

The national press and media in cities along the Ohio River praised Hall and Ashland for the way the crisis was being handled.

Gerald Meyers said: "The lawyers are turning over in the class-rooms at Yale and Harvard. Apologizing, that's an admission of guilt." He added: "The alternative is to stonewall and be accused of one of three things—ignorance, indifference or, worst of all, guilt. . . . Honesty during a crisis is in vogue in management these days. . . . Ashland is to be congratulated on how well they're executing it."[30]

"Hall was certainly honest about it. He was painfully honest, probably not too smart about it in a strictly legal sense," said Bruce Lazier, oil industry analyst for Prescott, Ball & Turben, New York. "John [Hall] was painfully honest, and I hope it doesn't cost them. The only real negative is why give up an admission that you screwed up? But I think Hall's admission is right."[31]

W. Tom Wiseman, the mayor of Defiance, Ohio, a city of 20,000 downstream from the spill, credited Ashland for its openness following a helicopter tour of the damage. "They did not express concern about their liability," he said. "They came right out and said 'We want you to know we want this thing resolved and we want to work with you.'"[32]

Headlines were positive with wire service stories:

"Ashland chief's honesty wins praise" —*The Cincinnati Enquirer*[33]

"Public, at least, likes Hall's honest regret; lawyers another matter"   —*The Herald Dispatch*, Huntington, West Virginia[34]

"Ashland getting praise for candor"—*Louisville Courier-Journal*[35]

"For Ashland's Hall, honesty was the best policy"
                    —*Akron Beacon-Journal*[36]

In an editorial, *The Pittsburgh Post-Gazette* wrote: "But the record must show that Ashland immediately notified the proper authorities so that containment efforts could begin quickly. Also, John Hall, Ashland's chief executive officer, forthrightly assumed the blame on behalf of the company and apologized to all harmed or inconvenienced by the spill. There was no ducking and bobbing about responsibilities over the spill itself. Furthermore, Mr. Hall has said the company will fully reimburse governments and agencies for the costs of the cleanup. He said Ashland will make donations to the Red Cross, the Salvation Army and volunteer fire departments as compensation for their outlays."[37]

The editorial writers for *The Herald-Dispatch* in Huntington, on the Ohio River, reminded its readers of the severity of the spill and the thousands of people being impacted, yet wrote, "Still, we can't help but say 'well done' to John Hall, Ashland's no-nonsense chairman and CEO who told reporters and photographers at a Tuesday press conference that the firm accepted full responsibility for what had happened. The polls show most Americans have scant regard for Big Business. And a big factor in that widespread public mistrust is that too many real-life businessmen come off looking every bit as shifty as television's J. R. Ewing. Not John Hall. . . . Hall's unusual candor has gone a long way toward making the best of a bad situation."[38]

Following the news conference, Hall had an editorial board meeting at *The Pittsburgh Post-Gazette* and then appeared on local television and radio. *Post-Gazette* staff writer Jim Gallagher added, "That kind of openness can give ulcers to corporate lawyers."[39] He wrote that by getting quickly on stage, Hall personally showed his concern. "What they're trying to do is win in the court of public opinion," he added.[40]

SATURDAY, JANUARY 9 [DAY 8]

As the spill continued to move downriver, Ashland president Charles Luellen called on the Wheeling emergency operations center and apologized to the people. "One reason that we are here today is to see what more we can do," he said. As the spill passed Steubenville, Ohio, the city resumed water treatment. Wheeling businesses were closed and depended on mobile water tanks from the National Guard.[41]

SUNDAY, JANUARY 10 [DAY 9]

Ice and cold weather slowed down the movement of the slick to one-half mile an hour as it virtually parked alongside Wheeling. The city's elaborate emergency plan all but collapsed as residents used too much water and pumps failed on barges delivering water to the city's filtration plant. Sistersville, a town of 2,000 downriver from Wheeling, stockpiled water in swimming pools, moved portable tanks to the hospital and nursing homes and loaded five 20,000-gallon rail cars for firefighters. Barge traffic and ice continued to hamper cleanup efforts.[42]

MONDAY, JANUARY 11 [DAY 10]

Mandatory water restrictions were lifted in Allegheny, Washington and Beaver counties. Pennsylvania's Lieutenant Governor credited "outstanding cooperation by all residents and business" for making it possible to officially end the water crisis in western Pennsylvania.[43] Cities and industries along the river were told to stay alert to the smell of diesel fuel near their intakes. The first 20 miles of the 40-mile-long slick was under the water surface. Then came a visible sheen on the water for another 20 miles.[44]

Hall continued to receive praise from the media. "Ashland Oil and John R. Hall, are to be congratulated on their honesty and willingness to accept the blame for the January 2 fuel spill near Pittsburgh," wrote the editors of *The Ironton Tribune*.[45] WTVN Radio in Columbus, Ohio, editorialized, "Credit where credit's due. . . . The company promised to pay for cleanup efforts. . . . many companies' first reaction would have been to stonewall in the face of such an incident. Ashland's open and honest approach should help the oil and chemical industries come to some conclusions about how to avoid a repeat performance."[46]

TUESDAY, JANUARY 12 [DAY 11]

Ashland's Roger Schrum told reporters that the company was paying expenses daily, was continuing to coordinate cleanup efforts with EPA, Coast Guard and Pennsylvania Department of Environmental Resources and had hired the Battelle Institute to investigate the accident.[47]

WEDNESDAY, JANUARY 13 [DAY 12]

Hall said he would open a Pittsburgh office Thursday to coordinate activities with various agencies, monitor environmental assessments and handle claims. Also, a firm experienced in handling oil spill claims would process claims from businesses and individuals. The company had spent more than $2 million to protect drinking water supplies dependent on the Ohio and Monongahela rivers.[48]

THURSDAY, JANUARY 14 [DAY 13]

The spill speeded up as it entered dams and locks, but then stagnated again on the river.[49]

FRIDAY, JANUARY 15 [DAY 14]

Officials in EPA's mid-Atlantic regional office in Philadelphia termed "inadequate" Ashland's spill prevention plan. "The plan appears to be more of a general plan useful at any of Ashland's facilities," said Janet Viniski. "It doesn't contain enough specifics." During an EPA briefing on Capitol Hill, Senate staff members are told that an estimated 830,000 people would be affected, mostly due to depleted water supplies.[50]

WEEK 3 (JANUARY 16–22)

Stories appeared in *Business Week* and *Newsweek*. The *Louisville Courier-Journal* wrote that Ashland Oil "may well emerge with a better public image than before the disaster." The story added that the firm "went by the book" in implementing its crisis communications procedures as the news was passed from the tank-farm workers up through the corporate hierarchy.[51]

On Wednesday, January 20, the company awarded $250,000 to the University of Pittsburgh's Center for Hazardous Materials Research for a year-long study to include a public information and education program on issues related to the spill's impact.[52] The company also opened a toll-free 800 claims line.[53]

While public relations professionals praised Ashland for its response, lawyers began advertising for customers to sue the company. City officials along the Ohio River praised Ashland for its cooperation during the crisis.[54] Law firms in Illinois and Pennsylvania advertised for victims to contact lawyers to find out whether they had legal claims. Paul M. Goltz, Pittsburgh attorney, said "The response has not been overwhelming." He said he was hired by a Wheeling hotel seeking $4,000 for expenses incurred in hiring experts to monitor how much drinking water was being used during the crisis and by a woman who missed a day of work when she was sick because of contaminated water.[55]

The litigious activity did prompt this letter to the editor:

'Nasty' attitude—"The recent water problem brought to light many nasty sides of Pittsburghers that I hope the national news did not pick up on. Before Ashland Oil gave $210,000 to begin payment for some of the services, many Pittsburghers and companies made a beeline for their lawyers. The people of Pittsburgh were inconvenienced but I do not see a need for this get-rich attitude that some have. I feel that Ashland Oil Co. may have made a few mistakes, and that it will have enough problems with the government agencies, and that the people of Pittsburgh should make the best with what they have."

—Ila Boyd, North Side[56]

WEEK 4 (JANUARY 23–29)

Allen Seiz, vice president of O'Donnell & Associates Inc., a Pittsburgh consulting engineering firm, told a Pennsylvania State Senate committee that the tank "very likely" ruptured because the steel became too brittle as a result of the cold weather.[57]

Cincinnati shut off its water intake valves at 10 P.M. on Saturday (January 23) four hours before the spill was expected to arrive. The river supplies drinking water for about 850,000 people, but the city had enough water in reserve for it to remain closed for up to five days. The spill was expected to pass the city in two days.[58]

Testifying before a U.S. House of Representatives subcommittee, Richard N. Wright, director for the Center for Building Technology of the National Bureau of Standards, said "A crack opened the tank. It probably split the whole height of the tank in something like one-ten-thousandth of a second. It was hardly a leak. . . . Good design, materials, inspection and testing prevent such fractures."[59]

A November 17, 1986, memo by Progress Services Inc. of

Monroeville, Pennsylvania, said X-rays showed that 22 of 39 welds on the tank were defective. This was strongly disputed by Larry Skinner, president of Skinner Tank Co. of Yale, Oklahoma. His company was hired to take down and rebuild the tank. Skinner said that his company had no reason to ignore such defects because "it would have taken us about half an hour and cost about $300 extra to fix that many welds." The Progress Services memo, which Ashland immediately gave to investigative agencies, was not written until a month after the welding was finished, raising questions about whether there was an unresolved dispute between the firm and Ashland on the welding job. Copies also were given to Battelle Laboratories.[60]

Hall said he and his senior management were not aware of the information until Friday, January 22. He also noted that the faulty welds were not in the area of the tank where the steel wall cracked and issued a statement that said "based on a preliminary review (of the documents), it appears that Ashland's normal practices regarding weld inspections were not followed. In addition, a number of the old welds may have been defective." The company reassigned to other positions three employees involved in moving the tank from Cleveland to the Pittsburgh area.[61]

As Congressional hearings continued, Tom Luken (D-Ohio) said he was "aghast" that EPA had relinquished its public responsibilities by allowing Ashland to control the cleanup. He was challenged by James Seif, EPA's regional administrator, who said EPA was ready to take control any time Ashland appeared ready to shirk its responsibility. Seif said he determined that Ashland had the resources and desire to clean up the spill and used the same contractors EPA would have hired.[62]

WEEK 5 (JANUARY 30–FEBRUARY 5)

In a January 27 news release, Hall said some employees might have known about defective welds more than a year before the tank collapse.[63] Later that week, at the annual shareholders' meeting, he said some questionable decisions were made by employees who built the tank. He said the company would inspect all 1,000 of its tanks.[64] The company took a 635,000-gallon rebuilt tank out of service in Evansville, Indiana, for testing.[65]

Hall told a Senate subcommittee: "We're embarrassed by this incident. However, we are proud of the valiant efforts our employees made to try to contain and clean up the spill and to help municipalities with water supplies. We already have paid $4 million to clean up the slick and provide drinking water for the 800,000 people who relied on the Ohio River."[66]

Continued rain and the series of locks and dams on the Ohio River helped move the spill along to Owensboro, Kentucky. Ashland announced it would begin a second stage cleanup on the Monongahela and Ohio rivers over the next three months under the review of the EPA.[67] Ashland stopped using a 3.3-million-gallon storage tank, also at Floreffe, when it discovered flaws in certain welded seams.[68]

WEEK 6 (FEBRUARY 6–12)

Heavy rains increased the water and current in the Ohio River and the oil slick dissipated out of existence. "We lost it after it left Evansville, Indiana," said Jeanne Ison of the Ohio River Valley Water Sanitation Commission in Cincinnati. "It's so diluted we can't track it anymore."[69]

The U.S. Attorney's office in Pittsburgh, conducting a criminal investigation into the spill, subpoenaed Ashland's records relating to the collapse of the tank.[70] The Pennsylvania Attorney General began one of at least a dozen separate investigations and studies.[71]

WEEK 7 (FEBRUARY 13–19)

The river cities began submitting bills for reimbursement. Cincinnati officials said they would bill $386,000, more than half of it for overtime pay for waterworks personnel. "Ashland Oil so far has been very cooperative and has been prompt in paying bills submitted to it," said Cincinnati City Manager Scott Johnson. The city of Ashland submitted expenses of $19,944.[72]

Pennsylvania State Senator D. Michael Fisher (R-Allegheny) accused Ashland Oil of trying to "stonewall" his committee's investigation of the spill. Company vice president Philip Block said he could not answer many of the committee members' questions but agreed to supply written answers within a few weeks. "At this time, we do not have all of the facts," he said.[73]

Hall received positive comments from a Senate subcommittee. "We commend you for coming here and making these statements. It's tough to 'fess up' like you have," Sen. Frank Lautenberg (D-N.J.) told him. Sen. John Chaffee (R-R.I.) agreed. "You have given us a candid statement, including some of your failings. That's unusual."[74]

WEEK 8 (FEBRUARY 20–26)

Water samples taken by the West Virginia Department of Environmental Resources and the Ohio River Valley Sanitation Commission revealed that one or more industries took advantage of the accident to dump their own chemicals in the river. There are 83 industrial discharge points along the 87 miles of the Ohio River from Pittsburgh to Wheeling. Edgar Berkey, then executive vice president of the University of Pittsburgh's Center for Hazardous Materials Research, said: "What these misdirected and misguided industrial people dumped are chemicals and materials far more harmful, far more biologically active, than the diesel fuel. They dumped dirty solvents because getting rid of them properly is expensive."[75] EPA's regional office in Philadelphia conducted a criminal investigation. "We received reports during the first two weeks after the spill that clandestine dumping had occurred," said Thomas Voltaggio, director of the Hazardous Waste Materials Division.[76] Editorial writers in river cities blasted the polluters, who may escape any punishment, for dumping chemical wastes .[77]

The Pittsburgh Post-Gazette wrote there could have been better coordination between agencies when the accident happened. Columnist David Guo noted the first message from the National Response Center was logged at 5:30 P.M. with "Sketchy rept (sic) of 100,000 diesel spill. Sloreffe (sic)." Chief Warrant Officer Joe B. Lindsey of the Coast Guard surmised that *Sloreffe* was probably

Floreffe. When he called Ashland at 5:33, 5:43 and 6:05 P.M., there was no answer since Ashland had shut off all power lines and the tank collapse knocked out phone lines. He got only an answering service at 6:16 P.M. at the Pennsylvania Department of Environmental Resources. At 6:20, 50 minutes after the alert from Washington, D.C., he got his first on-the-scene report from an Ashland towboat operator. Communications breakdowns are an inevitable part of emergency response. Reporter Guo felt many gaps were too long and too common and created significant delays. The legislative hearings said both the Coast Guard and EPA were at fault. The Pittsburgh public safety director said his men waited at least six hours for a floating boom barrier to contain oil. In total, there were only about a half dozen telephones at the four command posts. Each group focused on one piece of a four-part crisis. The city was handling the leading edge of the spill; the Coast Guard containment upstream; the county dealt with the gasoline leak and potential explosion; and local volunteers who knew the area were running the evacuation.[78]

MARCH 1988

Ashland reported that it was being examined by 55 government agencies and may face criminal charges as well as innumerable studies by public officials, academics and private companies.[79] EPA continued its investigation into hazardous chemicals dumped into the rivers following the oil spill, with no suspect.[80]

The company continued to receive praise. In *The Pittsburgh Post-Gazette*, Lieutenant Governor Mark Singel wrote: "Litigation is a fact of life, and it is likely that Ashland Oil will be in court for years. Ashland taught us, however, how a company *should* respond to an obvious error and its aftermath. Official and early statements from the company expressed more than regret—they assumed responsibility."[81] He also cited Ashland's public relations efforts having press liaisons always available and regular briefings held for updates and question-and-answer sessions. "This active press operation accomplished three things: It freed operations personnel from interruption; it kept the media and the public apprised of new developments and community water bulletins; and it reassured everyone that progress was being made," he wrote.[82]

A story in *Investor's Daily* quoted Lacy as saying: "There was never any question of whether we would tell the truth. The question was when."[83]

MAY 1988

A study by Battelle Institute, the world's largest private independent research organization, reported the failure was caused by a "brittle steel fracture, emanating from a dime-size flaw in the tank's bottom course steel plate." It also said: "Brittle steel fractures have been documented in older steel construction, resulting from a combination of stress and cold temperatures. . . . Welding of the steel plates during both its initial construction and reconstruction resulted in embrittlement of the steel surrounding the flaw. These factors, combined with cold temperatures and the stress placed on the tank as it was being filled near capacity created the conditions required for brittle fracture."[84] The Battelle report also noted:[85]

- The flaw was in the steel since its manufacture and prior to its original installation on or about 1940.

- X-rays of the welds indicated that certain old welds did not meet current standards but tests indicated the old welds were stronger than the steel plate.

- Had a full hydrostatic test been performed, the tank could have (1) withstood the test; (2) developed a slow leak; or (3) failed catastrophically.

Hall said that while the old steel used was in excellent condition, it did not meet industry standards and that all future tank construction will be done in full compliance with the material, welding and testing specifications of API 650.[86]

JULY 1988

Ashland signed a consent decree with the U.S. government agreeing to pay for the cleanup, reimburse the government

$680,000 in expenses and treat ground water for the next 30 years to be sure it is free of pollutants.[87]

SEPTEMBER 1988

A federal grand jury in Pittsburgh indicted Ashland on two misdemeanor violations of the Clean Water Act and the Refuse Act. The Justice Department said the counts were the most stringent that could be brought against the company and that the government was continuing its inquiry to see if any individual employees violated the law. The Justice Department estimated cleanup and environmental costs at $12 to $15 million.[88]

Ashland officials expressed displeasure with the Justice's decision to press criminal charges, pointing out its own efforts "to mitigate the spill's impact" and "the fact that the company quickly accepted responsibility for the incident." The company said it had spent $11.4 million already on the cleanup and that criminal provisions of the environmental protection statutes are used only in instances of deliberate pollution.[89] The company cited three other large chemical spills in the Midwest, none of which resulted in criminal charges. "This will impair rather than promote environmental compliance," said the company.[90]

OCTOBER 1988

The company pleaded not guilty and asked for a jury trial on criminal negligence charges.[91]

Ashland Oil accused Allegheny County authorities of perjury and obstruction of justice in the investigation that led to criminal charges. A civil subpoena it issued produced a copy of a May 19, 1986, memo signed by Chief Inspector Charles Kelly of the Allegheny County Fire Marshal's office and addressed to his supervisor, Lt. Norman Smilnyak, in the county's police bureau.[92]

Nearly 10 months after the incident and steadfastly maintaining that Ashland erected the tank without obtaining county approval implicit or otherwise, Deputy Fire Marshal Edward Babyak testified under oath in federal court that the company did have approval. Other county officials, Kelly and Fire Marshal Martin

Jacobs testified under oath that no approval for construction of the tank had ever been given. Babyak suggested in his testimony that if there were a cover-up, it would involve a higher-ranking official than Kelly or Jacobs. County Commission Chairman Tom Foerster ordered an internal probe by the county police bureau.[93]

In a speech at the Pittsburgh Press Club, Hall said the recent developments should raise questions about the thoroughness and objectivity of various investigations by state and federal authorities.[94]

CLOSING THE BOOK

In a March 1991 speech to the Center for Corporate Response Ability, Hall summed up the financial impact on Ashland, noting the company paid some 4,300 claims to individuals at an average cost of less than $87 per claim. He stated that "by February 1990, a little more than two years after the event, we reached an agreement to settle all outstanding issues for a maximum of $30 million, which included all previously paid claims and cleanup costs. Nearly all of this amount was covered by insurance."[95]

ASHLAND'S CRISIS STEPS

"We learned a lot of lessons from the spill," says Lacy. "When the tank collapsed, we didn't have a team and we didn't have a plan. We had to rely on our wits to get us through the crisis. We looked to the successful experience of other companies for guidance. Johnson & Johnson's handling of the Tylenol crisis taught us to show leadership, to stand up and be counted. To show concern. Take the heat. To do everything you can. And to do the right thing. What that said to us was to get involved, to get in deep and to be a factor in the solution," he adds. "So that's what we did. As a result, we've developed a recipe for crisis management." Here is Ashland's recipe for crisis management:[96]

1. Go to the site immediately.

2. Get firsthand information.

3. Marshal your resources and equipment to clean up the mess.

4. Contact governors and other local, state and federal officials

who need to know and who need to answer questions from their constituents. It's better for you to call them before they call you.

5. Offer restitution to third parties.

6. Call in third parties—scientists and similar experts—for advice and independent analysis.

7. Meet the press. Go to the media, even if you don't have all the answers. Tell them what you know and what you don't know.

8. Listen to your media relations staff; they are your eyes and ears on public opinion. The questions being asked by the press are the same questions being asked by the public. Because of this, many times the media relations folks have a better handle on the seriousness of the situation than do the operating people. Because it is the *public*—rather than your own operating people—that decides how big the problem really is, in terms of public perception.

9. Stay on the job until the danger is gone and the mess is cleaned up.

Using the Lesson Plan

Unfortunately for Ashland and Lacy, the company had a chance to apply the same techniques on September 16, 1990, when one of its tankers, the M.V. Jupiter, loaded with nearly 2 million gallons of gasoline, exploded and caught fire in the Saginaw River at Bay City, Michigan. President Luellen, Lacy, Schrum and other officials were immediately on the scene to talk with emergency response personnel and the media. Ashland called in professionals to contain the fire, limit the environmental damage, determine the cause and clean up the mess.

As it turned out, a ship passing in the channel was going too fast and created a trough that pulled the Jupiter from its moorings, stretching the product hose unloading fuel. The captain of the passing ship refused to talk to the media. Local television editorials praised Ashland.

Take a Lesson From Ashland

Gerald Meyers wrote in *The Los Angeles Times* that Ashland Oil is a good role model to follow in a crisis.[97] Too bad Exxon USA didn't take that advice when in March 1989 its Exxon Valdez ran aground. As philosopher George Santayana wrote in *The Life of Reason*, "Those who cannot remember the past are condemned to repeat it."[98]

Endnotes

Information to document this case history was provided by news clippings and internal reports from Dan Lacy, vice president, corporate communications, Ashland Oil, Inc., Ashland, Kentucky, and a case study, "Ashland Oil Inc.: Trouble At Floreffe" by Anne K. Delenhunt, Harvard Business School, Boston, Massachusetts, January 19, 1990.

1. "Reassembled oil tank collapses, sending slick far downstream," *Engineering News Record*, January 14, 1988, pg. 12.

2. "Spill on the Mon: A chronology," *Pittsburgh Post-Gazette*, January 4, 1988.

3. Reuters, various news reports, January 3, 1988.

4. Ibid.

5. Clare Ansberry, "Oil Spill in the Midwest Provides Case Study in Crisis Management," *The Wall Street Journal*, January 8, 1988.

6. Ibid.

7. Associated Press, "AOI oil spill cleanup on at Pittsburgh," *The Daily Independent*, Ashland, Kentucky, January 4, 1988.

8. Ibid.

9. Ibid.

10. Stephen Franklin, "Oil spill imperils water supply," *Chicago Tribune*, January 5, 1988, pg. 1.

11. Wolfgang Saxon, "Monongahela Oil Spill Threatens Water Supplies in Pittsburgh Area," *The New York Times*, January 5, 1988, pg. B1.

12. Ibid.

13. Ibid.

14. Clare Ansberry, *The Wall Street Journal*, op cit.

15. Ibid.

16. John Hall, opening remarks of press conference, January 5, 1988, Pittsburgh.

17. Ibid.

18. David Guo and Bill Moushey, "Ashland concedes it never had permit for

tank," *Pittsburgh Post-Gazette*, January 6, 1988, pg. 1; Bob Dvorchak, "Spilled fuel, search for cause spreading," *The Daily Independent*, Ashland, Kentucky, January 6, 1988, pg. 1; Associated Press, *The Plain Dealer*, Cleveland, Ohio, January 6, 1988, pg. A20; Catherine Chriss, "Chairman: Ashland lacked tank permits," *Lexington Herald-Leader*, Lexington, Kentucky, January 6, 1988, pg. 1A.

19. Clare Ansberry, *The Wall Street Journal, op cit.*

20. Dow Jones Wire, January 6, 1988.

21. Clare Ansberry, *The Wall Street Journal, op cit.*

22. Steve Kemme, "River cities cautious, not alarmed, over oil spill," *The Cincinnati Enquirer*, January 7, 1988, pg. 1A.

23. Don Black, Gannett News Service, "Conditions to be normal by the weekend," *The Cincinnati Enquirer*, January 7, 1988, pg. A6.

24. "Ashland Oil puts bad news behind," *USA Today*, January 7, 1988.

25. Associated Press, "Suite by 4 charges negligence by AOI," *The Daily Independent*, Ashland, Kentucky, January 7, 1988, pg. A1.

26. Michael Weisskopf, "Residents Fill Pools, Tubs as Spill Rolls On," *The Washington Post*, January 8, 1988, pg. 2.

27. David E. Malloy, "Ashland Oil fully insured, will 'do whatever it takes,'" *The Herald-Dispatch*, Huntington, West Virginia, January 8, 1988, pg. A1.

28. David Guo, "Weld, brittle steel suspected in spill," *Pittsburgh Post-Gazette*, January 8, 1988, pg. 1; Associated Press, National Wire, January 8, 1988.

29. Mark Belko, "County gets Ashland's 1st check," *Pittsburgh Post-Gazette*, January 9, 1988.

30. Earl Bohn, Associated Press, "What price honesty? Industry experts assess Hall's performance," *The Daily Independent*, Ashland, Kentucky, January 8, 1988.

31. Ibid.

32. Stephen Talbott, "Cooperation can limit spill liability," *The Plain Dealer*, Cleveland, Ohio, January 9, 1988, pg. B-6.

33. Earl Bohn, Associated Press, "Ashland chief's honesty wins praise," *The Cincinnati Enquirer*, January 8, 1988, pg. B-8.

34. Earl Bohn, Associated Press, "Public, at least, likes Hall's honest, regret; lawyers another matter," *The Herald-Dispatch*, Huntington, West Virginia, January 8, 1988, pg. A3.

35. Ben Z. Hersberg, "Ashland getting praise for candor," *Louisville Courier-Journal*, January 9, 1988.

36. Associated Press, "For Ashland's Hall, honesty was the best policy," *Akron Beacon Journal*, Akron, Ohio, January 10, 1988, pg. E-4.

37. "An overflow of good will," *Pittsburgh Post-Gazette*, January 8, 1988, editorial page.

38. "Ashland doesn't try to duck the blame," *The Herald-Dispatch*, Huntington, West Virginia, January 8, 1988, editorial pages.

39. Jim Gallagher, "Ashland scores high in public relations," *Pittsburgh Post-Gazette*, January 8, 1988.

40. Ibid.

41. Cass Peterson, "Best-Laid Plans Are Not Enough as Slick Arrives," *The Washington Post*, January 10, 1988.

42. Rae Tyson, "Water is flowing again in oil's wake," *USA Today*, January 11, 1988; United Press International, "Sistersville next stop for spill," *The Charleston Gazette*, January 11, 1988, pgs. A1, A12; Cass Peterson, "Wheeling Told to Save Water as Oil Lingers," *The Washington Post*, January 11, 1988; Associated Press, "Slick slowing down on trip downstream," *The Daily Independent*, Ashland, Kentucky, January 11, 1988, pg. A1.

43. Andrew Sheehan, "Crisis is over," *Pittsburgh Post-Gazette*, January 12, 1998.

44. Ibid.

45. Opinion, "Ashland Oil cleanup sign of good neighbor," *The Ironton Tribune*, Ironton, Ohio, pg. A4.

46. Editorial, WTVN Radio, Great American Television and Radio Co. Inc., Columbus, Ohio, January 12, 1988.

47. "Ashland Oil Co. Says Insurance Covers Pennsylvania Oil Spill," *Report for Executives*, Bureau of National Affairs, Inc., Washington, D.C., January 13, 1988, pg. A-2.

48. "Ready for claims," *The Herald-Dispatch*, Huntington, West Virginia, January 14, 1988, pg. B1; Associated Press, "AOI hires firm to help with claims," *The Daily Independent*, Ashland, Kentucky, January 14, 1988, pg. 15.

49. Associated Press, "Lt. governor wants action on river spills," *The Cincinnati Enquirer*, January 15, 1988, pg. C2.

50. Associated Press, "EPA: Oil Spill Plan Inadequate," national wire, January 15, 1988, 5:20 P.M.; "EPA Calls Ashland Anti-Spill Plan Inadequate," *The Washington Post*, January 16, 1988, pg. A-7.

51. Robert B. Irvine, "Candor, quick action on spill may improve Ashland Oil's image," *The Courier-Journal*, Louisville, Kentucky, January 17, 1988, pg. E-1.

52. "Pitt gets $250,000 to study spill," *The Pittsburgh Press*, January 21, 1988.

53. *Lexington Herald-Leader*, January 21, 1988, pg. B4.

54. Tom Daykin and Jim Jordan, "The Big Spill: Ashland has to ride the waves," Business Monday, *Lexington Herald-Leader*, Lexington, Kentucky, January 18, 1988, pg. 1.

55. Janice Bullard, "Lawyers Advertising for Oil Spill Claimants," *The Intelligencer*, Wheeling, West Virginia, January 19, 1998.

56. Editorial Page, *The Pittsburgh Press*, January 19, 1988.

57. Ralph Haurwitz, "Engineer says oil tank ruptured as its brittle steel broke in cold," *The Pittsburgh Press*, January 23, 1988, pg. A-5.

58. John Eckberg, "Oil slick should slide right by," *The Cincinnati Enquirer*, January 24, 1988, pg. 1.

59. Catherine Dressler, Associated Press, "Rare fracture caused oil tank to collapse, official says," *Lexington Herald-Leader*, Lexington, Kentucky, January 27, 1988, pg. B1.

60. Mark Roth, "Builder claims no notice of bad tank welds," *Pittsburgh Post-Gazette*, January 28, 1998, pg. 1; "Paper says Ashland knew of risk to Monongahela," *The Christian Science Monitor*, January 28, 1988, pg. 2; Associated Press, "Tank's weld defects a surprise, Hall says," *The Daily Independent*, Ashland, Kentucky, January 28, 1988, pg. 1.

61. Ibid.

62. Jim Ross, "Congressman" EPA 'too timid' in spill cleanup," *The Herald-Dispatch*, Huntington, West Virginia, January 27, 1998, pg. A1.

63. Associated Press, "Faulty welds found a year before spill," *The Herald-Dispatch*, Huntington, West Virginia., January 28, 1988, pgs. A1-A2.

64. "Ashland Targets Welds in Investigation of Fuel Spill," *The Oil Daily*, February 1.

65. Associated Press, "Ashland takes fuel tank out of service for testing," *The Pittsburgh Press*, January 31, 1988, pg. 13.

66. Reuter, "Ashland Pledges Thorough Cleanup of Oil Spill," *Investor's Daily*, February 5, 1988.

67. Associated Press, *The Daily Independent*, Ashland, Kentucky, February 2, 1988, pg. 11.

68. "Ashland stops using tank at spill site," *Lexington Herald-Leader*, Lexington, Kentucky, February 5, 1988.

69. Jim Ross, "ORSANCO loses track of slick," *The Herald-Dispatch*, Huntington, West Virginia, February 10, 1988.

70. Reuters, "Ashland Oil records on spill subpoenaed," *Lexington Herald-Leader*, Lexington, Kentucky, February 8, 1988.

71. Earl Bohn, Associated Press, "Slick disappearing, but spotlight remains bright on Ashland Oil," *The Sunday Independent*, Ashland, Kentucky, February 7, 1988, pg. 29.

72. Associated Press, "River cities begin submitting cleanup statements to AOI," *The Daily Independent*, Ashland, Kentucky, February 19, 1997, pg. 13.

73. Tara Bradley-Steck, Associated Press, "AOI 'stonewalling' spill probe, panel told," *The Daily Independent*, Ashland, Kentucky., February 13, 1988, pg. A1, A14.

74. Patrick Crow, "Ashland's redemption," Watching Washington, *Oil & Gas Journal*, February 15, 1988, pg. 29.

75. Marylynne Pitz, "High levels of pollutants are found in Ohio River water," *Pittsburgh Post-Gazette*, February 22, 1988, pg. 6; Associated Press, "Dumped chemicals show up in river samples," *Sunday Gazette-Mail*, Charleston, West Virginia, February 21, 1988; Associated Press, "Some industries dumped chemicals in Ohio River after spill, official says," *The Sunday Independent*, Ashland, Kentucky, February 21, 1988, pg. 16; Associated Press, "Experts Say Plants Used Spill as Cover To Dump Pollutants," *The New York Times*, February 22, 1988; Associated Press, "Illegal Dumping Under Cover of Spill?," *The Washington Post*, February 22, 1988.

76. Don Hopey, "EPA to investigate illegal pollutants in spill," *The Pittsburgh Press*, February 24, pg. 1; Associated Press, "EPA Gets Reports Of Illegal Dumping Into Ohio After Spill," *The New York Times*, February 25, 1988.

77. "Worse than an oil spill," editorial, *The Pittsburgh Press*, February 23, 1988; "No sympathy for polluters," editorial, *The Daily Independent*, Ashland, Kentucky, February 25, 1988, pg. 14; "Sabotage on Ohio River," editorial, *Akron Beacon Journal*, Akron, Ohio, February 23, 1988, pg. A4; "Criminal polluters at work," editorial, *Lexington Herald-Leader*, Lexington, Kentucky, February 23, 1988, pg. A8.

78. David Guo, "Vital hours were lost to poor coordination," *Pittsburgh Post-Gazette*, February 23, 1988.

79. Thomas Easton, "Wake of massive spill stains Ashland Oil," *The Sun*, Baltimore, Maryland, March 20, 1988, pg. D-1.

80. Don Hopey, "EPA still seeking chemicals reported in Ohio River," *The*

Pittsburgh Press, March 11, 1988; Associated Press, "U.S. Rebuts Rumors of Poison Dumping," *The New York Times*, March 12, 1988, pg. 9.

81. Mark S. Singel, "Good grades for crisis reaction," editorial pages, *Pittsburgh Post-Gazette*, March 4, 1988.

82. Ibid.

83. Art Hagoplan, "Executives Promote Honesty as Best Policy," *Investor's Daily*, March 2, 1988, pg. 1.

84. "Ashland Releases Battelle Study On Diesel Storage Tank Collapse," news release by Roger Schrum, Ashland Oil Inc. Communications Department, May 26, 1988.

85. Ibid.

86. Ibid.

87. Ralph Haurwitz and Janet Williams, Scripps Howard News Service, "Prosecution mean to punish AOI, warn others, officials say," *The Daily Independent*, Ashland, Kentucky, September 17, 1988.

88. Janet Williams and Ralph Haurwitz, "Ashland indicted in Mon diesel fuel spill," *The Pittsburgh Press*, September 15, 1988, pgs. A1, A6; Rick Wartzman, "Ashland Faces Criminal Counts From Fuel Spill," *The Wall Street Journal*, September 16, 1988, pg. 38; Reuters, "Ashland Indicted in Pa. Oil Spill," *New York Newsday*, September 16, 1988; Ruth Marcus, "Ashland Oil Is Indicted in Pennsylvania Oil Spill," *The Washington Post*, September 16, 1988; "Ashland indicted for Monongahela oil spill," *USA Today*, September 16, 1988; "Ashland Oil charged with criminal acts over spill," *Lexington Herald-Leader*, Lexington, Kentucky, September 16, 1988, pg. 3.

89. Ibid.

90. Ibid.

91. "Firm Enters Innocent Plea on Environmental Charges," *The Wall Street Journal*, October 7, 1988, pg. C14; "Ashland Oil says it's not guilty of criminal negligence in spill," *The Herald-Dispatch*, Huntington, West Virginia, October 7, 1988, pg. C2; Associated Press, "Ashland Oil pleads not guilty in tank collapse," *Lexington Herald-Leader*, Lexington, Kentucky, October 7, 1988, pg. C17.

92. "Ashland Oil Obtains Copy Of Approval for Fuel Tank," *The Wall Street Journal*, October 21, 1988, pg. A7; "Ashland accuses local investigators," *The Courier-Journal*, Louisville, Kentucky, October 21, 1988, pg. B3; David Guo, "Deputy fire marshal found key oil-tank memo," *Pittsburgh Post-Gazette*, October 22, 1988; Earl Bohn, Associated Press, "Ashland Oil finds proof in spill case," *The Herald-Dispatch*, Huntington, West Virginia, October 21, 1988, pg. A1; Editorial, "Ashland's new evidence," *The Pittsburgh Press*, October 22, 1988.

93. Ibid.

94. Ralph Haurwitz, "Ashland chairman questions quality of tank inquiries," *The Pittsburgh Press*, October 28, 1988.

95. "Pittsburgh Oil Spill," remarked by John R. Hall, chairman and chief executive officer, Ashland Inc., to the Center for Corporate Response Ability, New York, March 6, 1991.

96. Dan Lacy, "Issues In Crisis Management, speech, Ashland Oil Inc.

97. Gerald C. Meyers, "Perrier's Crisis Management," *The Los Angeles Times*, February 25, 1990.

98. John Bartlett, *Bartlett's Familiar Quotations*, 14th edition, 1968, Little, Brown and Company, Boston, pg. 867.

CHAPTER TEN

WHAT DEATH MEANS
TO HEALTHCARE

There is nothing like a higher-than-normal incidence of unexplained deaths, an outbreak of infectious bacteria such as staphylococcus or the kidnapping of a baby from the nursery to set the crisis team in action at a hospital, nursing home or healthcare facility.

In addition to problems unique to the industry, healthcare providers also are vulnerable to workplace violence, sexual harassment, food poisoning and natural disasters. Institutions dependent on public funding need to develop a positive image and counter negative perceptions.

Any facility caring for the elderly must be concerned about investigative reporters going under cover or using techniques with hidden cameras to document mistreatment and misdeeds. While the guilty should be exposed, those who may have been wrongfully accused must know how to respond. HMOs are being challenged whether or not patients are getting the necessary attention deserved.

In Washington, D.C., Congress and the White House hope to save $3 billion over five years by cutting payments to hospitals that transfer patients to lower-level care after short stays. It is one of the few Medicare cost-saving measures that both parties agreed upon. Today, about 40 percent of elderly patients use inpatient nursing, rehabilitation or home health services, many after shorter hospital stays. Medicare doesn't realize any savings from a shortened stay at the hospital and also has to pay the added cost of recuperative care somewhere else. Lobbying by the providers was intense.[1]

In the midst of this, Allegheny University Hospital for Women in Philadelphia ran full-page newspaper ads with the headline, "Finally, there's another sign that stands for women" with a bold "A" in a shield.[2] One ad ran in black and white, but another was in color with a scarlet "A" on a blue shield. Was the hospital seeking out Hester Prine as a patient? Had the creative team never read *The Scarlet Letter*? Allegheny subsequently filed for bankruptcy and its leaders are being investigated for possible financial mismanagment.

Mergers and Downsizing

The increase of managed care, corporate medicine and other economic forces spurred dramatic changes in hospital services, resulting in painful downsizings and an unprecedented wave of mergers and alliances. From 1994 to 1997 about 900 hospitals nationally have been part of a merger or acquisition.[3] While administrators see reduced overhead and enhanced services, physicians find themselves competing for dwindling dollars, being taken over by larger groups and even battling with former colleagues while patients get bounced from doctor to doctor.

In the mid-1980s, four hospitals in the western suburbs of Philadelphia — an area known as the Main Line — formed one of the areas' first hospital networks. It was called the Main Line Health System. For the hospitals — Lankenau Hospital, Bryn Mawr Hospital, Paoli Memorial Hospital and Bryn Mawr Rehabilitation Hospital — it was a system in name only. For eight years, until 1994, there was no perceived need to unify the administrative or medical staffs. Until then, only human resources, legal and some general administrative areas had unified.[4]

In the fall of 1994, the president of Bryn Mawr Hospital was given the additional role of president of Lankenau Hospital and, in 1996, was appointed president of Paoli Memorial Hospital. The joint presidency was just the beginning of the combination of administrative departments. Late in 1993, Bryn Mawr laid off 300 workers, the first in the hospital's history, spreading rumors about its future. The community thought the hospital would close. Main Line Health's public affairs department embarked on a major program of community and employee information meetings to reassure both employees and the public that both hospitals would remain open. Hospital executives explained the benefits of combining Bryn Mawr and Lankenau Hospitals' services and the reasons for the combinations. They emphasized that the changes were being made so that both hospitals would remain vital and thriving in an era of vast healthcare changes.[5]

A New Affiliation

In 1995, one of Philadelphia's major teaching hospitals, Thomas Jefferson University Hospital, and Main Line Health, agreed to affiliate and become part of an umbrella entity called Jefferson Health System. Creating a single Main Line Health medical staff was needed even before the affiliation took place. A unified staff became a necessity even though there was no plan to unify Main Line Health with the Jefferson physicians. The public affairs staff worked hard to reduce the anxiety by again scheduling numerous employee and physician meetings plus community information meetings. Considering all of the changes, hospital officials felt that the unification went as smoothly as could be expected. While the process took two years, only three doctors voted against unifying the staff.[6]

When the process of unifying the medical staffs of the four Main Line hospitals actually began, several medical groups came together with relative ease. But it was a painful process for the neonatology physicians because they had different philosophies that they could not reconcile. Unification was a big challenge since Main Line Health officials simply stated the objective but did not tell their physicians how to do it.[7]

Change Not Easy to Accept

Change is never easy to accept, and this was especially difficult. The hospitals served the community for nearly a century in exactly the same way in the same locations. But healthcare changes of the '90s required some change. For nearly three years, to the writing this book, administrators continued to explain the benefits of the reorganization both internally and externally. Through community meetings, briefings for government officials, newspaper ads containing open letters to the community, employee information meetings and an active speaker's bureau, the hospital diligently informed all constituencies of the reasons for the changes and the benefits of affiliation. Through all the discussion of unified administrative staffs and medical staffs and hospital affiliations, the patients appear to have been satisfied with their care. Results of patient-satisfaction surveys continue to remain extremely favorable.

There is still a way to go in making sure that all of the employees, the physicians and the general public know the changes that have and will continue to take place, the reasons why and the benefits. In managing change, communications can't end.[8]

Murder in the ICU?

During a 22-month period from 1993 to 1995, patients died at triple the usual rate at Vermillion County Hospital in Clinton, Indiana. In March 1997, Indiana State Police released the names of 147 patients who died in the hospital's four-bed intensive care unit and "may have been the victims of a crime, or crimes, including murder."[9]

A single unusual death in a hospital can put it into a crisis mode, but an extraordinarily high number of deaths in a small facility can soon put it on network television. Adding to the complexity of the crisis was the fact that a number of the patients seemed to be progressing and then died unexpectedly. Many were elderly and had serious medical problems.

Intensive care nurses repeatedly warned the hospital's president that something was wrong. Only after seeing the high number of deaths in 1994 did administrators contact law enforcement officers. Investigators focused on Orville Lynn Majors, a licensed practical nurse at the hospital, who was listed as having treated 130 of the 147 patients. The Indiana State Police and Indiana Health Department both received anonymous letters that said "an angel of death" was at work in the hospital.[10]

State Attorney General Files Complaint

The attorney general filed a complaint with the nursing board alleging that Majors "contributed to the unexpected deaths" of 26 patients. In February 1996, the board suspended his license for five years, ruling that his "nursing behavior jeopardized the health, safety and welfare of the public" because he had overstepped his authority as a nurse by administering drugs and performing other duties for registered nurses and physicians.

Majors' lawyer pointed out that his client is a nurse with a history of excellent employee reviews and the investigation had already cost $1 million with no charges having been filed. Majors proclaimed his innocence on two nationally syndicated talk shows and denied doing anything wrong. Yet he stood accused by the community of mass murder. He wanted his suspended nursing license back and filed lawsuits against the state and hospital for character assassination.[11]

The state health department fined the hospital $80,000 for lax management procedures and the Joint Commission on Accrediting Healthcare Organizations withdrew accreditation.[12]

Another PR-Attorney Confrontation

When the story broke, the hospital retained Borschoff Johnson & Co., Indianapolis, to handle crisis communications. "A demoralized staff was confused, angry and being bombarded with hard questions from friends, family and national news media," said Myra Borschoff. "The lawyers wanted to clam up the press—they didn't want anybody to answer any questions and that was not the right approach."[13]

"Such crises can be nightmares because many hospital attorneys do not realize that these cases are usually decided in the court of public opinion long before they reach a court of law," says Larry Smith of the Institute for Crisis Management.

In 1989, Daniel Drake Memorial Hospital in Cincinnati made national headlines when a nurse admitted to, and was subsequently convicted of, killing 24 patients. Drake subsequently changed its name as did Vermillion when it signed an agreement with Union Hospital in Terre Haute, Indiana. It is now called West Central Community Hospital and was re-accredited unconditionally for three years in January 1997.[14]

On December 29, 1997, following a 33-month investigation, Majors was arrested and charged with the murder of six patients. State police examined 165 deaths and exhumed the bodies of 15 patients, all of whom died from injections and who were under his care. His attorney called the arrest "a travesty." Some 65 families have filed a class-action lawsuit against the hospital alleging negligence in supervising Majors.[15]

An affidavit describes how co-workers said he would refer to patients' families with disgust, calling them "white trash" and "dirt," made fun of poor people and told them "I'm just sitting here waiting for the woman to die." Police seized potassium chloride from Majors' van and a number of syringes and needles from his former home. Potassium chloride is used to control irregular heartbeat. In high concentrations it can kill. The prosecutor said there are no plans to seek the death penalty but Majors could received 40 to 60 years in prison for each charge.[16]

Medical Terrorism

In October 1993, California Pacific Medical Center in San Francisco learned that an employee of eight years told a friend he had been fantasizing for some time about infecting patients with AIDS-tainted blood. The employee, a blood-drawing technician, even kept a list of "victims." The employee tried to extort $1 million from the hospital in return for his silence.

Realizing how misinformed and apprehensive the public is about HIV and AIDS, the medical center immediately took action to head off a crisis. A private investigator was hired to tighten security and recommend methods to improve blood-drawing procedures. Social workers and related staff planned to educate the community about all issues related to AIDS. A toll-free hot line was established, the hospital began a counseling program, and free AIDS testing was given to any patient believed to have had blood drawn by the technician during the time he was employed at the hospital.[17]

A medical ethicist advised on the crisis and local public health officials and legal authorities were consulted. AIDS experts at the hospital, health department and local universities collectively concluded that it was nearly impossible to transmit the HIV virus during a blood-drawing procedure, as contrasted with an injection.

Concern About a Media Frenzy

A media frenzy was expected when the public announcement was made. The hospital wanted to demonstrate its candor and openness. A video B-roll was produced in less than 12 hours and news releases and media briefing materials prepared for a news conference. The employee contacted the *San Francisco Chronicle* with his version of the story. The hospital focused the story on facts rather than emotion. It wanted to remove sensationalism from media coverage by focusing on safety and to reach the greatest number of patients who may have been tested by the employee.[18] Other target audiences included:

- Patients who may have had blood drawn by the employee.

- Employees who would interact with the public and were as misinformed as the public.

- Benefits coordinators for large contracted employer groups.

- Affiliated healthcare providers who were a part of the hospital's healthcare delivery system and who would be expected to provide information and answers to their patients.

All network television affiliates covered the news conference and used the video B-roll that demonstrated the safety of the blood-drawing procedures. Nearly every story emphasized the safety of the procedure and positioned the story as an act of terrorism and a "hoax."

What medical center officials anticipated to be a multi-day story was given scant attention by the media after one week. Rob Morse, a columnist with the *San Francisco Examiner,* wrote this in response to the hospital's actions: "This week a hospital is fighting to keep its most important therapeutic commodity, trust. San Francisco has been hit by a bomb scare to the bloodstream, and the people at California Pacific Medical Center had to announce it. Unlike a bomb scare, you can't clear the room. Instead, they filled a room with cameras and spoke the dread initials, HIV. All they could do was add two reassuring numbers: zero HIV transmissions from blood tests and 1-800-220-CPMC. Rationality may work, once past the fear."[19]

Reducing Budgets and Minimizing Layoffs

With the increasing cost of healthcare, Presbyterian Medical Center of Philadelphia was faced with a $5 million deficit. Administrators knew they could manage their medical and clinical services, but they also knew they lacked the specific experience needed to cut costs in other departments — 330 employees in foodservice, environmental services, engineering and maintenance, materials management and security — without sacrificing dozens of jobs.

They hired a management company to run four nonclinical departments and a security firm to manage hospital security. The companies were expected to hire most existing hospital personnel to preserve as many jobs as possible.[20] The public relations department developed a plan to communicate the changes to the staff and community. The announcement was to be made in less than three weeks and the changes were to take effect the same day the announcement was made. Presbyterian hired Anne Klein & Associates, Philadelphia-area public relations counselors, to develop the communications program. The assignment was strategic planning and writing, plus preparing hospital executives to communicate with various audiences.

Rumor Control Essential

Timing was critical. The first 10 days had to be carefully orchestrated. The announcement had to be communicated so employees did not walk out, act out or talk out in an inappropriate manner to patients, to the community, to the press or to any audiences. Rumor control was essential. The hospital had to function as normally after the announcement as it had before.[21]

Top priority was information-gathering interviews with hospital executives to learn details about the publics affected and their anticipated response, plus other hospital staff members and outside audiences not directly affected and their anticipated response. Because the outsourcing was non-negotiable, no employee was involved in the process. Surveys showed there was a strong possibility that employees would be shocked, sad, insecure, angry and feel "sold out." The hospital was well-liked in the community, the CEO had great credibility and no department had morale problems. Employees had twice rejected union representation. However, research uncovered the fact that union sign-up cards were again being distributed.

The public relations goal was to protect the hospital's reputation as a caring and well-managed institution that provided high-quality healthcare. Six objectives included gaining acceptance of the outsourcing process by all employees, minimizing disruption to normal hospital operations, retaining loyalty of key audiences, assuring that any media coverage was fair and accurate, and avoiding unfounded rumor.[22]

Build on Credibility and Loyalty

Based on research, the communications strategy incorporated mangement's credibility and the employees' loyalty. Face-to-face meetings would be important. All audiences would hear the news early in the day. Communications had to be caring and express concern. The CEO would have a visible role in making the announcement and be available throughout the day.

Logistics was one of the toughest assignments. The communications process required tight scheduling. Volumes of printed information, scripts and Q&As were prepared. Key messages were critical. Executives had two days of presentation and media training. The hospital planned for staff availability 24 hours a day, including psychiatrists, psychologists and the chaplain. Executive management was available throughout the day to answer questions. They walked the corridors and were in the employee cafeteria.

The program was successful as measured against the objectives. Employees were surprised and shocked, but no one acted out any unpleasant or inappropriate behavior. Patient care was not compromised. The hospital functioned normally. The hospital's goal was to save jobs. Of the 330 employees, only 19 jobs (6 percent) were lost. No employees walked out.

Media Coverage Not an Objective

Gaining extensive media coverage was *not* an objective. The goal was only to secure fair and accurate coverage, avoiding unfounded rumor. Only two newspapers ran the story and both were fair and accurate. There were no rumors.

Although the hospital is non-union, the union made the move a union issue. In an organizing attempt, Presbyterian employees again rejected the union, 222 to 53. The objective of gaining acceptance of the outsourcing process, including from those outsourced, was met. Gaining acceptance meant "understanding," not "approval."

There were no repercussions. The program goal was "to protect the reputation of the hospital as a caring and well-managed institution that provides high-quality healthcare." Its reputation remained intact. There was no drop in patient admissions or physician referrals.[23] Presbyterian has since become a member of the University of Pennsylvania Health System.

"Find Baby Kerri"

The prevention of kidnapping incidents has become a major focus with hospitals. In 1988 to 1989, 50 babies were kidnapped from hospitals in the United States. Because of cost containment factors, healthcare staff are faced with managing risks of greater proportion than previously when all babies stayed in the nursery and were only seen infrequently by the mother and father. There also is the factor of family structure and unmarried or unwanted fathers that complicates the issue.[24]

Alta Bates Medical Center in Berkeley, California, had the first kidnapping in its 86-year history on Friday, June 12, 1992, with the abduction of Baby Kerri. On Tuesday, the hospital called in the San Francisco public relations firm of Kamer/Singer & Associates Inc. A press conference was scheduled the following day with a physician urging whomever had Kerri to seek competent medical attention for the one-week-old infant.[25]

A meeting was scheduled for Albert L. Greene, president of Alta

Bates, with the Berkeley police chief on Thursday, to stress the hospital's priority and to keep open a line of communications between the two organizations. Greene held a press conference to discuss steps being taken, including a $25,000 reward and a planned community outreach effort.

The campaign was designed to quickly reach the suspect or anyone who might have information about the abduction and motivate them to come forward. In addition to the media, many publics were targeted with specific programs: business and residential areas adjacent to the hospital; hospitals and medical offices throughout California; Alta Bates physicians, staff and other volunteers; local businesses, especially large employers; transit agencies and other operators of well-traveled public places; elected officials; and law enforcement agencies.[26]

Intense Public Information Effort

By Saturday, 350,000 flyers and posters were produced, and distribution began with door-to-door calls and through community organizations. A professional organizer oversaw volunteer recruitment. Actress Whoopi Goldberg did a public service announcement urging the baby's safe return. It was shot, edited and dubbed on June 23 and shown at a press conference with the Berkeley Police Department. The PSA was given widespread media coverage.

On June 25, door-to-door mobilizations were held in Berkeley, San Francisco and San Jose. Flyer distribution numbers exceeded those of the previous weekend and media coverage continued. During all this, the hospital and its agency worked under extreme pressure and, with two law enforcement agencies, had to maintain confidentiality and counter rumors and execute an aggressive outreach effort without taxing care at the hospital. To insure a consistent message, regular internal meetings and updates were scheduled.

The volume of media calls strained the public relations staff. In the first two weeks more than eight press conferences were held and 10 press releases issued. Subjects included new leads, likely medical needs of the baby and the reward.

In September, three months after the abduction, Baby Kerri was safely recovered and reunited with her mother. Alta Bates not only maintained, but improved its reputation as a high-quality, caring hospital, dedicated to the community.[27]

A Summary Checklist for Healthcare Facilities

Anne Sceia Klein, APR, Fellow PRSA, president of Anne Klein & Associates, says management of a healthcare facility should consider a few of the possible "issues" crises they could confront:

- Unexplained patient deaths.
- Employee sabotage.
- Sexual harassment charges leveled by or at a hospital employee.
- Anti-abortion picket violence.
- Medicare or Medicaid fraud.
- Hospital staff member, especially a surgeon, with AIDS.
- Anti-animal research protests.
- Sexual advances by a doctor toward a patient.
- Flash fire.
- Misappropriation or misuse of funds.
- Loss of accreditation.
- Unusually high death rates.
- Charges of inept or corrupt management.
- Mishandling of medical waste.
- OSHA violations.
- Pollution from the hospital incinerator.
- Inadequate staff education and preparedness.

"The implication is clear: no hospital administrator can afford to think 'it can't happen here.' Like the giant chemical firms, oil companies and pharmaceutical manufacturers, hospitals are facing difficult, volatile issues today," says Klein. "If a hospital doesn't have a crisis communications plan to go along with its crisis management plan, now is the time to start putting one together."

She adds that while the CEO will guide the crisis management team, the hospital's public relations director will be the primary person to develop the crisis communications plan. "Whether you develop your crisis communications plan in-house or engage a public relations firm to help you, the time, effort and money spent in preparing for the worst will be well worth it."

Endnotes

1. Alice Ann Love, Associated Press, "Hospitals fight change in Medicare's flat fee," *The Philadelphia Inquirer*, July 26, 1997, pgs. D1, D7.

2. *Philadelphia Weekly*, July 2, 1997, pg. 2.

3. Marian Uhlman, "Hospital mergers are causing new set of ills," *The Philadelphia Inquirer*, July 14, 1997, pg. A1.

4. Anne S. Klein, APR, Fellow PRSA, Anne Klein & Associates, Marlton, New Jersey, documents, correspondence and discussions, February 26, 1998.

5. Ibid.

6. Ibid.

7. Ibid.

8. Ibid.

9. James Meek, "High-Profile Incidents at Hospitals Are Often Decided in Court of Public Opinion," *Healthcare PR & Marketing News*, April 3, 1997, pgs. 1, 5, and Daniel LeDuc, "Hospital's wave of deaths raises suspicion," *The Philadelphia Inquirer*, July 8, 1997, pgs. A1, A7.

10. Ibid.

11. Ibid.

12. James Meek, *op cit.*

13. Ibid.

14. Ibid.

15. Charles Hoskinson, Associated Press, "Nurse charged in unexplained hospital deaths," January 4, 1998, and Judy Pasternak, *Los Angeles Times* News Service, "Ex-nurse charged with giving 6 patients fatal injections," *The Philadelphia Inquirer*, December 30, 1997, pg. A2.

16. Ibid.

17. Public Relations Society of America, Silver Anvil entry, 1994.

18. Ibid.

19. Ibid.

20. Anne S. Klein, APR, Fellow PRSA, Anne Klein & Associates, Marlton, New Jersey, documents, correspondence and discussion, February 26, 1998.

21. Ibid.

22. Ibid.

23. Ibid.

24. James T. Turner, "Infant Abductions in Health Care: Critical Incident Response,: *Journal of Police and Criminal Psychology*, pg. 2.

25. Public Relations Society of America, Silver Anvil entry, 1993.

26. Ibid.

27. Ibid.

CHAPTER ELEVEN

FOUL! IS THIS ANY WAY TO PLAY THE GAME?

Sport bridges age, race, gender, nationality and religion. In some countries, it even is a religion. Today it is one of the most powerful marketing tools. Companies worldwide recognize the extent to which sport pervades domestic and international lifestyles and use sport to promote and market products, services and corporate images.

An entire book, perhaps even several volumes, could be written about crises in sports. Some comical. Some sad. Some where people never learn. Professional, amateur and collegiate, few sports have not been affected. Even chess; even little league competition.

The earliest recorded crisis in sports involved the Olympic Games which began in 776 B.C. The festivals were held every four years and continued following the subjugation of Greece by the Romans in 146 B.C. Nearly 300 Olympiads were held for 1,200 years until A.D. 393, when Roman Emperor Theodosius ended them because of rampant corruption. During the fifth century B.C., cities began to reward their athletes with prize money, and later cases were cited where athletes accepted money from an opponent in exchange for conceding the victory.[1]

Some names always seem to be in the news involved in controversy. Owners and players alike. Dallas Cowboys. George Steinbrenner. Dennis Rodman. Marge Schott. Lawrence Phillips. Mike Tyson. Even officials responsible for the conduct of sport.

Columnist John Leo, of *U.S. News & World Report*, writes about the high tolerance a sports fan must have today and how many tried not to notice the charges of drug abuse, spousal abuse and rape brought against various stars on the 1986 World Championship New York Mets baseball team. And how football's Lawrence Phillips played despite 50 fines for team offenses and six brushes with the law, including a conviction for beating up a woman and dragging her down a flight of stairs by her hair.[2]

Leo also discusses the case of Latrell Sprewell of the Golden State Warriors who was suspended for attacking and threatening to kill his coach, P. J. Carlesimo. The team suspended Sprewell for 10 games and terminated his four-year $32 million contract. The league then suspended him for a year. The players' union backed Sprewell, who later held a news conference, issued a formal apology and presented himself as a victim. Johnnie Cochran, one of O. J. Simpson's attorneys, came to Sprewell's defense and complained of a "lack of due process" and "rush to judgment," and said the suspension would deprive his client of $8 million. Tony Kornheiser of *The Washington Post* wrote: "Nobody's talking about choking the coach anymore, are they? Now they're talking about 'fundamental fairness' for the player."[3]

Who Can You Trust?

Can you trust a basketball referee who cheats on income tax? People responsible for officiating the conduct of a sport should have the highest standards of ethics and integrity. Four referees of the National Basketball Association were indicted for tax evasion for allegedly taking first-class airline tickets given them by the league, downgrading them to cheaper fares and then pocketing the difference without reporting the gain as income.[4]

Do Announcers Really Tell It Like It Is?

Even sports announcers have crises, generally creating their own problems. Frank Gifford was tabloid material when he had an extramarital affair unbeknownst to his wife, television star Kathie Lee. In any crisis you want closure as quickly as possible. Gifford's problem was brought back into the spotlight months later when *Playboy* magazine did a cover story, interview and photo spread on Suzen Johnson, who told her side of the affair she had with him.

Things turned out quite differently for NBC's Marv Albert, whose 30-year career broadcasting Knicks basketball and Rangers hockey games made him a New York legend. In May 1997, he was accused of forcible sodomy, sexual assault and biting Vanessa Perhach, a Virginia woman with whom he had a 10-year relationship.[5]

The third day of the trial Albert surprised everyone by accepting a plea bargain. Judge Benjamin N. A. Kendrick asked Albert, "Are you in fact guilty of this crime?" Albert replied, "Yes." The prosecution agreed to drop a felony charge of forcible sodomy which could have resulted in a jail term of five years to life.[6]

Only hours after Albert pleaded guilty and publicly thanked NBC for its support, he was fired from his $2-million-a-year job with the network.[7] Sports columnist Mike Lupica took a jab at Albert's publicity representative, Howard Rubenstein, writing: "How has Rubenstein's advice worked out for him so far? He's the one who told him back in May to hold a press conference and deny everything." Rubenstein responded that Lupica "didn't have all the facts" in his column.[8]

Within a week after sentencing, Albert began a talk show tour that included interviews with ABC's Barbara Walters on *20/20*, CNN's Larry King, Katie Couric on *The Today Show* and David Letterman. The Letterman interview lasted 19 minutes and was the longest ever for the late-night host. Albert called his accusers "liars," said Perhach "was trying to extort me," and that another woman's accusation was "a complete fabrication." He also said he doesn't need the court-ordered therapy he is undergoing, saying "I really feel that's been overrated."[9]

Yes-s-s-s

Albert was back in business by July 1999 when he was rehired by NBC for a multiyear deal after Fox Television was getting ready to make him an offer. He will announce pro basketball and cover boxing and hockey in the Olympics.[10]

Even Owners and Players on the Same Team Have Sex Problems

Charlotte Hornets star Anthony Mason was charged in New York with statutory rape involving two teen-age girls. Queens District Attorney Richard A. Brown said two girls under 16 years of age told police that Mason and one other person at a party had sex with them.[11]

And in Charlotte, North Carolina, George Shinn, owner of the Hornets professional basketball team, was sued by a 28-year-old Charlotte woman who told police that Shinn forced her to perform oral sex at his Tega Cay home on September 5.[12] Prior to the suit being filed, "sources" said the woman wanted $5 million to drop her alleged charges, but Bill Diehl, Shinn's attorney, said "I unequivocally deny the solicitation of anything from anybody."[13]

Don't All Cowboys Carry Guns?

In recent years Dallas Cowboys football players have encountered off-field lawsuits, drug charges and assault charges. In July 1997, Coach Barry Switzer was arrested and subsequently fined $75,000 by the team owner for carrying a gun through an airport metal detector. During the controversy involving Cowboys' star Michael Irvin's indictment for possession of cocaine and marijuana and his arrest in an Irving motel with a former teammate and two women who described themselves as self-employed models, an editorial in *The Dallas Morning News* stated that "like it or not, Mr. Irvin holds a privileged, high place in our community. That position obligates him to behave civilly and decently—if he is to maintain that position. This does not mean that he and other stars must necessarily forswear alcohol, attend church and give liberally to charity. But this does mean that one must not curse viciously in public. . . . It also means a player should not be caught in the presence of illegal drugs and other illegal activities."[14]

No Crisis. *An Incident Over in Two Days*

Steve Everitt, center for the Philadelphia Eagles, did everything right after being arrested in south New Jersey and charged with speeding, drunken driving and possession of drug paraphernalia.

He had been with several teammates at a Monday night professional wrestling event and was on his way home at 12:37 A.M.[15]

The story broke Tuesday and Everitt did not speak with reporters. Eagles team officials issued statements to the media:
"Whenever a player is involved in an incident, alleged or otherwise,
it is embarrassing to the organization. . . . Our players have to understand that they represent this organization and the city of
Philadelphia at all times, whether they are on or off the field. Our
players have to conduct themselves properly and be accountable for
their actions all the time. They are professionals and, while they certainly live their lives in a fishbowl, that comes with the territory."[16]

The next day, against the advice of his lawyer, Everitt met with
the media. "I'd just like to take this time to apologize for the embarrassment and distraction that I've placed on many people the
last couple of days . . . ," Everitt said. "I realize now that my actions affect a lot more people than just myself."[17] The previous season the Eagles had signed Everitt to a five-year, $11.5 million pack-
age, including a $2 million signing bonus.

A newspaper described Everitt as a soft-spoken man who is as
serious about painting as he is about football, who funds college
scholarships in both disciplines, helped pay for an art therapy program at a hospital and has been a spokesman for the United Way.[18]
The incident never became a crisis. It was over in two days. Everitt
took a page out of the crisis communications book and told all and
asked forgiveness.

I'm "Only Joking"—Is the Mike Off?

Coaches and players, youth and adults alike need media training if
they are going to have any contact with journalists. When Tiger
Woods won the Masters, golfer Fuzzy Zoeller praised the "little
boy" for driving and putting and suggested that Woods' menu at
the 1998 Masters Champions Dinner not include fried chicken and
collard greens. Kmart ended his longtime sponsorship.[19] Zoeller,
who said he was only joking, withdrew from a tournament the following week, apologized publicly for his remarks and expressed
his personal concern to Woods.

John Calipari, former head coach of the New Jersey Nets professional basketball team, called beat writer Dan Garcia of the *Newark Star-Ledger* a "(expletive) Mexican idiot." Calipari said he was "only joking." "I guess I'm still learning how the system works," he said. Fred Kerber, sportswriter of the *New York Post* didn't buy it. "He's still learning?"[20] Garcia sought $5 million in compensatory and punitive damages for suffering "extreme humiliation and emotional distress," but the case was dismissed.[21] By going to court, Garcia continued to take his case to the public and the coach and team did not have closure until the judge's ruling.

New York Mets pitcher Jason Isringhausen, thinking his microphone was off after a press conference, called his team's director of media relations a "Jew boy." His defense was that he was "only joking." "We all talk to Jay like that," he said. "Jay is our favorite person in the world."[22]

Steinbrenner and the Commissioners

George M. Steinbrenner, owner of the New York Yankees, had problems with two commissioners of baseball—Bowie Kuhn and Fay Vincent. In 1990, Vincent banned him from baseball for alleged dealings with gambler Howard Spira for information that would make player Dave Winfield look bad. In an yet unpublished manuscript of his autobiography, Vincent relates a phone conversation where Steinbrenner asks him: "Where is it in the Constitution that says I have to tell the truth to the press? It's not illegal to lie to them, is it?" Vincent replied: "No, George. But not many people think in those terms."[23]

Steinbrenner pleaded against a suspension fearing it would damage his relationship as vice president of the U.S. Olympic Committee. Although the penalty was intended as a lifetime exile, Vincent paroled Steinbrenner in time to start the 1993 baseball season.[24] Yet, in his book, Vincent writes: "He's disruptive, corruptive, corrosive, boorish and embarrassing. If George wanted out, I was happy to show him the door." In another excerpt, Vincent says Steinbrenner "embodied sleaze" and dubbed him "baseball's worst recidivist." According to the chapter, the late Bart Giamatti, former baseball commissioner who died in 1989, called the Yankees owner the "Typhoid Mary" of baseball saying, "Wherever he went, disease followed."[25]

Crisis in the Stadium

An athlete's worst fear is being attacked. A promoter's or organizer's worst fear is not only an attack on an athlete, but a riot in the stadium or some kind of terrorist attack. Today no sport is untouchable and no event entirely safe. Every sports management executive and event director must have a crisis plan in place.

Security concerns for athletes first became well-known during the 1972 Olympic Games in Munich. Terrorists invaded the Olympic Village and killed 11 Israeli athletes and coaches. The April 1993 attack on Monica Seles has become the most prominent symbol of what has become the plague of sports in the 1990s. Then skating had to deal with the attack on Nancy Kerrigan coming off the ice after practice.[26]

Soccer is a sport that has been plagued with violence and death. In 1964, nearly 300 spectators were killed in Peru in a brawl following a disputed referee's call. In Scotland, in 1971, 66 people were crushed to death at the exits. A 1985 riot in Belgium killed 39 people. Violence still erupts in Italy, Spain, Germany and the Netherlands. The United States made a concentrated effort and had security at the maximum when it hosted the 1994 World Cup. There were no major incidents.[27]

Security experts are working with architects and designers to plan safety into new stadiums and arenas. With its on-field advertising billboards surrounding the playing field, soccer has created a moat-like barrier between the crowd and the athletes and officials.

Even Fans Are at Risk

Even fans, photographers and security guards are in danger. A photographer and a security guard were slightly injured from shattered glass during an October 25, 1997, hockey game at the Nassau Coliseum when a player went headfirst into the glass behind the goalie's net. Three nights earlier at Madison Square Garden, a pane of glass was knocked loose and fell and hit actress Janet Jones, wife of superstar Wayne Gretzky. Jones suffered a mild concussion and required three stitches in her lip.[28]

Late in the 1997 football season, the Philadelphia Eagles and city of Philadelphia took a proactive stance to turn Veterans Stadium into a thug-free zone during NFL games. After a national television audience saw violence in the stadium during a Monday night football game, Mayor Ed Rendell and Eagles owner Jeffrey Lurie announced an action plan that included:[29]

- To discourage any kind of intimidation, more police patrolling the stadium, some undercover wearing apparel of the visiting team, and the sale of beer banned after the start of the third quarter.

- Two municipal judges on site during games to immediately collect fines on the spot or jail offenders. This is an extension of Philadelphia's "night court" program to discourage "quality of life" crimes that include underage drinking, public drunkenness and disturbing the peace. Two holding cells were constructed on the first floor of the stadium.

Municipal Court Judge Seamus McCaffery said offenders now will be arrested, handcuffed and taken directly in front of a judge. "If you're found guilty, you'll receive a significant fine," he added. "And if you don't pay, you will be sent to jail."[30]

Going for the Gold

In 1990 when he was president of the U.S. Olympic Committee, Robert H. Helmick, a Des Moines attorney, set new ethical standards for the organization's volunteers, officers, directors and paid staff. Only one year later Helmick, an unpaid volunteer, came under the scrutiny of Mike Dodd, an investigative sports reporter for *USA Today*. On September 5, 1991, Dodd broke the story about potential conflicts of interest because clients doing business involving Olympic sports paid Helmick for his services.[31] By the time Dodd finished his investigation, it was found Helmick had received more than $275,000 in legal work from clients with

Olympic ties. He quit as USOC president two weeks after Dodd's first story and in December resigned his lifetime position on the International Olympic Committee.[32]

USOC bylaws state an officer shall not participate in any evaluation or transaction in which he has a financial interest and that the organization's properties, services, opportunities, authority and influence are not to be used for private benefit. "Everything the president of the USOC does, even tangentially, should be disclosed because it could be deemed a conflict or an appearance of conflict," said William E. Simon, former secretary of the treasury and USOC president from 1981 to 1985.[33]

Helmick's professional relationships in 1990 reported by *USA Today* were:

- Turner Broadcasting paid him to advise on obtaining rights to the 1991 Pan American Games in Cuba. Unless approved by the U.S. Department of Treasury, it is against the law for a U.S. company to have a commercial transaction with Cuba.

- Bob Seagren, former Olympic pole vaulter, paid him to regain status for golf as an Olympic sport. Seagren formed the U.S. Golf Federation with Robert Helmick Jr. The International Olympic Committee's Program Committee, on which the younger Helmick was serving, approved sports for Olympic competition.

- Ron Meyers & Associates paid $25,000 to promote bowling to Olympic sport status.

- Lifestyle Marketing division of Saatchi & Saatchi, $14,500, which seeks sponsors for the USOC and represented Barcelona in television negotiations for the 1992 Olympics.

While there was no apparent sports connection, the Romanian government paid $75,000 for advice on improving U.S. relations. Regarding his not disclosing the relationships, Helmick told Dodd, "There's no reason for me to." However, Howard Miller, a former vice president of ITT and former treasurer of the USOC, criticized Helmick's administrative expenses and for not disclosing the business relationships. "There is no reasonable basis to allow that man to remain and continue to use the organization for his own benefit," he said.[34]

Authorities on ethics say Helmick should have avoided any business relationships with Turner Broadcasting and federations seeking to have their sports on the Olympic program. "It's clear Mr. Helmick is making money by using his perceived political clout. That's troublesome. Whether it crosses the line is questionable, but it's skirting close to the ethical line," said Gary Roberts, sports law specialist and vice dean of the Tulane Law School."[35]

A Divided Response

Some people lined up supporting Helmick and felt he did no wrong, while others called for him to step down."It appears to be diametrically opposed to the code of conduct and ethics . . . which requires public disclosure of any apparent conflict of interest," said the late F. Don Miller, former executive director of the USOC. "I would find in my mind the appearance to be a violation of public trust."[36]

Support came from Mike Plant, chairman of the Athletes Advisory Council and a member of the USOC's executive committee, "I feel there isn't a conflict of interest there." And Turner Broadcasting President Terry McGuirk said, "As far as I can see, Bob Helmick is as pure as the driven snow when it comes to dealing with us. He recuses himself from any potential conflict."[37]

Telling the Executive Committee

Prior to his meeting with the executive committee of the USOC, Dodd spent several hours interviewing Helmick, asking him about every questionable business relationship. Saturday, September 7, Helmick, denying any wrongdoing, met with his colleagues to "walk through each deal." Helmick told the committee he had terminated and would refrain from any private business perceived as a conflict of interest. During the weekend meeting, he disclosed he received more than $150,000 in two other business deals:

- More than $150,000 from TIVI Amsterdam, the marketing firm of Romanian Ion Tiriac, that represented FINA, the international swimming federation for the sale of rights to world championships in 1991, 1994 and 1998. Helmick was president of FINA from 1984 to 1988.

- An undisclosed sum from TransSports, a Seattle travel business, to lease dock space in Barcelona for a luxury liner that could house 7,000 guests during the 1992 Olympics. Helmick's son, John, an attorney, was brought in and asked if his father could help secure the slip. Helmick said he withdrew when Barcelona interests insisted the USOC become part of the deal.[38]

And More Charges

On September 17, U.S. Skiing, the governing body for Alpine and Nordic skiing, called for Helmick's immediate resignation. The federation also called for the resignation of USOC executive director Harvey Schiller, the No. 2 man behind Helmick and in charge of day-to-day operations at the Colorado Springs headquarters. Howard Peterson, president of the ski federation, charged that Schiller used his position to try to get free ski equipment and "gold passes" and allow unlimited skiing at major resorts. Ski officials turned down the request and said they were told USOC grants would be increased if the passes were provided. Schiller said that he had no control over the grant procedure and was "only joking" when he sent a note to the ski federation writing, "Somewhere in this grant is a captured payment on a USA ski pass."[39]

USOC vice president George Steinbrenner told the reporters that the "cheap shots" had "better stop." He then added, "My advice is Howard Peterson better start worrying how his skiers do in Albertville (1992 Winter Olympic Games). This is bull. It makes me wonder what personal agenda they have."[40]

Instead of opening a book on crisis management and putting an end to the crisis, Mike Moran, public relations director for the USOC, threatened to deny Tom Kelly, U.S. Skiing's director of communications, an official appointment at the 1992 Winter Olympics in Albertville, France, for privately commenting about the Helmick controversy. Moran said he didn't want Kelly on his "team" of press officers but would give him a credential to represent the ski federation.[41]

Helmick Resigns

On September 17, two weeks after Dodd first broke the story, Helmick resigned. "I have reached the decision to resign with deep regret," he told *The Des Moines Register*. "But it is time that we put the focus of our attention back on the athletes where it belongs. I hope *USA Today* puts as much attention on the athletes in Barcelona as they did on Harvey Schiller and myself.[42] . . . [The] recent trial by media has made it impossible for me to continue to function effectively . . . I just cannot allow this organization . . . to be paralyzed by this situation. There has not been a single piece of, quote, evidence, unquote, since all this media nonsense began."[43]

William J. Hybl, CEO of the El Pomar Foundation in Colorado Springs, was named interim president to fill the 15 months remaining on Helmick's term.[44] It took Hybl only a week to recommend sweeping changes in disclosure, review and ethics policies.[45]

Just One More Deal . . .

When special counsel Arnold Burns, a former U.S. deputy attorney general, gave his report to the executive committee, it revealed another unreported business deal. Three days after signing a licensing agreement with the USOC, Impel Marketing, makers of trading cards, retained Helmick as a consultant. Six weeks later Helmick countersigned the Impel deal for the USOC. His fee was more than $50,000, but he cashed only $30,000 before his disclosure.[46] The theme was "quid pro quo" which Burns translated, "one thing in return for another." The report said Helmick "repeatedly violated" the USOC's conflict-of-interest rules in work as a paid consultant. Helmick said he disagreed with many of the report's conclusions and Burns' "interpretations."[47]

The Reign Ends

Three months after Helmick's ethics conflicts became public, he resigned from his lifetime appointment to the International Olympic Committee.[48] Some people believe the Helmick crisis could have been contained as an incident if he had been forthcoming, told Dodd everything in the very first phone call, did not hold back disclosing any potential improprieties and asked for forgiveness. The story, instead of being over in a week, continued for four months. It tarnished Helmick's reputation and embarrassed the U.S. Olympic Committee and the International Olympic Committee. In fact, had responsibility been admitted and accepted and a support campaign developed, he may not have had to relinquish either of his Olympic positions.

Where Is Baron Pierre de Coubertin When We Need Him?

More Olympic controversy erupted in December 1998. Marc Holder, Swiss member of the International Olympic Committee and a member of the executive board, alleged widespread corruption with bribes paid by cities wanting to host the Olympics. Holder, who is an attorney, said he believes 5 to 7 percent of the 105 voting IOC members solicited bribes through agents and were involved in bid campaigns for the 1996, 1998, 2000 and 2002 Summer and Winter Games.

As IOC members resigned and were asked to resign, investigations continued into alleged financial misconduct by the Salt Lake City group that won the bid for the 2002 Winter Games. Holder described as a "bribe" the $500,000 scholarship fund set up by organizers that benefitted relatives of six IOC members.[49]

Silence Is Not Golden in Atlanta

Following the bombing at Atlanta's Centennial Olympic Park in 1996, the husband of the woman killed said he can't understand why Olympic officials haven't called him. John Hawthorne of Albany, Georgia, also said authorities seemed to minimize the death of his wife, Alice, by emphasizing that only one person was killed in the blast. His 14-year-old stepdaughter was injured by bomb shrapnel and the Hawthorne's home was burglarized.[50]

"To be perfectly blunt, I cannot understand why they haven't called," he told Associated Press Television. "I am not sure what is so pressing that could not allow them a few minutes to either make a phone call or something. I'll just leave it at that." A. D. Frazier, chief operating officer for the Atlanta Olympic Committee said: "Is that the case? I'm sorry I didn't know that to be true, and I'm glad to have that brought to my attention, if so."[51] It would have been most appropriate for Billy Porter Payne, head of the Atlanta committee and an attorney, to personally express compassion and sympathy for the Hawthorne family. But there was also no statement when the FBI cleared Richard Jewell in October 1996 of being the prime suspect in the bombing.

As the keynote speaker at the 1992 conference of the Public Relations Society of America in Orlando, Florida, Payne boasted that Atlanta would be "twice as big at Los Angeles." When reminded that Los Angeles had a profit of $250 million, there was no response. Atlanta has not reported revenues that exceed expenses. Payne's group has a $17 million contingent liability owed to the U.S. Olympic Committee as part of a marketing agreement that must be paid before there would be any surplus. While the USOC expects to receive some of the $17 million, no one expects Atlanta to report a surplus.[52] What happened to the $500 million projection?

When the Athletic Program Brings Shame to an Institution

Jan Kemp, an English instructor at the University of Georgia, put the academic integrity of its athletic program on trial in January 1986. When she accused the university of giving athletes preference in a remedial program, her contract was not renewed. She sued, claiming she had been penalized for speaking out. The strategy of university lawyers was to prove her contract was not renewed because of incompetence, not because she spoke out against university practices.[53]

Hue Henry, counsel for Kemp, wanted the jury to hear about the remedial program and the athletic program and U.S. Judge Horace Ward agreed. What stunned people in the courtroom the following morning was the opening statement by O. Hale Almand, the defense counsel. "We may not make a university student out of him, but if we can teach him to read and write, maybe he can work at the post office rather than as a garbage man when he gets through with his athletic career," Almand said, referring to athletes in developmental studies. Jerry G. Footlick, author of *Truth and*

Consequences: How Colleges and Universities Respond to Public Crises, believes Almand may have intended to make the point that three or four years' exposure to higher education, even without graduation, would help anyone.[54]

Footlick notes that Kemp and her attorney kept the case in the public eye for months, ensuring that it would be front-page news for the entire trial. "They gave informal press conferences at recesses, lunch breaks and the close of the court day. They returned reporters' telephone calls," he writes. "The men who ran the university didn't know what hit them."[55]

But Athletic Shame in the Ivy League?

Anyone who doesn't think an athletic scandal can happen in the Ivy League need only to look at Penn, which forfeited five of its 1997 season football games because it used an ineligible player. The story surfaced when Sandra Marrow, mother of all-Ivy League defensive tackle Mitch Marrow, called the athletic department to ask if her son was on track to graduate and whether his tuition bill would be reduced to reflect his part-time status. When Marrow dropped a course in September he was one short of what is considered a full load at Penn for a student athlete and was immediately ineligible to participate in any games or practices. Weekly reports sent to the athletic department by the university's registrar showed Marrow to be a part-time student.[56]

In November, the athletic department and two professors worked to bend the rules by arranging an independent study course for Morrow the day before the final game of the season against Cornell. Two professors in the history department accused the athletic department of a "sleazy" maneuver to preserve Marrow's eligibility. A Wharton School professor approved the independent-study, but this was overturned by a dean of the School of Arts and Sciences. The athletic department was faulted for not immediately informing the university's president or provost of the problem, as well as the Ivy League and the NCAA.[57]

Football coach Al Bagnoli said he knew nothing of the problem because confidentiality rules prevent him or any member of his staff from checking academic records of a player. Steve Bilsky, the athletic director, said Penn had no choice but to forfeit the games, while interim provost Michael Wachter said if the university had not done so voluntarily, "it would have been imposed on us."[58] During the entire controversy, there was complete silence from the president's office. The one person out front with the media and public was Stanley Chodorow, the outgoing provost. He did ask that the Ivy League honors for Marrow be vacated.

Columnist Melissa Dribben took Penn to task saying Marrow should have known he was over the line and, "More important, his adviser should have known it. His coach, as well. They all plead ignorance, if not innocence." She writes that Marrow blames one professor for creating the uproar out of anti-Semitism, yet the professor's wife is Jewish. "The athlete had a history of dishonesty and was previously suspended for one semester for plagiarism," she adds. "It's not hard to see how the athletic department could let a little thing like a dropped course slip," noting that Marrow is 6'5", weighs 285, can bench-press 500 pounds and has a 41" vertical leap.[59]

But are there pressures to win even in the Ivy League? Penn fired its softball coach after the spring season and its volleyball and men's soccer coaches after the fall season because they did not produce a sufficient number of wins. "We want to achieve, we want to do better," said athletic director Bilsky.[60]

What's One Man's News Is Another Man's Trouble[61]

Barry Switzer, former coach of the Dallas Cowboys, has a history of crises. This crisis happened when Switzer was the head football coach at the University of Oklahoma. In February 1989, a story broke about several of Switzer's football players involved in criminal acts including an alleged gang rape, one player shooting another, and the star quarterback charged with selling cocaine. David Swank, dean of the law school who was serving as interim president, did an interview with CBS sports anchor James Brown during halftime of a college basketball game. Sooner alum John Meek, a Washington, D.C., public relations counselor, was appalled and embarrassed by Swank's answers and general performance in explaining the problems with the school's football program. "He was a swarthy, balding man who seemed shifty-eyed and uncertain in answering Brown's questions," Meek added. As a member of the NCAA's Committee on Infractions, Swank probably was better-equipped to discuss the issue of big-time college sports programs than almost any university president.[62] Meek thought what had been communicated from Norman had made matters worse instead of better.

Switzer returned Oklahoma to its national prominence as a college football power and led the Sooners to win three national championships. The school's recruiting and deportment record had been spotless except for a slap-on-the-wrist, two-year probation in 1955. "In a state that seemed doomed forever to wear the mantle of 'Okies,' poor shiftless dirt farmers on their way to California, having a winning football team at their primary university provided a lot of bragging rights. This was especially true for the hordes of Sooner graduates who now were heading not for California but to jobs in the oil patches of Texas."[63]

The Emergence of Black Athletes in the South and Southwest

As Barry Switzer came on the Sooner scene a major change was about to take place in college sports in the South and Southwest, and he very possibly was the one person who could have best pulled off this transition at OU. The change was the integration of Black players into college athletic programs. "Switzer had grown up in a highly dysfunctional family in rural Arkansas," says Meek. "Unlike Bill Clinton, another Arkansan who partially had grown up in a small town, Switzer's youthful friends were as likely to be Black as White. So when the opportunity came to begin recruiting top Black football players for OU, primarily at Texas high schools, the new Oklahoma coach not only knew how to talk the talk but also how to walk the walk."[64]

He built his record of three national championships and numerous major post-season bowl victories not with middle-class White kids, but with Black players from the lower income areas and ghettos of Dallas and Houston. Among the Switzer-era Black stars were Heisman winner Billy Sims, Joe Washington and J. C.

Watts, a former quarterback who now is a U.S. congressman from Oklahoma and a rising star in the Republican Party.

In the Switzer era, the players lived in suites in Bud Wilkinson House—the only school in the then entire Big Eight Conference that so isolated their athletes from the rest of the student body. It was in the privacy of these suites that the shooting of one player by his best friend and the gang rape of a 20-year-old virgin had taken place.[65]

Meek told Rick Linn, a vice president in the OU development office, that if the school wanted professional public relations help from him and his partner, Jim Hartz, a Tulsan who had been co-host of NBC's *Today Show* with Barbara Walters from 1974 to 1977, they were available.

Linn said Swank had asked the school's Board of Regents to let him hire a public relations firm and his request was rejected. Meek and Hartz not only offered to do the work without a fee, but to pay their own expenses.

An Offer That Couldn't Be Refused

On Friday, February 24, Swank cleared his calendar for Meek and Hartz and asked Switzer; Donnie Duncan, athletic director; and Donna Murphy, director of OU's public relations office to do the same. The CBS interview, and the fact that campus officials had clammed up, created a media frenzy. Calls from major media demanding more information were stacking up in the offices of Swank, Switzer, Duncan and Murphy. The "war room" group agreed nothing should be said until they had developed a strategy.

The year before, Oklahoma had been charged by the NCAA with numerous recruiting violations. Now on probation, the Sooners were suspended from appearing on television for two years and severely cut back on the number of athletic scholarships they could provide. The probation, combined with the alleged crimes, gave the public a perception that the coaches and players were out of control. And all of this under Switzer, who Meek believes either did not know or care what was happening in his football program so long as he was winning.

First Correct the Problem

Meek and Hartz had not come to Norman to help the institution explain away the incidents. Meek believed that the way out of the crisis was to make the appropriate changes to correct the problem and then to tell the world about these changes. Neither had previously met any of the OU officials. Meek analyzed the situation and spared no one in his critique. He told Swank his CBS interview was awful. Swank said he was blindsided by CBS, who told him "not to look at the camera during the interview." This was the opposite of what Swank should have done.

To Switzer, who had given an interview to *USA Today* earlier in the week in which he called the players indicted in the rape "animals," Meek said, "Coach, just a few weeks ago those 'animals' were the stars of your team. You ought to keep in mind that no matter how disgusted you feel, in this country people are still innocent until a court proves them guilty. That kind of comment is not helping you or the university. . . . Barry Switzer clearly had never had anyone talk this way to him," added Meek. "But to his credit, he seemed to realize we were there to help. He listened and offered no excuses." Saturday morning Dr. Tom Hill, an Olympic bronze-medal winner who had been brought in to work with athletes on their deportment, joined the team along with Fred Gipson, the school's legal counsel. Meek and Hartz set up a "meet the media" seminar to rehearse Swank, Switzer and Duncan for future television and other interviews.

"Switzer was the star. Not only did he have the experience of having hosted his own weekly television program on Oklahoma football for years," said Meek, "he had all the answers. He accepted his role in the failure of the players because being lenient was his style. At the same time, since none of the three crimes had any connection to one another, he did not see any particular step he or his staff could have taken to have prevented them from occurring."

Get Other Input for a Plan

While developing his plan, Meek sought out his contacts throughout the state to see how they felt about Switzer. A key strategy was to first get the story about the changes OU was making out to the people of the state and then to the national media. Not one person felt that Switzer was the bad apple in the barrel. As the coach himself admitted, his problem was in cutting too much slack both with his assistant coaches and the players.

To launch the offensive, he proposed a special half-hour program on Oklahoma Public Television in which Swank, Switzer and Duncan would be interviewed by Hartz. It was a given that Switzer's job was on the line and maybe Duncan's as well. In spite of Swank's statements to the contrary, Meek's friends told him he really wanted to be named president. Meek knew there was a major selling job to be done with Oklahomans. Swank said he had to consult with his regents before he could make further moves.

On February 28, Meek faxed his plan to Donna Murphy, the principal staffer responsible for carrying it out. At no time while in Norman had Switzer or Swank brought the Oklahoma sports information director into the meetings or even mentioned his name. This crisis was in fact about restoring the reputation of a university, not about football players. Meek and Hartz thought if the university bought the plan and everyone had their act together, Swank, Switzer and Duncan should do nothing in the next week or two but deal with every media person who would listen to their story. The television networks were important, but so were such programs as Larry King's three-hour talk show on Mutual Radio.

The Plan for the Sooners

Meek started his plan with seven general observations:

1. *Keep what has happened in the athletic program in perspective.* It is a crisis. But tragic and unfortunate as the recent incidents have been, the institution has continued its major function of providing an education to the students.

2. *Say, repeat, and repeat again and again that criminal behavior will not be tolerated on the OU campus.*

3. *Accentuate the positive.* At this point it is probably too late (even if it were possible) to give a defensive explanation of why the alleged criminal acts by football players happened

because the coincidence of the three straight alleged felonies appear to defy explanation. Therefore, we recommend that OU officials talk about the changes that have been approved by the regents and are being carried out. The public always wants to see *perceived* wrongs corrected, and now that that has been done OU can begin to communicate the story.

4. *Don't blame the media for the problems.* Be smart and use the media instead to work the university out of this situation.

5. *Avoid any statement that presumes guilt of the five student athletes charged with felonies.* It clearly is a tragedy for them, the alleged victims and this great university. No more need be said until the criminal justice system has run its course.

6. *Recognize that the university has been a victim of circumstances, regardless of how its athletes are housed, given second chances or made to live in the national sports media spotlight.* We do not believe on the basis of all information made available to us that OU officials created an atmosphere for this kind of alleged behavior.

7. *Make your own audiotape of every interview.* This is an accepted practice today.[66]

He then outlined a comprehensive plan for communicating with the Oklahoma constituents, especially state government officials and alums, and the national media. But the regents vetoed the idea of the half-hour special on Oklahoma Public Television. There seemed to be a feeling it would be best to go the route of the national media.

Meek, who had served in Washington as press secretary to two Oklahoma senators, felt this was a mistake. He believed the influence of *The Daily Oklahoman* in Oklahoma City and *The Tulsa World* would determine both Switzer's and Swank's future. He subscribed to the late House Speaker Tip O'Neill's philosophy that "all politics are local."

The next day Murphy told Meek they decided to launch their public relations offensive that night on ABC's *Nightline*. The thinking was the David Swank would be interviewed by Ted Koppel. The other guest was a *Sports Illustrated* writer who had done a cover story on football scandals at OU, Colorado and other campuses. But the cover featured the drug-dealing OU quarterback handcuffed in a jailhouse-orange jumpsuit.

Meek believed that Swank had done well in the mock interviews staged in his office. But he also felt it was a big mistake to put him up against Koppel and the *Sports Illustrated* reporter. He felt Switzer was the person to go on *Nightline* because he not only knew all the answers but could hold his own with the two journalists. Swank was dead set on doing the interview. When the program was over, Swank had done a credible job as far as the national audience was concerned, but he had not been strong enough in taking advantage of each opportunity to talk about the changes OU had put in place to prevent such incidents in the future.

"I knew that in Oklahoma his performance likely would be judged another major media failure. And so far as being named president, he was dead meat," Meek continued. "Switzer would not have taken any of the Koppel jabs sitting down. Considering his record, he had much to be proud of in his football program. As the major culprit in the eyes of most of the media, Switzer would have done a masterful job of defending himself."[67]

What Next?

"Swank's *Nightline* appearance bombed with Oklahomans. Swank and Switzer were never really in synch on how to work their way out of the crisis and both kept maneuvering to save themselves. Switzer resigned as coach on June 19. In time, Swank was replaced by former University of Houston president Richard L. Van Horn. Swank's next crisis would be as the "boss" of Anita Hill, a young woman on his law school faculty who made international news during the U.S. Senate hearings on the confirmation of Clarence Thomas as a Supreme Court Justice.

When his book was published in 1990, Switzer credited Meek and Hartz for their efforts. He noted that the weekend "war room" sessions cost him a free trip, courtesy of Nike, to Hawaii with his girlfriend and strongly implied their efforts to "coach" the coach on how to dress and talk were somewhat of a joke. After all, he wrote, he had spent hundreds of hours before television cameras as host of *The Barry Switzer Show*.[68]

Two years later, Meek ran into Switzer at a Washington reception during President Clinton's first inaugural. Twice since the book has come out, he has encountered and been warmly greeted by the coach. "In case you never figured it out, Barry," Meek told him, "Hartz and I were really down there mainly to save your ass. We though you were getting a bum rap." Meek said Switzer was genuinely apologetic. "I didn't really mean what I said about you guys in the book," he told Meek. "I was just trying to get back at David Swank."

"One of the points I stressed in the 'meet the media' seminar was that Switzer should stop giving interviews off the field dressed in polo shirts and start wearing a jacket and tie," said Meek. "The idea was that if OU was going to be businesslike about cleaning up its football program, he should look businesslike. I told him 'Ross Perot is a billionaire who can wear anything he wants to wear but always wears a suit and tie.' If you want to be taken seriously, start wearing a coat and tie." When Barry Switzer faced some 200 members of the media the day he resigned as coach of the Oklahoma Sooners, he wore a dark suit and a tie.

Wrapping It Up

Asked to analyze the OU crisis situation and its aftermath from the perspective of eight years later, Meek had these observations:

"First, while Hartz and I had access to all the top officials at OU who should have been involved, apparently the major calls were being made by the regents. I think the regents, no matter how sincere their interest, were a world apart from Swank, Switzer and Duncan who were sitting on the hot griddle. I never heard of a university regent ever being blamed for losing a key football game or a student being killed or injured from some prank in a frat house.

"Second, the regents should have allowed Swank to hire a public relations firm to help the university through its crisis and to restore its good name. The OU public relations office simply did not have either the staff or experience to carry out the plan developed for them. Nor were we asked to provide further assistance.

"Third, I believe the effort we made to assist the university basically was a waste of time and money. OU got our services free, so there was no feeling of the need to get their money's worth as there would have been had they hired a firm at $20,000 to $30,000 a month."

Missed Opportunities to Win Public Support

According to John Gerdy, former associate commissioner of the Southeastern Conference, of all the components of higher education, college athletics possesses all of the resources to make a difference—media exposure, education resources, tremendously talented coaches and student athletes, and a national audience that idolizes athletes. "They are all there. We must not waste these resources," he says.[69]

However, some college and university presidents and administrators have had trouble dealing with the appropriate role athletics should play in their academic institutions. A group of senior university advancement professionals, sports information directors, athletic directors and athletic conference officials met in Chicago in early 1994 to discuss these issues and how college sports programs reflect our society and its values.[70]

A few well-publicized scandals surrounding the academic and fiscal integrity of athletic programs, as well as the personal conduct and behavior of student athletes, coaches and alumni, have tarnished an overwhelming number of good athletic programs across the country and exacerbated these complaints.[71] A five-part series in 1993 in the *Chicago Tribune* documented how universities compromised by admitting academically unqualified student athletes and then kept them eligible for competition.[72]

"If athletics are to be viewed as more than just the entertainment arm of higher education, they must demonstrate how they can contribute more fully to improving the public's perception of higher education," says John Gerdy. "Administrators have not fully appreciated the tremendous opportunity that televised games could provide to effectively promote the value, mission and goals of higher education. Corporate America recognized the power of television to sell its products and services. Higher education should seize the same opportunity."[73]

The proliferation of cable television and new sports networks has created an insatiable appetite for sports events. From almost mid-August to mid-June college and university sports events are televised — football, men's and women's basketball, baseball, soccer, volleyball and other sports. Higher education has not used television as a powerful medium to win public trust. Research done in 1992 for the NCAA revealed that 53 percent of the total American public, 65 percent of men and 43 percent of women, follow college sports and that most people who follow college sports follow them on television by a 2 to 1 margin over those who attend games in person.[74]

During televised football games, most networks give the school 30 seconds to use for an institutional promotional spot. No two networks are the same since the television contracts for football are negotiated by individual conferences, with the exception of Notre Dame's exclusivity with NBC. The rules vary as well for post-season bowl games.[75]

The NCAA controls basketball. When it negotiated a $1 billion contract with CBS to televise the Division I men's basketball tournament, it made no provision for institutional promotional spots for the competing schools. In fact, the NCAA took all of the promotional spots for its own use. No consideration was given to individual schools when it extended CBS's right in December 1994 for another eight years at a cost of $1.75 billion.[76]

During the 1995 NCAA Division I men's basketball championships, the NCAA had 104 opportunities to tell its story and that of its member schools. CBS had 26 television sessions to cover the 63 basketball games. The NCAA was given two minutes of time in each session (a total of 52 minutes). Rather than airing 104 30-second spots, the NCAA had 90 promotional spots of varying lengths, none directed to winning the public's trust for higher education or collegiate sports.[77] The cost for a sponsor to buy one 30-second commercial in all 26 sessions would have been $5 million, so the total commercial value of all the airtime was in excess of $20 million.[78]

In 1992 Lou Harris & Associates reported that an overwhelming 81 percent of the media surveyed and 55 percent of the general public gave a negative rating to the NCAA's effectiveness in deterring violations.[79] Television spots would be an excellent opportunity to educate fans and boosters, and athletes and their families, on compliance. "The NCAA has enacted such a bizarre, Byzantine tangle of rules as to make it practically impossible at time to tell what is right and wrong," writes Russ Gough, assistant professor of philosophy and ethics at Pepperdine University. "Lacking common sense, compassion and, above all, clarity, the NCAA rule book — all 512 pages and 2½ pounds of it — has gained a notoriety to match that of the IRS Code.[80]

"The NCAA needs a separate commission to get word to the general public on compliance. They are heavy on enforcement and violations, fines and punishment, but they're very light on education and communication."[81] Rather than educating the American public on compliance, talking about the values of higher education or addressing issues in Chapter 12, the NCAA aired spots to help prevent drug and alcohol abuse. No guidelines or recommendations are provided to individual institutions regarding the spots they produce for football and other telecasts.

Sportswriter Ira Berkow of *The New York Times* believes networks can do a better job of humanizing the athlete and showing he is a student. During the 1995 NCAA men's basketball championships, CBS identified each athlete's academic major. "Once in a while we read a visual on the screen that informs us that the young man at the free-throw line is majoring in something or other. But that's the end of it," writes Berkow. "Take us into some of their classrooms. More important: Make it honest. From the heart. The real deal."[82]

Berkow also writes: "CBS has made a huge commitment to bringing these activities to its huge, primetime television audiences, and does so with all the artistry and technical skill of the 21st century. . . . What if just five minutes of a five-hour telecast were devoted to what these kids are truly supposed to be all about?"[83]

Berkow shouldn't have to ask. This should be a *given* in any broadcast and insisted upon by the NCAA, the various conferences and schools.

Who Makes the Rules?

According to *The Kansas City Star*, the NCAA has one set of rules that govern athletes and a completely different set of rules for itself. The manual for cities hosting a Division I men's basketball Final Four requires that gifts be delivered nightly to the hotel rooms of NCAA officials. According to John Parry, athletic director at Butler University, these mementos cost Indianapolis about $25,000. At a minimum, gifts for each official included a Samsonite suit bag, a Final Four ticket embedded in Lucite, a Limoges porcelain basketball and Steuben glass.[84]

The newspaper reported that in the last 23 years NCAA revenues increased almost 8,000 percent and its contract with CBS for the Division I men's basketball tournament is bigger than any single professional sports league's network deal. It said that sports generate almost $2 billion in annual revenue just for the top 305 Division I schools—twice the money the Department of Defense pays colleges and universities for research. The average college in the 100-plus power schools in Division I-A makes $4 million annually on football and men's basketball. "I don't see that we are money-hungry," responded NCAA executive director Cedric Dempsey.[85]

Hollywood—That's Entertainment!

Hollywood can provide tremendous impact in delivering a message. The impact can be positive or negative. Scores of feature films and movies for television—good and bad alike—have been produced about collegiate and professional sports. In 1993 two motion pictures glamorized every negative stereotype the American public perceives of college sports.

One was a Disney movie about football called *The Program*. Trying to emulate the hero of the movie, two teenage boys from Pennsylvania and New York died as a result of a scene from the film.[86] *Blue Chips* is a story about the best college basketball team money can buy. The script was 12 years old when producer Bill Friedkin made it into a movie. Friedkin told a Chicago sportswriter that he believes the movie's story line is valid and that the payoffs and bribes to players and parents take place at all major colleges and universities.[87]

It would have been very difficult for the film companies to produce either film without the cooperation from a number of universities who allowed filming on their campuses and in their stadiums and arenas, and even the use of actual game uniforms. *The Program* was shot on the Duke campus and in the University of South Carolina's stadium and used team uniforms from Georgia Tech, Michigan, Iowa and Mississippi State. When Arthur Haley's *The Moneychangers* was made into a television miniseries, there was no cooperation from any bank. Detroit certainly did not cooperate when *Wheels* was made into a movie for television. And a public utility consortium went so far as to buy all motion picture and television rights for *Overload* to prevent it from ever reaching the broad public.

Through its member schools, it would have been easy for the NCAA to mount an aggressive campaign to set the record straight on both movies — that this is not the standard practice on American campuses. NCAA officials were conspicuously silent, not even writing op-eds for major newspapers. Its public relations committee didn't even want to discuss the subject. Some colleges and universities went so far as to have joint promotions with the producers of *Blue Chips* when the film was released in their city.

Once a feature motion picture is made, the damaging misperceptions will be told and retold over a period of at least five or six years and generally much longer. One film, about an sniper assassin on the campus of the University of Texas-Austin, was being shown on cable television more than 20 years after it was produced.[88]

Don't We All Wish . . .

One very popular organization that has avoided any type of crisis is the Orlando Breakers. Coach Hayden Fox and his team, their owner, players, coaching staff and even mascot are an example for all to follow. What a wonderful world sport would be! Thank you, *Coach*. Thank you, Hollywood.

Endnotes

1. C. Robert Paul, Jr., "History of the Ancient Olympic Games 776 BC-393 AD, Part I," *The Olympic Games*, revised March 1984, U.S. Olympic Committee, Colorado Springs, Colorado, pgs. 1-3.

2. John Leo, "On Society — Basketball: Unfair to thugs," *U.S. News & World Report*, December 22, 1997, pg. 22.

3. John Leo, *op cit.*; Joel Stein, "Tell Men Behaving Badly," *Time*, December 15, 1997, pg. 91; and David DuPree, "Stern 'very comfortable' with Sprewell's penalty," *USA Today*, February 6, 1998, pg. 6C.

4. "NBA ref pleads guilty to fraud, resigns," *The Philadelphia Inquirer*, pg. D3.

5. Gary Mohoces, "A provocative preview," *USA Today*, September 23, 1997, pg. 3C; Rudy Martzke, "Broadcaster's family, media attend opening day of case," *USA Today*, September 23, 1997, pg. 3C; Steve Wulf, "Oh, No! For the Yes Man," *Time*, October 6, 1997, pgs. 44-45; Dorian Friedman, "He's out of the game," *U.S. News & World Report*, October 6, 1997, pg. 8.

6. Michael Janofsky, *The New York Times*, "Plea Bargain Halts Marv Albert Trial," *San Francisco Chronicle*, September 26, 1997, pg 1 and Debbie Becker, "Shocking trial ends with plea," *USA Today*, September 26, 1997, pg. 3C.

7. Michael Heistand, "Plea, firing raise marketability doubts," *USA Today*, September 26, 1997, pg. 3C, and Debbie Becker, "Albert fired after guilty plea," *USA Today*, September 26, 1997, pg. 1.

8. "Rubenstein Criticized by Lupica," *Jack O'Dwyer's Newsletter*, October 23, 1997, pg. 5.

9. W. Speers, "Newsmakers," "Albert denies nearly all and pooh-poohs therapy," *The Philadelphia Inquirer*, November 7, 1997, pg. E2 and Peter Johnson, "Inside TV," "Marv Albert gets warm 'Late Night' welcome," *USA Today*, November 13, 1997, pg. 3D.

10. "People in the News," *U.S. News & World Report*, July 12, 1999, pg. 12.

11. "Sportsworld," *The Virginian-Pilot*, Norfolk, Virginia, February 8, 1998, pg. C5.

12. Ibid.

13. Associated Press, "Shinn sought settlement, lawyer says," *The Virginian-Pilot*, Norfolk, Virginia, October 4, 1997, pg. C3.

14. "Michael Irvin — Athletes play in a unique universe," editorial, *The Dallas Morning News*, April 4, 1996.

15. Phil Sheridan, Gary Miles and Robert J. Terry, "Birds' Everitt is arrested in S. Jersey," and Timothy Dwyer, "It's the latest thorn in Ray Rhodes' side," *The Philadelphia Inquirer*, November 5, 1997, pgs. E1-2.

16. Ibid.

17. Phil Sheridan, "Deep Contrition," *The Philadelphia Inquirer*, November 6, 1997, pgs. E1-2.

18. Phil Sheridan, Gary Miles and Robert J. Terry, *op cit.*, pg. E-2.

19. "Media Overlooked Zoeller's Comments," *Jack O'Dwyer's Newsletter*, April 30, 1997, pg. 2.

20. Alison Stateman, Trendwatch, "No Laughing Matter," *Public Relations Tactics*, July 1997, pg. 2.

21. Michael James, "Calipari's Yule gift," *The New York Daily News*, December 25, 1997, pg. 71.

22. Ibid.

23. Richard Sandomir, "Court Papers Contain Vincent's View of Steinbrenner," *The New York Times*, August 10, 1997, pg. S6.

24. Ibid.

25. Ibid.

26. Barry Wilner, Associated Press, "An athlete's worst fear now is a personal attack," *Oakland Tribune*, Oakland, California, December 26, 1994.

27. Robert Millward, *op cit.* and James A. Michener, *op cit.*, pgs. 531-532.

28. "Sports In Brief," *The Philadelphia Inquirer*, October 26, 1997, pg. C3.

29. Phil Sheridan, "Eagles, city plot tighter coverage for fan offenses," *The Philadelphia Inquirer*, November 21, 1997, pgs. 1, A10.

30. Ibid.

31. Mike Dodd and Rachel Shuster, "Helmick says clients were OK; critics disagree," *USA Today*, September 5, 1991, pg. 2C.

32. Mike Dodd, "Ethics committee's top concern is policy," *USA Today*, January 7, 1992, pg. 14C.

33. Mike Dodd and Rachel Shuster, *op cit.*

34. Ibid.

35. Greg Boeck, "Ethics experts: Deals 'skirt line,'" *USA Today*, September 6-8, 1991, pg. 1C.

36. Mike Dodd, "Relationships surprise IOC colleagues," *USA Today*, September 6-8, 1991, pg. 1C.

37. Ibid.

38. Rachel Shuster and Mike Dodd, "USOC's Helmick confirms two more deals," *USA Today*, September 12, 1991, pg. 3C.

39. Mike Dodd and Rachel Shuster, "Olympic officials face new heat," and Greg Boeck and Mike Dodd, "USOC's Schiller denies ski pass charge," and Mike Dodd, "U.S. Skiing points finger at USOC," *USA Today*, September 18, 1992, Pgs. 1A, 1C, 3C.

40. Ibid.

41. Mike Dodd, "U.S. Skiing points finger at USOC," *USA Today*, September 18, 1991, pg. 3C.

42. Greg Boeck and Mike Dodd, "Embattled Helmick resigns," *USA Today*, September 18, 1991, pg. 1C.

43. "How the controversy developed," *USA Today*, September 18, 1991, pg. 3C.

44. "USOC committee quick to make interim pick," *USA Today*, September 24, 1991, pg. 9C.

45. Gene Policinski, "New USOC president proposes ethics changes," *USA Today*, October 1, 1991, pg. 11C.

46. Rachel Shuster and Steve Woodward, "Helmick deals called 'one thing for another,'" *USA Today*, November 25, 1991, pg. 3C.

47. Ibid. and Rachel Shuster and Steve Woodward, "USOC: Fees to Helmick violated rules," *USA Today*, November 25, 1991, pg. 1C.

48. Mike Dodd, "Helmick resignation 'took a lot of courage,'" *USA Today*, December 5, 1991, pg. 3C.

49. Stephen Wilson, Associated Press, "IOC official alleges Olympic-site bribery," *The Philadelphia Inquirer*, December 13, 1998, pg. C4.

50. Associated Press, *The Dallas Morning News*, August 1996.

51. Ibid.

52. Correspondence and telephone calls October-December, 1997 between the author and William J. Hybl, president, and John L. Samuelson, chief financial officer, U.S. Olympic Committee, Colorado Springs, Colorado.

53. Jerry K. Footlick, "Campuses Under Siege," *CASE Currents*, Council for Advancement and Support of Education, May 1997, pg. 32, and *Truth and Consequences: How Colleges and Universities Respond to Public Crises*, Oryx Press, 1997.

54. Ibid.

55. Ibid.

56. Ralph Cipriano, "Penn forfeits football games," *The Philadelphia Inquirer*, January 3, 1998, pg. 1; Joe Juliano, "Coach denies he knew of violation," *The Philadelphia Inquirer*, January 8, 1998, pg. 2; Mike Jensen, "Marrow case points up a crack in Ivy wall," *The Philadelphia Inquirer*, January 11, 1988, pg. 1.

57. Ibid.

58. Ibid.

59. Melissa Dribben, "Penn forgot a key lesson," *The Philadelphia Inquirer*, January 5, 1998, pg. 1B.

60. Mike Jensen, *op cit.*

61. Finley Peter Dunne, "The News of a Week," *Observations by Mr. Dooley*, 1902, *The International Thesarus of Quotations*, compiled by Rhoda Thomas Tripp, Thomas Y. Crowell Company, New York, 1970, pg. 431, No. 622-1.

62. John Martin Meek, discussion, notes, correspondence and memorandum to Rene A. Henry, October 1997.

63. Ibid.

64. Ibid.

65. Ibid.

66. Ibid.

67. Ibid.

68. Barry Switzer, *op cit.*

69. John R. Gerdy, "Restoring Trust in Higher Education: Athletics' Role," *The College Board Review*, No. 170, Winter 1993/94, pg. 32.

70. Nordy Jensen and Sarah Hardesty Bray, *Communicating About Intercollegiate Athletics*, Council for Advancement and Support of Education, 1994, pg. 1.

71. Nordy Jensen and Sarah Hardesty Bray, *op cit.*, pg. 1.

72. Ed Sherman and Barry Temkin, "Perilous Balance," *Chicago Tribune*, December 5, 1993, pg. 1.

73. John R. Gerdy, "How Televised Sports Can Further the Goals of Higher Education," *The Chronicle of Higher Education*, December 7, 1994, pg. A52.

74. Lou Harris & Associates, Executive Summary of a research report for the National Collegiate Athletic Association, 1992.

75. Rene A. Henry, *op cit.*, pg. 10.

76. Debra E. Blum, "All Part of the Game," *The Chronicle of Higher Education*, February 24, 1995, pg. A39.

77. Letter of April 17, 1995 from Kathryn M. Reith, director of public information, National Collegiate Athletic Association, Overland Park, Kansas, and telephone conversation of April 17, 1995 with Amy Sackler, CBS Television Sports, New York.

78. Telephone conversation of April 20, 1995 with John Brooks, CBS Network Television Sales, New York City.

79. Lou Harris & Associates, *op cit.*

80. Russ Gough, "Tangle Up by the NCAA," *The Washington Post*, August 1, 1994, editorial page.

81. Transcript of meeting of a blue ribbon panel on NCAA Compliance and Communications, Houston, Texas, June 28, 1994, pg. 184.

82. Ira Berkow, "Do College Players Read Books?," Sports of The Times, *The New York Times*, March 30, 1992.

83. Ibid.

84. "Reports detail gifts accepted by NCAA," *USA Today*, October 6, 1997, pg. 3C.

85. Ibid.

86. Michael deCourcy Hinds, "Not Like the Movie: A Dare to Test Nerves Turns Deadly," *The New York Times*, October 19, 1993, pg. 1.

87. Telephone conversation with Ed Sherman, sportswriter, *Chicago Tribune*, December 11, 1994.

88. Rene A. Henry, *op cit.*

CHAPTER TWELVE

INSTITUTIONAL ARROGANCE IN THE IVORY TOWER?

There's trouble in River City . . .[1]

- A coed files a date rape complaint. The administration stonewalls the media, investigates and keeps everything confidential. The victim and her parents disagree with the college's actions. Finally the woman and her parents hold a press conference and publicly tell their story. The president, an attorney, says "no comment." The young woman becomes the cover story of national news magazine. Now she is on the speaker's circuit damning the college.

- Two distinguished chemistry professors are always at odds. Dr. A's research includes cold fusion and transmutation of metals. Dr. B is angry because he wasn't honored with a Nobel Prize and campaigns to have Dr. A's "distinguished professor" title taken from him. Dr. B wages his case in the media, further embarrassing the school. The department chairman, dean, provost and president do not get involved. The reputation of the university suffers.

- The parents of a high school senior tell the university that its admissions officer, a man, made improper sexual advances to their son and offered to trade sex for his admission. The attorneys tell the president to say nothing and pay off the family. The parents become furious when the admissions officer is not fired, but only transferred to another campus office. An investigative reporter is stonewalled, misled and has no success in uncovering the story. Further investigation finds that other admissions officers and even the director sought sexual favors from prospective students, and even a mother, in return for admission and scholarships. It is only a matter of time until someone goes public with the story.

- The president comes home early from a business trip and finds his wife having sex in their bed with a member of his board of trustees.

- The football coach dies from a heart attack while having sex with a prostitute in a downtown hotel.

- The vice president of business services is indicted by the grand jury for soliciting free trips and other favors while negotiating contracts to privatize the bookstore.

- Two star football players are accused of gang rape. The football coach says they are innocent and refuses to suspend or reprimand the players. The coed wants justice. The attorneys say to keep it all under wraps.

- The chancellor is again arrested for drunk driving. The joke around town is that if you want an appointment to see him, you better meet in the back seat of a police car because he is spending more time there than in his office.

- The university's superstar journalism professor is charged with plagiarism. The leadership of the faculty pressures the president to take no action because they believe in time it will be forgotten.

- During an annual banquet honoring student athletes, an assistant athletic director publicly insults the newspaper's publisher. The athletic department official is angry because a reporter did not run a publicity release he sent them. The publisher immediately walks out of the banquet. The president has to intervene before any apology is made.

- The public university is criticized by an African-American state legislator because a penalty given a fraternity for holding a party with racial overtones was not as severe as critics hoped. The student newspaper tells the legislator to stay out of university affairs and publishes a racist political cartoon. This provokes the entire Black Caucus of the legislature. One legislator insists the president resign. The governor demands an apology from the newspaper. The journalism department adviser supports the student editors under First Amendment rights. In the end, the administration apologizes for the actions and naïveté of its students and future journalists.

- The college had an unwritten policy to conceal liquor purchases by having its supplier provide double receipts for "soft drinks and ice." The district attorney calls a number of university employees before the grand jury, including the executive assistant to the president, two deans, two vice presidents, the director of athletics and several department heads. All are indicted and plead guilty, no contest or are convicted. The continuing story reads like a daytime soap opera and tarnishes the ethics and integrity of the university over a period of months.

- An audit of the College of Engineering finds two professors double-billed travel expenses. While being reimbursed for speaking engagements or other projects, they also billed the public university in amounts in excess of $12,000. Since both are responsible for bringing in research dollars, the dean of the college fights to conceal any misdoing. The district attorney is kept at bay and the professors are allowed to make full restitution without any penalties.

- One of the state's leading sportswriters follows up on a story and calls a university attorney at his home to inquire about a lawsuit involving an athlete. The attorney chastises the sportswriter for calling him at home. The journalist apologizes and says, "The hearing was scheduled for tomor-

row and I want to be sure I have the correct information."
The attorney responds, "When did you ever care about having anything accurate." The attorney refuses to apologize
and the general counsel sees nothing wrong with the arrogance and rudeness. The head of university relations, a
coach and the athletic director apologize.

- An animal rights group plans a protest and demonstration
over the use of laboratory animals on campus. The dean of
the medical school has T-shirts printed and wants to have a
counter "get in your face" demonstration. The head of university relations has to seek help from the president to avoid
a crisis.

- A graduate student accuses her doctorate adviser of demanding sex for academic favors. She reports it to the
department head who does nothing. She then takes it
to the dean, who follows suit. Her dissertation is not
approved. She hires an attorney who files suit and releases
the story to the media.

All are true stories. Every crisis happened. Most could have
been avoided.

Higher Education Is Losing Public Trust

Public trust in higher education has been steadily declining during
the past decades. Louis Harris & Associates has been tracking confidence in public institutions since 1966. It reported that in 1992
only 25 percent of the public polled had a great deal of confidence
in the people running higher education as compared to 56 percent
in 1966.[2]

"Higher education may have been the last great institution in
American society to enjoy unstinting public trust—but no more,"
writes Anthony DePalma. "The loss of public trust has been most
dramatic in higher education. Until the end of the 1980s, the state
university systems had enjoyed more than 30 years of steady financial support."[3]

Criticism has been broad and has come from outside as well as within the academic community. One biting critique of university teaching came in 1988 with Charles Sykes' book *ProfScam: Professors and the Demise of Higher Education*.[4] This was followed by two other books in 1992: *How Professors Play the Cat Guarding the Cream*, by Richard Huber, and *Impostors in the Temple*, by Martin Anderson. CNN did a devastating feature on its network on March 15, 1993 — *The Absent Professor*.[5]

Derek Bok, president emeritus of Harvard University, believes that the erosion of public confidence is due in part to higher education's failure to communicate its goals. "There is no one able to communicate a compelling vision of what we are trying to accomplish for our students," says Bok. "We have been the victim of much exaggeration and distortion. We have not convinced the public or ourselves that we are doing all we could."[6]

When there is no response to criticism, the public can only assume the charges are correct. Often a president will not want to make a decision and have a committee take the responsibility. In other cases, attorneys will take a "no comment" approach. The university must listen to its public relations professional.

"There is a growing perception that higher education is not responding effectively to the problems that face our society," says John R. Gerdy, former associate commissioner of the Southeastern Conference. "Society expects our nation's colleges and universities to provide leadership in addressing such issues. Reversing the decline in public trust is the most fundamental challenge facing higher education today,"[7]

Why Such a High Incidence of Crises?

Professor Carole Gorney of Lehigh University points out that colleges and universities are microcosms of society and, as such, are vulnerable to a staggering number of potential crises, the same as any large city or small town. "Higher education institutions have to deal with crime and violence, fires, power outages and natural disasters," she says. "Like corporations, they are accountable for endowment investments, employee relations and managing funds. The science laboratories have the same potential for creating environmental accidents or generating activist criticism as any chemical plant. Such situations become true crises only when they are mismanaged. Categorize potential crises and list specific anticipated problems within each category. Never rely entirely on the news media to communicate your messages to key publics." [8]

This author polled a select group of college and university presidents regarding crises in higher education and here are their responses:[9]

- The leading causes of crises are racial discrimination and racial unrest, sexual harassment and intercollegiate athletics. Athletics problems included crimes committed by athletes and failure to comply with National Collegiate Athletic Association regulations.

- Crises are exacerbated by not being honest with the media, not being prepared to deal with a crisis, and stonewalling or a "no comment" response.

- Most do little to isolate an incident and prevent it from becoming a crisis.

- Periodic media training for all possible institutional spokespersons ranks high.

- The presidents stated nearly unanimously that crises affect image and reputation. Some respondents actually believed their institutions were "immune" from having a crisis.

- When a crisis happens, presidents want the most qualified individual or team to help, but all too often action is taken after the fact when an immediate response is needed.

- The presidents believed the general counsel should be a member of the bar and the chief medical officer a member of the AMA; they felt it was not important for the head of university relations to be a member of a comparable professional organization, such as the Public Relations Society of America.

Why So Many Crises?

Crises in higher education can be attributed to the following:

1. CEOs less prepared than their counterparts in corporate America.

2. The institutional culture of higher education with tenure, work ethic, turfs and a *laissez faire* attitude compared to for-profit and nonprofit organizations and governments.

3. A lack of strong executive leadership.

4. Individuals with the wrong disciplines — fundraisers, lawyers and academicians — heading advancement and public relations. Or when the individual is highly qualified, that person does not have total support from the CEO when dealing with others in the academic family.

5. The head of public relations without direct access to the president.

6. Reacting passively, not at all or having a "no comment" syndrome.

7. Unmitigated arrogance.

Because of the financial pressures and spiraling costs, recent trends have been to hire fundraisers as the advancement or public relations executive. Most fundraisers know how to bring in money but have no training or experience in public relations disciplines, especially crisis communications. Some observers believe that too great an emphasis is being placed today on fund raising, rather than cost cutting. "Few institutions have grasped the importance of building a powerful public affairs office that is staffed with skilled, experienced, and well-remunerated professionals who can tell an institution's story in the best ways and protect it in times of crises," writes Jerrold K. Footlick, a former *Newsweek* editor for 20 years and now a professor at Queens College in New York.[10] An individual's ability to pick up a $100,000 gift or write a brilliant speech or op-ed is not going to prepare an institution to prevent a crisis or deal with one when it hits.

Keep Alumni and Development Apart From Public Relations

Placing alumni, public relations and development all under one leader is a common practice at many colleges and universities. This can be a disaster if the person heading the three very different departments is not skilled in the disciplines required for each.

Having a completely separate and independent alumni organization provides many benefits for an institution. An alumni office independent of the institution may not be subject to certain Freedom of Information Act requests. It also can pay for items that cannot be purchased by a public university. Alumni can be an extremely powerful constituency.

Another problem is the way the educational practice divisions of executive search firms and university search committees look at qualifications for the person to head public relations. A mistake is to believe that a journalist is the answer. Few journalists have ever created and implemented a comprehensive public relations or crisis campaign and most are skilled in only one of the media areas — television, radio, newspapers or magazines. Other executive recruiters and campus committees also place more emphasis on candidates having a Ph.D. or master's degree rather than being members of or recognized by the Public Relations Society of America, such as by being accredited or elected to the College of Fellows. When seeking the head of advancement or public relations, the president and his search committee would be better served using the corporate division and its public relations search specialist at an executive search firm rather than the educational practice division.

Problems Facing Higher Education

Here are a few issues that institutions need to address to rewin the public's trust:[11]

- The increasing use of teaching assistants in classrooms rather than full-time professors (in addition to the quality of the teaching assistants). A television feature on CNN showed classroom instructors at the University of Texas-Austin who could hardly speak English.[12]

- Overcharging the government for research and unauthorized overhead items.[13]

- Teaching students in the classroom versus doing research.[14]

- Undergraduate education versus graduate and professional programs.[15]

- The workloads of professors. A number of state legislatures are looking into faculty workloads. The stae of Arizona found that if professors taught four, rather than two, courses a semester, it could save $10 million a year per campus. In Missouri, one-half of the faculty statewide spent the majority of their time doing something other than teaching.[16] What if every professor at every college and university just taught one class each semester?

- The elitist attitude of many institutions. Some people look at many of our schools as snob factories.[17]

- Administrative waste and inefficiency. Between 1975 and 1985, administrative staffs grew 60 percent while faculty increased less than 6 percent. Between 1980 and 1990, college students between the ages of 18 and 24 dropped from 30 million to 26.8 million.[18]

- The length of time it takes to get a degree. Four years no longer is the norm at many schools. Some students cannot get courses when needed to graduate on time. Others take the minimum course load to seek higher grade point averages. With increased tuition costs, other students need to work at full- or part-time jobs to pay for their education expenses.

- The rising cost of tuition. From 1979 to 1993, tuition increased at public colleges 211 percent and at private colleges 242 percent, in contrast to the consumer price index rise of 75.4 percent. The U.S. National Center for Education Statistics projected costs to double in 10 years and increase by more than 150 percent in 15 years. Why won't higher education explain to an American family that the cost of a four-year college education today is more than $110,000 but will increase to $206,000 in 10 years?[19] Another survey revealed that between 1985 and 1995, tuition and room and board at private institutions increased 91 percent, and 82 percent at public institutions. The average graduate has an indebtedness of $13,788.[20]

- Tuition price fixing.[21]

- Deceptive marketing and promotional practices to seek students by inflating SATs and graduation rates to get higher rankings in various guidebooks such as *U.S. News & World Report, Money* and *Barron's Profiles and American Colleges.*[22]

- Tenure is difficult to explain and justify to the American public. Only in higher education is someone guaranteed a job for life after working seven years.[23]

- Plagiarism and intellectual fraud.[24]

- Students graduating with degrees and not prepared for the workforce.[25]

- Political correctness and its not being put into perspective.[26]

- Hazing incidents, harassment and student misbehavior.[27]

- Athletic scandals, which run the gamut from violating the rules of the NCAA to athletes themselves behaving like common thugs.[28]

- Conflicts of interest and ethics with university presidents and chancellors, deans and faculty members sitting on boards of directors of outside organizations or having outside income-producing interests.[29]

A Need for Strategic Planning and Marketing

Higher education needs to practice what it preaches. Its institutions have produced the nation's leaders in marketing communications and strategic planning. Colleges and universities have a valid story to tell to motivate the public from being adversaries to being advocates. Following the *Time* magazine cover story "How Colleges Are Gouging U,"[30] Stephen D. Haufe of Clinton, Iowa, wrote the following letter, "When the trust placed in colleges evaporates in the face of unreasonable costs, the ivory towers will collapse under their own weight."[31]

A strategically planned marketing communications program would be best undertaken by one association or a consortium of associations representing the country's colleges and universities. William Honan, educational writer for *The New York Times*, criticized academic leaders for not speaking out. "Today, almost no college or university president has spoken out significantly about . . . healthcare, welfare reform, or dozens of other issues high on the national agenda," he wrote. "A generation ago . . . college and university presidents . . . called for the reform of American education, proposed safeguards for democracy, sought to defuse the Cold War, urged moral standards for scientific research and addressed other important issues of the time."[32]

Changing Perception Into Reality

Higher education has failed to convince the American public how hard professors work. Sarah Hardesty Bray at the Council for Advancement and Support of Education held a one-day workshop in Washington, D.C., for public relations leaders in higher education to discuss how to better communicate faculty workloads. No one had the research or data needed to undertake a program. One participant pointed to a story about how a history professor at the University of Virginia spent his week. The professor, Edward Ayers, responded to a series of stories that had run in state newspapers questioning how little time some college professors spend in the classroom.[33] Ayers went on the offensive and broke down how he spent 55 hours at work in an average week:

5 Teaching classes.
10 Talking to students.
3 Doing committee work.
1 Talking to groups outside the classroom.
3 Preparing for lectures.

5 Preparing for discussion classes.
1 Writing letters of recommendation for undergraduates.
6 Reading student papers.
6 Helping graduate students who are writing books or teaching undergraduate courses.
15 Judging manuscripts for journals, writing letters for others' tenure
    and promotion, working on books and research projects.

He did a great job of explaining to his adversaries how he spent
his week.[34] However, the audience reached was very limited. The
story should have been told to the national media.

During the workshop, the author suggested that different comparisons could be used depending on the target audience. If a state
legislator demanded more productivity, it could be pointed out that
paying a professor only for the time in a classroom would be like
paying a legislator only for the time spent voting on legislation,
rather than meeting and corresponding with constituents, serving
on committees, cutting ribbons at public events, attending political
ceremonies, fund raising and other such functions.

Where Does the Money Go?

An investigative reporting team from *Boston Magazine* and the
Boston Channel 4 "I-Team" decided to look into what they considered how "local universities were fleecing people with their lav-
ish excesses and outrageous salaries." The team cited that while
Boston University's tuition, fees, room and board rose 6.9 percent
in 1997, or more than triple the rate of inflation, its trustees created a position of chancellor for former president John Silber, paid
him $400,000 in salary plus $204,212 in benefits, with an entitle-
ment to one year's leave at full pay. Silber also borrowed money
from the university at interest rates ranging from zero to 5 percent
and negotiated two loans that total $500,000 on which he pays in-
terest, but which will be completely forgiven and considered outright gifts if he remains chancellor through May 31, 1999. Silber,
who is 71, can continue to live on campus even when he steps
down as chancellor and since he did not take sabbaticals during his
25 years as president, he can collect an estimated $1.3 million.[35]

The investigative team noted that Jon Westling, who succeeded Silber as president, never worked outside of academia, is paid $305,000 in salary and $56,229 in benefits and lives rent-free in a university house. Additionally the school spent $60,168 for membership in country clubs, $1.2 million in lobbying, and $72,796 to have an annual trustees' meeting at an Arizona resort owned by one of the trustees.[36]

Not to be outdone in salaries, when John A. Curry resigned as president of Northeastern University in Boston, he received $995,358 in an early retirement, salary, benefits and a severance package for the 1995–1996 year, making him the most highly paid college president in the nation.[37] Some governing boards also felt that some salaries were too high. Dr. Peter Diamandopoulos, president of Adelphi University, was near the top of the list with his $421,070. He and the trustees of Adelphi were dismissed in February 1997 by the New York State Board of Regents.[38]

Are Students Prepared for the Job Market?

What could be more frustrating than a parent or student investing $100,000 in a college education and not finding a job except in a fast food operation or retail store? A college degree is no guarantee of employment even though hiring picked up in the late '90s. There are cycles where jobs just are not available for graduates in certain fields. According to the U.S. Bureau of Labor Statistics, nearly 18 million college graduates are expected to join the labor force between 1992 and 2005, but there will be only about 14 million jobs during that period of time requiring college degrees. The same data show that in 1992, about 20 percent of those with a bachelor's degree earned less than $21,241, the median salary for all high-school graduates.[39]

The other side of the coin is that some graduates may not be as prepared as their predecessors. They do not have the education of their predecessors. A 1994 survey by the Department of Education showed that more than half of American college graduates can't read a bus schedule and 56.3 percent were unable to figure out how much change they should get back after putting down $3 to pay for a 60-cent bowl of soup and a $1.95 sandwich.[40]

U.S. employers with international operations expect college graduates to have international knowledge and second language skills.[41] "European college graduates are multilingual and understand cultural diversity. U.S. graduates are monolingual and don't have a clue or any sensitivity for other cultures," says consultant James Harvey. "Professors are not up-to-date on the state-of-art techniques, especially those used in business."[42]

In April 1997, for the first time, applicants for new teaching jobs in Massachusetts were tested for basic competence in reading, writing and a subject area. Of 1,795 recent or soon-to-be graduates, 59 percent failed.[43]

Higher education needs to say why graduates are not prepared for the workplace. What if Congress passed a "Truth in Education" bill the way we have "Truth in Lending" legislation? For example, an enrolling student interested in a degree in public relations would be told by the school, "Your chances of being employed in your field of choice upon graduation in four years are one chance in 27," or whatever an accurate projection might be. A ratio would be given for other disciplines. Universities would find students not enrolling in some courses or programs and heavier loads in others. Higher education would be held accountable.

Crime on Campus. What Is the Truth?

The 1990 Student Right-to-Know and Campus Security Act requires schools to file an annual report with the U.S. Department of Education on campus crimes. But what does a parent or student want to know? Crimes actually committed on the campus, or in the immediate vicinity of a campus? How safe is the campus and its environs?

The University of Pennsylvania was audited by the Department of Education following testimony at a congressional subcommittee that many schools deliberately understate their annual crime figures to promote image and enrollment.[44] The investigation coincided with a federal civil suit filed a year earlier by a former student who says that she was raped in a Penn high-rise dormitory in 1994. The university reported no rapes that year. The federal definition of a campus is: "Any building or property owned or controlled by an institution, within the same reasonably contiguous geographic area, and used by the institution in direct support of, or in a manner related to, the institution's educational purposes."[45]

The university interpreted that definition to include crimes committed on its campus proper but not incidents on city streets and sidewalks of its 262-acre campus. In its 1995 report, Penn listed 18 armed robberies on campus compared with the Philadelphia Police Department's 181. Excluded were robberies in front of Penn's popular food court and the shooting of a student on the sidewalk outside its dental school. Penn responded to critics saying that it counts crimes the way other schools do.[46] The former Penn campus police chief admitted she lumped many sexual assaults and suicides into a category ambiguously called "personal incidents."[47] Penn violated laws and regulations requiring publication of complete and accurate campus crime statistics. Federal auditors said Penn had to amend its reports already on file and improve its compliance with federal law.[48]

Following an attack on a female student in November 1998, Penn's student body passed a resolution calling on the administration to boost security and also began handing out bright red bull's-eye stickers that asked, "Am I a Target?" The resolution called for installation of more lighting, for consolidating night classes in a few central buildings and for security to require anyone in nonresidential campus buildings to wear his or her Penn ID card visibly after 10 P.M.[49]

Security on Campus Inc., King of Prussia, Pennsylvania, is a watchdog group and probably the nation's leading voice on college safety. "Colleges don't comply, but instead, manipulate their statistics," says Ben Clery, president of the organization whose sister was murdered by a fellow student in her dorm room at Lehigh University in April 1986. "One loophole colleges use is to channel student-on-student crimes like drug dealing and rape into campus judicial systems meant to handle matters like plagiarism."[50]

Such proceedings remain private, police are never contacted and the crimes aren't reflected in college crime reports. "Another way colleges avoid the act is to give crimes misleading names. There used to be no specific reporting category for 'simple assault' so a school would put simple assault in a category such as a liquor violation," Clery adds.[51]

Dealing With Sexual Assaults

In 1990, Rogers & Associates, Los Angeles, developed a national public information campaign for its client, the Rape Treatment Center of Santa Monica Hospital Medical Center in Santa Monica, California. Research indicated that rape is the most prevalent violent crime committed on college campuses; that 90 percent of campus rapes go unreported; more campus rapes occur at the beginning of the school year than at any other time; and college students are more vulnerable to rape than any other age group.[52]

The campaign was directed to college students, their parents, college administrators and faculty, campus security personnel, print and broadcast media, law enforcement officials, state and federal legislators and the general public.

A press conference was held in Los Angeles Tuesday morning, September 4, 1990, at 10 A.M. to allow television news networks to feed the story to eastern affiliates in time for evening broadcasts. Press materials for the media kit and a question-and-answer briefing paper were prepared for the media-trained center spokespersons. The materials were sent to 2,500 media outlets that included 2,000 college newspapers and radio stations. Media coverage included NBC's *Today Show,* CBS's *Morning News, Inside Edition, Entertainment Tonight, Time, USA Today, TV Guide* and a cover story in *People.*[53]

The campaign components included public awareness materials such as print, television and radio public service announcements, posters and bulletin boards and the following:

- *Campus Rape,* a compelling film hosted by *L.A. Law* television series stars Susan Dey and Corbin Bernsen. It included a 10-page discussion guide and provided workshop presenters with background information to stimulate post-film discussions.

- *Sexual Assault on Campus: What Colleges Can Do,* a report which outlines programs and policies colleges can adopt to reduce the incidence of sexual assaults on campus and provide support for victims.

Since many of the gang rapes on campus involve college athletes, the NCAA was asked to support the campaign. To date there is no record that the NCAA used any of its available free network television time in sports events to promote rape prevention.

While developed for higher education institutions, these concepts are adaptable to any company or organization. The campaign is something every school could redo at the beginning of every school year. Each campus sexual attack has the potential to become a major crisis. How an institution deals with the problem and how honestly it reports crime statistics will determine whether or not the problem becomes an embarrassing crisis.

Community Relations or Money Pressures?

The University of Pennsylvania outraged residents of Bucks County north of Philadelphia when it proposed to sell a 211-acre farm which it received as a donation in 1973 to use as an arts center. Penn expects to receive about $5.5 million for the property, which is on the edge of an agricultural zone and 1,000-acre farmland preserved by state and country easements.[54]

Penn's spokesperson, Dean Gary Hack, said "We have a responsibility to do what's in our best interest. Who buys the property and what they use it for is not our concern."[55] In its 1995 federal tax return, Penn reported a surplus of $182.8 million, but its annual report for the same period, using a different set of accounting rules, still showed a substantial surplus — $63.4 million. Its endowment rose 25.9 percent in 1996 to more than $2.1 billion.[56] A private institution, Penn also received $35.47 million in public funds in 1997–1998 from the Commonwealth of Pennsylvania.[57]

Congressman James Greenwood (R-Pa.) who worked to preserve the farm, said he did not expect the university to give away the property and take a loss, but to recognize its obligation to give the community an opportunity to mutually resolve the situation. He was joined by State Representative David Steil (R-Bucks Co.) who wants the university to give the township the first opportunity to buy the property.[58] Money should not be an issue superseding community relations based on the school's endowment and income. Also, Penn's Judith Rodin ranked third on the list of top-paid college presidents, with salary and benefits of $453,029 in addition to a house on campus.[59]

Research—Money and Controversy

Science comes in many forms. There is good science, bad science, junk science, political science and, of course, science fiction. Research means considerable income for many large universities. With it, however, comes controversy.

After seven years of court action, the University of Michigan paid $1.67 million in damages to Dr. Carolyn Phinney, a researcher in psychology who said her work had been stolen by her supervisor. The case also was unusual because the jury awarded damages for retaliation by university officials as well as for fraud. In April 1997, the appeals court upheld the jury's 1993 award, ending the case that began in 1988.[60]

Phinney was doing part-time research at Michigan's Institute of Gerontology while finishing a postdoctoral fellowship at the Institute for Social Research. Her supervisor, Dr. Marion Perlmutter, a recognized researcher in aging, suggested Phinney write up her findings and other research in applications for research grants. Perlmutter promised Phinney she would be listed as the first author on papers resulting from her work as well as gain a job at the institute. According to Phinney, once Perlmutter had the information, she claimed the work was her own. The lawsuit contends that Phinney complained to university officials, but Dr. Richard Adelman, director of the institute, threatened Phinney and told her that if she did not drop the matter against her senior colleague she would be dismissed. Perlmutter then dismissed Phinney from her laboratory. After a year of negotiation failed, Phinney sued.[61]

Following the decision, Phinney said, "I believe what happened to me was intellectual rape." According to Lisa Baker, associate vice president for university relations at Michigan, "The university remains convinced that the decision . . . was in error. The university continues to stand behind our personnel in this matter and believe they acted appropriately."[62]

In the summer of 1990, in the wake of a scandal involving the validity of a scientific paper published by a group that included the former president of Rockefeller University, two cases of alleged research fraud, apparently unrelated to each other, surfaced at California Institute of Technology. Caltech had just completed a policy for self-regulation for scientific misconduct and immediately launched an inquiry. Both individuals were sanctioned.[63]

"Because Caltech did everything by the book and the situation would be hard to paint as a scandal, the local media weren't interested," says Robert L. O'Rourke, assistant vice president for public relations. "Caltech officials' willingness to talk openly ensured accurate coverage of the story. Our decisive handling of the situation was praised. *The New York Times* mentioned the case as an example of 'how it should be done' in an article of controversial research."[64]

What Is Being Politically Correct?

In the 1960s some campuses banned speeches by people like Herbert Aptheker, Gus Hall and Ernest Mandel who were communists, alleged communists or people just more politically active. Recent problems have involved speeches by right-wing Israeli politicians, rap artist Sister Souljah, literary critic Camille Paglia, former Los Angeles Police Chief Daryl F. Gates and even distinguished public figures like Ambassador Jeane Kirkpatrick.[65]

Businessman and philanthropist William E. Simon believes many colleges and universities are alienating their donors with political correctness. The former Secretary of the Treasury writes: "Activist professors who control many of our universities are openly contemptuous of America and its way of life and are determined to use the classroom to overturn it."[66]

Simon cited the case where faculty members at Lafayette College endorsed a resolution to withdraw an invitation for then U.N. Ambassador Jeane Kirkpatrick to speak at commencement. Simon served as a member of the board at Lafayette and earlier had defended Jane Fonda's right to speak on campus. Because of the controversy, Ms. Kirkpatrick declined to participate and the school had no commencement speaker. He noted that this incident preceded the departure of Robert Higgs, a distinguished economist, who left the University of Washington to come to Lafayette as an endowed William E. Simon Professor. "Higgs left after being ostracized by his 'politically correct' colleagues for his free-market views," Simon says.

There Is No Level Playing Field

Simon notes an incident at Harvard where faculty members protested Pulitzer Prize-winning columnist George Will teaching a class as a visiting professor of government. Will earned a Ph.D. in political philosophy at Princeton and taught at Michigan State University and the University of Toronto. "The same professors applauded when filmmaker Spike Lee taught a Harvard class in 1992," he continues. "Apparently, there are some kinds of 'diversity' the apostles of 'tolerance' find intolerable."[67]

Handling Controversial Speakers

While there is no way to restrict or eliminate controversy when controversial speakers come to campus, there are guidelines to follow to prevent a crisis. CASE held a forum and published an issues paper with tips and tactics to follow before, during and after the event.[68]

Advance planning and communicating are critical, at all times remembering the First Amendment. Robert M. O'Neil, a law professor at the University of Virginia, wrote the following: "Past decisions by the Supreme Court have made clear that speakers cannot be barred because their views are offensive or divisive, or even because someone fears their appearance might cause a riot. . . . only policies based on grounds other than the content of speakers' messages may be cause to cancel invitations to outside speakers."[69] It is important to have a policy regarding the First Amendment, free speech and dissent, and specifically how it addresses any speaker that comes to campus.[70]

In advance of a controversial speaker it is important to work closely with the sponsoring group. Identify key constituencies, advocates and adversaries, and keep them informed and have a system in place for handling inquiries and complaints. Contact other institutions where the speaker has been on campus. Work with all groups to stress civility. Create a plan to distribute tickets. Communicate to internal audiences. Work closely with campus security and prepare for heightened media interest. Have a policy for media access and possible demonstrations.[71]

Following the event, be prepared for continuing media coverage and to communicate with key opinion leaders and various constituency groups. Educational forums may be needed if the speaker stirred up issues that require further examination or espoused hatred of a particular group. Most of all evaluate and try to improve on the plan for the next event.[72]

Dragging a Crisis Out More Than Four Years

In January 1993 a student at the University of Pennsylvania touched off a national incident that was in the media and not resolved until September 1997. Eden Jacobwitz, a freshman, leaned out his sixth-floor dormitory late one evening and yelled down to five Black sorority members whom he thought were talking too loudly and bothering his studying. The story went national when he yelled out: "Shut up, you water buffalo. If you're looking for a party, there's a zoo a mile from here."[73]

The women charged Jacobwitz with racial harassment under Penn's hate-speech policy. Jacobwitz insisted his use of the phrase "water buffalo" was roughly translated from the Hebrew word for foolish person. The women dropped the charges in May 1993 saying they couldn't get a fair hearing because of the media coverage. Penn abandoned its hate-speech code later that year. The incident has been debated regarding political correctness and free speech.[74]

In February 1996 Jacobwitz sued, alleging university officials conspired with the five women to pursue racial harassment charges against him that they knew were false, inflicting emotional distress. Jacobwitz graduated from Penn and entered Fordham University Law School. In September 1997 Penn, admitting to no wrongdoing, paid him $50,000 to settle the lawsuit and his attorney "under $10,000" to cover part of his expenses.[75] "The incident shouldn't have lasted longer than an hour," says Jacobwitz. "Instead, it took four or five years."[76]

So How Much Is Overhead?

For every dollar the federal government spends with a university to support basic and applied research, the institution can charge an overhead expense for items such as utilities and maintenance. In mid-1991 large, distinguished research universities throughout the country were being charged with bilking the federal government on research contracts to the tune of millions of dollars. Stanford was at the forefront of the corruption scandal that included University of California-Berkeley, California Institute of Technology, Carnegie-Mellon, University of Chicago, Columbia, Cornell, Dartmouth, Duke, Emory, Harvard Medical School, University of Hawaii, Johns Hopkins, MIT, University of Pennsylvania, Pittsburgh, Rutgers, Southern California, Washington and Yale.[77] Many major research universities were caught in a "guilt by association" situation.

Federal auditors found Stanford University had one of the highest overhead rates, adding 74 cents for every dollar it received in federal funds.[78] In fact, it was estimated that Stanford may have overcharged taxpayers $480 million for research costs during the 1980s.[79]

The "research" expense that gained the most notoriety was $184,286 in depreciation charges for the *Victoria*, a 72-foot yacht used on weekends by members of the Stanford Sailing Association, which included faculty, staff and alumni.[80] Other charges included $707,737 for the administrative costs of running a commercial shopping center for profit; $17,500 for a wedding reception for Donald Kennedy, the university's president and his new wife; $400 for a floral arrangement for the dedication of the Stanford stables, and "research" expenses at president Kennedy's residence that included $1,610 to install a shower curtain and two window shades in his bathroom, $2,000 a month for fresh flowers and $2,910 for a pair of antique chairs.[81]

The university initially denied everything to a Congressional subcommittee. Then Donald Kennedy told his faculty that he found "especially disturbing" the "ugly and erroneous implications that as president . . . I have somehow been living extravagantly, partly at public expense."[82] While agreeing to eliminate some charges, such as flowers and the piano in his house, Kennedy publicly said he found "nothing improper in their inclusion"[83] and denied that the university had done anything wrong.[84]

The investigation, congressional hearings and negative national publicity combined with the cost of outside attorneys in addition to the in-house university staff of 25, a $600,000 monthly bill for outside accountants and a shortfall in the university budget of $95 million for the next two years, brought increased pressures on Kennedy. William F. Massy, who had been Stanford's chief financial officer since 1977, suddenly resigned. On July 30, 1991, Kennedy announced that he would resign at the end of the next academic year. On March 19, 1992, he left.[85]

250 Universities Subject to Audit

While 250 universities had been notified they were subject to audit and investigation, 14 were investigated in detail. Some of the charges for "research" included:

- University of Texas — a dozen engraved crystal decanters from Neiman-Marcus;[86]

- Pittsburgh — the president charged his golf club membership, opera tickets, a trip his wife took to Grand Cayman Island and travel to "football matches" in Dublin;[87]

- Cornell — Steuben glass and part of the costs of construction of a new alumni club in New York;[88]

- MIT — $75,000 in salary and benefits for the president's cook, $23,137 to a law firm to lobby Congress and $68,000 in legal expenses to defend David Baltimore against charges of scientific fraud;[89]

- Dartmouth — $20,490 for a chauffeur used by the school's president, James Freedman, and his wife, $60,343 for expenses involved in terminating employees and $55,470 in legal fees to defend the college against a civil rights lawsuit brought by the student newspaper, the *Dartmouth Review*.[90]

In the wake of the investigations, Michigan withdrew $5.9 million in research charges. The university wrote off decorations for the Christmas tree in the president's office and an excursion to the 1989 Rose Bowl game.[91] But close to home was Congressman John Dingell (D-Mich.). When he announced his committee's investigation of Stanford's research bills, he was openly attacked by faculty members who compared him to Joe McCarthy and said he had a vendetta against science.[92] During his committee hearings in March 1991, Dingell lambasted Stanford for excess and arrogance and accused it of exhibiting "a brazen 'catch me if you can' attitude similar to that found in the defense industry."[93]

To Pollute or Not to Pollute—That Is the Question

Colleges and universities face a new challenge today, being in compliance with state and federal environmental laws and regulations. Many presidents and chancellors are finding it not only very expensive, but very embarrassing. How can you justify spending hundreds of thousands of dollars in fines and corrective actions and at the same time raise tuition and fees? Or ask a state legislature or friends and alumni for more money to correct the pollution? Or not invest in energy-saving, budget-saving programs. This becomes even worse if the institution teaches or gives degrees in environmental sciences. These are crises facing many higher education CEOs.

The University of Georgia may have to spend as much as $2.62 million to clean up a toxic waste site near the State Botanical Garden where it buried laboratory waste and dead animals for 10 years until 1979, when it stopped because of federal laws.[94] Boston University paid a penalty of $253,000 and agreed to spend $518,000 to remedy its violations for polluting the Charles River. The University of New Hampshire was cited for 15 violations of hazardous waste management laws and a penalty of $308,000. Yale paid fines of $69,570 for mishandling and mislabeling hazardous chemicals. It will cost in excess of $1 million to clean up contaminated groundwater on a former fire-training site at Penn State. Virginia Tech was cited for improper use and storage of pesticides and the University of Virginia for improper storage and disposal of hazardous waste. Georgetown was fined for illegally removing and handling asbestos.

There can be scores of violations at any physical plant — leaking underground storage tanks, PCBs in transformers, old boilers spewing dirty air into the atmosphere, decomposing asbestos, contamination of groundwater from pesticides and animal waste and mishandling and mislabeling of hazardous materials.

Many environmental problems can be attributed to deferred spending on maintenance. This is not "unfunded maintenance," but "dumbfunded maintenance." In some cases, institutions even believed they were not part of the regulated community and that they did not have to comply with state and federal laws.

Presidents and chancellors need to eliminate turfs within their institutions and team up professors who teach environmental courses with those responsible for facility maintenance. They also need to follow the lead of business and industry and reduce costs by making their campuses more energy efficient. Institutions who have taken advantage of the Energy Star Buildings^{SM} and Green Lights® programs of the U.S. Environmental Protection Agency have found quick paybacks and a new source of revenue.

The University of Cincinnati invested $2.96 million to realize $1.38 in annual savings. At the University of Missouri, a project that cost $1.68 million resulted in $515,235 annual savings. Florida International spent $1.53 million and is saving $218,879 each year. Even smaller schools like Delaware State, saving $648,000 a year, are finding the voluntary programs very profitable. In addition to the cost savings, the institutions can point with pride how this new approach helps prevent air pollution by reducing harmful gases such as nitrogen oxide, sulfur dioxide and carbon dioxide. These pollutants contribute to smog, acid rain and global climate change. It is a win-win situation. CEOs who are not taking advantage of these programs will soon have to answer students, their parents, members of their board and, for public schools, the state legislature, every time they want to raise tuition and fees or ask for more public financial support.

Prioritize the Campus Crisis Plan

"Before setting out to plan for specific emergencies, decide on the priorities of the institution," say two members of the administration at Oglethorpe University in Atlanta, Georgia. Andrew A. Altizer, assistant dean of community life, and Robert M. Hill, director of public relations, wrote, "Every university will have a different set of priorities, and once decided, those should be the guidelines for the rest of the plan."[95] They list the following as a typical set of priorities:

- Protect the health and lives of the students.
- Protect the health and lives of university personnel.
- Protect and maintain the university's image.
- Protect university property.
- Communicate clearly to internal and external constituencies.
- Follow up with counseling or other necessary steps to restore well-being on campus.
- Resume business as usual.
- Evaluate the crisis and update procedures as needed.

Keeping the priorities in mind, once a crisis committee is assembled it should brainstorm to come up with any crisis likely to strike campus. Altizer and Hill say it is better to anticipate an emergency that never happens than to assume the institution is safe from any particular crisis. They list the following, in alphabetical and not probability order, as potential campus crises at Oglethorpe:[96]

- Bomb threat.
- Chemical or radiation spill.
- Civil disturbance.

- Death of a student.
- Earthquake.
- Epidemic or contagious condition.
- Explosion, downed aircraft on campus.
- Fire — academic/administrative building.
- Fire — residence hall.
- Fire — student center/dining hall.
- Food poisoning.
- Gas leak (strange odor).
- Hurricane.
- Medical emergency.
- Nuclear threat.
- Power outage.
- Rape on campus — acquaintance.
- Rape on campus — stranger.
- Snow or ice storm.
- Suicide.
- Terrorist/hostage.
- Threat to individual or group.
- Tornado.
- Violent crime.

Endnotes

1. Rene A. Henry, *Could This Happen on Your Campus*, paper, July 1997.
2. Anthony DePalma, "Universities Grope for Lost Image," *The New York Times*, April 5, 1992, editorial page.
3. Ibid.
4. Linda Stewart, "Under Siege," *The Dallas Morning News*, December 8, 1992.
5. Rene A. Henry, *How to Use Sports to Sell Higher Education*, paper for

the American Marketing Association Conference on Higher Education, Chicago, November 12-15, 1995, pg. 1.

6. Carollyn J. Mooney, "Bok: To Avoid Bashing, Colleges Must Take a Leadership Role on National Problems," *The Chronicle of Higher Education*, April 8, 1992.

7. John R. Gerdy, "Restoring Trust in Higher Education: Athletics' Role," *The College Board Review*, No. 170, Winter 1993/94, pg. 23.

8. Carole Gorney, "Crisis Management — How to plan ahead for potential crises," *AS&U*, January 1990, pg. 20a.

9. Rene A. Henry, "Highlights of Crisis in Higher Education Survey," May 1997.

10. Jerrold K. Footlick, "Doing the Right Things," *Case Currents*, Council for Advancement and Support of Education, Washington, D.C., May 1997, pgs. 31, 34.

11. Rene A. Henry, "Education and Society — A United Front," speech at Council for Advancement and Support of Education District IV Conference, March 28, 1994, Houston, Texas.

12. Cable News Network, "The Absent Professor," Transcript No. 269, Segments 3 and 4, March 15, 1993, and Linda Stewart, "When students teach students," *The Dallas Morning News*, March 16, 1993, pgs. 20-21A.

13. Martin Anderson, "Institutional Corruption," *Impostors In The Temple*, Hoover Institution Press, Stanford, California, pgs. 167-179.

14. Carolyn J. Mooney, "Critics Within and Without Academe Assail Professors at Research Universities," *The Chronicle of Higher Education*, October 28, 1992, pg. A17.

15. Cable News Network, *op cit.*, Segment 3 and Gordon C. Winston, "The Decline in Undergraduate Teaching," *Change*, September/October 1994, pgs. 9-15.

16. Robert L. Jacobson, "Colleges Face New Pressure to Increase Faculty Productivity," *The Chronicle of Higher Education*, April 15, 1992, Pg. A31; Allan M. Winkler, "Explaining What Professors Do With Their Time," *The Chronicle of Higher Education*, July 15, 1992, pg. B2, and Cable News Network, *op cit.*

17. Martin Anderson, *op cit.*, pgs. 2-16.

18. Colleen Cordes and Dylan Rivera, "Trimming Academic Pork," *The Chronicle of Higher Education*, September 8, 1995, pg. A36; "Universities Grapple With Productivity," *Newsline*, National Association of State Universities and Land-Grant Colleges, February 1994, pg. 1; Erik Larson, "Why Colleges Cost Too Much," *Time*, March 17, 1997, pgs. 46-56; Carl Horowitz, "Where Higher-Ed Funding Goes," *Investor's Business Daily*, November 7, 1995, pg. 1; Shawn Tully, "Finally, College Start To Cut Their Crazy Costs," *Fortune*, May 1, 1995, pgs. 110-114.

19. Carl Horowitz, *Investor's Business Daily, op cit.*; Shawn Tully, *Fortune, op cit.*; *Financial World*, March 15, 1994; and *The International Herald Tribune*, March 5, 1994.

20. "Financial facts," *U.S. News & World Report*, September 8, 1997, pg. 77.

21. Martin Anderson, *op cit.*, pg. 167.

22. Steve Stecklow, "Cheat Sheets — Colleges Inflate SATs And Graduation Rates in Popular Guidebooks," *The Wall Street Journal*, April 5, 1995, pg. 1.

23. Amanda Bennett, "Tenure: Many Will Decry It. Few Deny It," *The Wall Street Journal*, October 10, 1994, pg. B1.

24. Martin Anderson, *op cit.*, pg. 133.

25. Robert J. Samuelson, "The Wastage In Education," *Newsweek*, August 10, 1998, pg. 49.

26. William E. Simon, "Rewriting History—Universities alienate donors with political correctness," *The Dallas Morning News*, Viewpoints Section, September 17, 1995, pg. 5J.

27. Jacqueline Stenson, Medical Tribune News Service, "Drinking, greeks go hand in hand—Harvard study finds real party animals," *The Dallas Morning News*, July 11, 1995, pg. 6C and Leigh Hopper, "As Greeks hold 'rush,' traditions are debated," *Austin American-Statesman*, Austin, Texas, August 30, 1995, pg. A12.

28. Martin Anderson, *op cit.*, pgs. 179-187; Daniel Golden, Sports, *The Boston Globe*, four-part series, September 10, 11, 12 and 13, 1995; Mike Rubin, "Illegal Procedures," *Village Voice*, New York, January 16, 1996, pg. 27; Dave Anderson, "Real College Champions Are the Ones Who Graduate," *The New York Times*, July 6, 1995, Sports, pg. 1; Robbie Morganfield, "It i$ more than ju$t a game, college boo$ter$ $ay," *Houston Chronicle*, Houston, Texas, September 3, 1995, pg. 37A; Nordy Jensen and Sarah Hardesty Bray, *Communicating About Intercollegiate Athletics*, Council for Advancement and Support of Education, Washington, D.C., 1994.

29. Editorial, "Ethics for universities," *Austin American-Statesman*, Austin, Texas, November 26, 1995, pg. E2.

30. *Time*, March 17, 1997, cover.

31. Stephen D. Haufe, "Letters," *Time*, April 7, 1997.

32. William H. Honan, "At the Top of the Ivory Tower the Watchword Is Silence," *The New York Times*, July 24, 1994, pg. E5.

33. Edward L. Ayers, "What we do all week," *Commentary* magazine, *The Virginian-Pilot & The Ledger-Star*, Norfolk, Virginia, January 23, 1994, pg. 1.

34. Ibid.

35. Jon Marcus, "Ripped Off! Inside the Higher Ed Racket," *Boston Magazine*, November 1997, pgs. 54-59, 104-110.

36. Ibid.

37. William H. Honan, "Best-Paid College Leader Is at Northeastern U.," *The New York Times*, October 19, 1997.

38. Ibid.

39. Wendy Bounds, "Graduates Learn Diplomas Aren't Tickets to Success," *The Wall Street Journal*, October 10, 1994, pg. B1.

40. John Leo, "The answer is 45 cents," *U.S. News & World Report*, April 21, 1997, pg. 14.

41. "What Employers Expect of College Graduates: International Knowledge and Second Language Skills," *Education Research Report*, Office of Research, Office of Educational Research and Improvement, U.S. Department of Education, July 1994, pg. 1.

42. James Harvey, speech, *op cit.*

43. Robert J. Samuelson, *op cit.*

44. Michael Matza, "Auditors to eye Penn's campus-crime data," *The Philadelphia Inquirer*, June 9, 1997, pg. A1.

45. Ibid.

46. Ibid.

47. Ibid. and Michael Matza, *op cit.*

48. Michael Matza, "U.S. Agency faults Penn's crime reporting," *The Philadelphia Inquirer*, February 10, 1998, pg. B1.

49. James M. O'Neill, "Penn students speak out for security on campus," *The Philadelphia Inquirer*, November 20, 1998, pg. B2.

50. "Campus Crime: Hear No Evil, See No Evil, Report No Evil," *Philadelphia Magazine*, March 1998, Pgs. 51, 160.

51. Ibid.

52. Rogers & Associates, Los Angeles, California, executive summary of entry in Silver Anvil competition of the Public Relations Society of America, New York, 1991.

53. Ibid.

54. Rena Singer, "Penn plan to sell farm angers some," *The Philadelphia Inquirer*, October 2, 1997, pg. B3.

55. Ibid.

56. Erik Larson, "Why Colleges Cost Too Much," *Time*, March 17, 1977, pg. 52.

57. Letter of May 21, 1997 to the author from Barbara L. Senier, director of the Bureau of Postsecondary Services, Department of Education, Commonwealth of Pennsylvania.

58. Rena Singer, *op cit.*

59. William H. Honan, "Best-Paid College Leader Is at Northeastern U.," *op cit.*

60. Philip J. Hilts, "University Forced to Pay $1.6 Million to Researcher," *The New York Times*, August 10, 1997, pg. 13.

61. Ibid.

62. Ibid.

63. Ibid.

64. Ibid.

65. "Coping With Controversial Speakers," *A CASE Issues Paper for Advancement Professionals*, Council for Advancement and Support of Education, Washington, D.C., May 1994, No. 17.

66. William E. Simon, *op cit.*

67. Ibid.

68. "Coping With Controversial Speakers," *op cit.*

69. *Chronicle of Higher Education*, February 16, 1994.

70. "Coping With Controversial Speakers," *op cit.*

71. Ibid.

72. Ibid.

73. Associated Press, "Former student settles suit over 'water buffalo' case," *The Philadelphia Inquirer*, September 9, 1997, pg. B1.

74. Ibid.

75. Ibid.

76. Ibid.

77. Martin Anderson, *Impostors in the Temple*, Hoover Institution Press, Stanford, California, 1996, pg. 169.

78. Martin Anderson, *op cit.*, pg. 170.

79. Martin Anderson, *op cit.*, pg. 170, from Jeff Gottlieb, "Overcharge Estimate Climbs," *San Jose Mercury News*, November 15, 1991, pg. B1.

80. Martin Anderson, *op cit.*, pg. 171, Joe Shurkin, "Sailboat Costs Charged in Error to Government," *Stanford University Campus Report*, December 5, 1990, pg. 1; John Wagner, "In Troubled Waters," *Stanford Daily*, December 5, 1990, pgs. 1, 20.

81. Martin Anderson, *op cit.*, pgs. 171-172; and Tracie Reynolds, "Stanford Research Out of the Ordinary," *Peninsula Times Tribune*, March 13, 1991, pg.

1; Jeff Gottlieb, "Congressional Probers Grill Stanford Leaders," *San Jose Mercury News*, March 14, 1991, pg. lA; John Wagner, "House Subcommittee Lambasts Stanford," *Stanford Daily*, March 14, 1991, p. 19; John Wagner, "University Cuts Bill for Indirect Costs," *Stanford Daily*, January 24, 1991, pg. 1.

82. Martin Anderson, *op cit.*, pg. 172; Donald Kennedy, remarks delivered at the April 3, 19091, meeting of the faculty senate, *Stanford University Campus Report*, April 10, 1991, pg. 15.

83. Martin Anderson, *op cit.*, pg. 175; Diane Curtis, "Stanford Centennial Year Marred by Allegation," *San Francisco Chronicle*, December 24, 1990, pg. A7.

84. Martin Anderson, *op cit.*, pg. 175; Andrew Pollack, "Under Audit, Stanford Will Repay U.S.," *The New York Times*, January 24, 1991, pg. A12.

85. Martin Anderson, *op cit.*, pg. 177-178;

86. Martin Anderson, *op cit.*, pg. 173; Philip J. Hilts, "U.S. Warns 250 Campuses of Audit on Overhead Costs Linked to Grants," *The New York Times*, May 10, 1991, pg. A10.

87. Martin Anderson, *op cit.*, pg. 173; "More Universities in Trouble: 12 Prestigious Schools Accused of Overcharging Government," *San Francisco Chronicle*, May 10, 1991, pg. A3.

88. Martin Anderson, *op cit.*, pg. 173; Colleen Cordes, "Allegations of University Abuses of Overhead System Continue as House Panel Releases a New List of Embarrassing Items," *San Francisco Chronicle*, May 10, 1991, pg. 20; Martha Graham and Tracie Reynolds, "Stanford to Repay Government," *Peninsula Times Tribune*, May 9, 1991, pg. A1.

89. Martin Anderson, *op cit.*, pg. 174; Jeff Gottlieb, "Congress Reports More Universities Overcharged U.S.," *San Jose Mercury News*, May 9, 1991, pg. A27; *Chronicle of Higher Education*, April 24, 1991, pg. A27, May 1, 1991, pg. A20 and May 15, 1991, pg. A20; *Stanford Daily*, April 23, 1991, pg. 10.

90. Martin Anderson, *op cit.*, pg. 174; Hugo Restal, "Dartmouth Accused of Abusing Grants," *Dartmouth Review*, May 15, 1991, pg. 7.

91. Martin Anderson, *op cit.*, pg. 173; "Michigan University Billing Questioned," *San Francisco Chronicle*, September 11, 1991, pg. A3; Colleen Cordes, "Draft Report Cites More Questionable Billing for Research Overhead," *Chronicle of Higher Education*, September 18, 1991, pg. A33.

92. Martin Anderson, *op cit.*, pg. 175-176; Christopher H. Schmitt and Jeff Gottlieb, "How Stanford Turned Grant Expenses into Big Money and Big Controversy," *San Jose Mercury News*, March 10, 1991.

93. Martin Anderson, *op cit.*, pg. 176; Opening statement of the Hon. John D. Dingell, chairman, Subcommittee on Oversight and Investigations, March 13, 1991.

94. Associated Press, "Cleanup of toxic waste site may cost UGA $2.62 million," July 3, 1999.

95. Andrew A. Altizer and Robert M. Hill, "Crisis on Campus: How to Develop an Emergency Action Plan," *Campus Law Enforcement Journal*, March/April 1997, pgs. 11-15.

96. Ibid.

CHAPTER THIRTEEN

DEALING WITH VIOLENCE IN THE WORKPLACE

Every company, organization and institution should have, at a minimum, a crisis management plan in place and ready in the event of violence in the workplace. Violence and murders in workplaces are increasing at an alarming rate in the U.S. Now schools, school boards and school districts must be prepared for violence by students.

According to the National Institute for Occupational Safety and Health, 20 people are murdered on the job each week in the United States.[1] This represents a 33 percent increase in just four years. A study by the institute in 1994 reported than an average of 15 people are murdered on the job each week.[2] A report by the National Safe Workplace Institute found there were 111,000 violent workplace incidents in 1992 costing employers $4.2 billion.[3] Homicide was the leading cause of work-related deaths for women and the third leading cause of facilities for men according to the 1994 report by the National Institute for Occupational Safety and Health.[4] And it continues to get worse.

The numbers of workers who are physically threatened, harassed and attacked also are increasing. According to a study by Northwestern National Life Insurance Co., between July 1992 and July 1993, 2.2 million full-time workers were physically attacked on the job, 6.3 million were threatened with violence and 16.1 million were harassed.[5]

Jobs with the highest incidence and risk of homicide are:[6]

1. Driving a cab.

2. Working in a liquor store.

3. Being a police officer.

4. Working in foodservice.

5. Working in a gas station.

6. Working in a grocery store.

7. Working in a jewelry store.

8. Working in a hotel-motel.

9. Working in a barbershop.

10. Working in a courthouse.

Robbery is the motive in most murders at food and drink establishments. About 10 percent are attributed to disgruntled employees and domestic violence that carries over into the workplace. Liquor stores, restaurants, gas stations and grocery stores that are open late at night and early in the morning are especially vulnerable because they deal in cash and depend on a transient labor force.[7]

In workplace homicides, 97.5 percent of the people responsible for the murders are men, average age of 36, who use firearms in 81 percent of the cases. In one-fourth of the incidents the person responsible for the violence commits suicide.[8]

No Workplace Is Completely Safe

A student defending his thesis before a panel of professors at San Diego State University opened fire in a university classroom and killed three faculty members who obviously didn't agree with the thesis. When the university refused to comment, the media interviewed a maintenance worker and two people who had been in the classroom when the shooting began.[9] San Diego State missed an opportunity to tell its story and show compassion for the loss of three members of its family.

There has been a high incidence of violence among postal workers. In 1986 a disgruntled postal worker killed 14 people and turned the gun on himself at the U.S. Postal Service office in Dearborn, Michigan. In October 1991, a terminated employee from the Ridgewood, New Jersey, post office killed his former supervisor and her boyfriend in the supervisor's home. He then returned to his former post office and killed two co-workers. In November 1991, an employee fired from the Royal Oak Post Office in Royal Oak, Michigan, killed three former co-workers and wounded six others before shooting himself in the head.[10]

In 1991 domestic violence spilled over to the Avis Rental Car counter at Dallas' Love Field. A boyfriend, who was a former employee, went to the airport to see his old girlfriend. Two employees ended up in serious condition after being shot, and the girlfriend escaped by being hidden in a toilet by a friend. The love triangle incident had nothing to do with Avis until it became the physical site of the incident. The employees became an integral part of the story. The shooting interfered with normal business operations and jeopardized the positive image enjoyed by the company. The company responded immediately with concern for the shooting victims and their families, established a briefing room for the media at the airport and managed control of the news.[11]

When he was Secretary of the U.S. Department of Labor, Robert Reich issued guidelines designed to reduce workplace violence and homicides for the healthcare and social services industry where he noted two-thirds of workplace violence occurs. "Healthcare and social service workers often face aggressive patients, visit clients' homes in dangerous neighborhoods, encounter violent situations in hospital emergency rooms or face other dangerous situation," Reich said. He added that guidelines will be developed for other industries, including the night retail industry.[12]

The Occupational Safety and Health Administration's "Guidelines for Workplace Violence Prevention Programs for Health Care and Social Service Workers" can be obtained by sending a self-addressed label to OSHA Publications, P.O. Box 37535, Washington, D.C. 20013-7535. Recommendations include:

- Install metal detectors to identify weapons.

- Install alarm systems or panic buttons.

- Use bright and effective lighting systems.

- Use curved mirrors at hallway intersections or concealed areas.

- Allow for two exits and arrange furniture to prevent entrapment.

The Labor Department's data show the rate of workplace violence for private industry is three cases for every 10,000 workers. However, for residential-care employees it is 47 cases per 10,000 and for nursing and personal care facilities, 38 cases per 10,000.[13]

Public relations professional Carla L. Ferrara of the Property & Casualty Communications office of CIGNA Corporation, Philadelphia, points out a number of factors that could account for the increase in workplace violence:[14]

- Rising drug and alcohol abuse.

- Layoffs and firings because of corporate downsizing.

- Rise in stress levels among remaining workers.

- Violence on television.

- Domestic abuse coming into the workplace.

- Availability of firearms.

Bullets Kill More Than E. Coli or Salmonella

Two of the 20 people killed at work each week in this country are employed in the foodservice industry. Two of the worst incidents involved gunmen who entered restaurants and went on a killing rampage. In October 1991, a gunman entered Luby's Cafeteria in Killeen, Texas, and killed 22 diners before killing himself. In July 1984, a man shot 21 people to death in a McDonald's in San Ysidro, California. The San Antonio-based Luby's Cafeterias waited five months before reopening its restaurant while McDonald's chose to raze the restuarant and deed the land to the city for a park.[15]

Several fast-food restaurants, including Kentucky Fried Chicken and McDonald's, believe the presence of police officers will deter crime. They have installed special booths in their restaurants that police can use to write their reports. In 1992, the 3,500-restaurant Hardee's chain instituted a "zero tolerance violence" program that includes an anonymous, toll-free tip line and employee training. According to Francis D'Addario, loss prevention director for Hardee's, as a result, robbery-related violence decreased an estimated 83 percent during the five years through August 1997.[16]

When a manager and two employees were murdered in the back room of a Starbucks coffee shop in the fashionable Georgetown section of Washington, D.C., in July 1997, the Seattle-based chain placed guards at eight of its area stores. It offered a $50,000 reward for information leading to a conviction. The company's president immediately flew to Washington to be on the scene and available to the media and families of the victims. Starbucks issued a statement saying it is "committed to providing the safest possible environment for employees and customers."[17] This contrasted with a multiple homicide at Humperdink's restaurant in Addison, Texas, where the Tacoma, Washington-based RAM International Ltd. declined to comment on the incident, not even showing remorse for the victims. The company owns four Humperdink's restaurants in the Dallas area.[18]

Restaurants should have a crisis plan in place for dealing with tragedies, according to David Margulies of Margulies Communications Group, Dallas, Texas. The plan should designate the company spokesman when tragedy strikes. "You don't want a situation where every employee is suddenly speaking for your organization," he says. "The details of the crime should be left to the police. If a police officer describes what happened, that projects the image that this is a crime—it happened at my restaurant, but it could've happened anywhere else," Margulies said.[19]

Margulies said a crisis plan should provide for counseling workers and customers. He also suggests not charging customers for their meals, offering to drive them home or call a cab, and contacting them later that day or the following day to be sure they are all right.[20]

Employee Assistance Programs

Human resources departments at many companies and organizations have employee assistance programs that can provide invaluable support for employees following a disaster and also help at risk employees to alleviate violence.

Following the shooting of an employee by her estranged husband in one of its hospitals, Alliance Health System activated its Critical Incident Stress Debriefing Team. This team is headed by a psychiatric nurse and a social worker and provides grief counseling and crisis debriefing for traumatized workers. The team also went to Oklahoma City to help local hospital workers work through their anger, stress and grief after the bombing of the federal building.[21]

Through prescreening, personnel managers can identify "at risk" individuals. After personnel managers have assessed an applicant's psychological tendencies toward violence, they are in a better position to lessen their organization's vulnerability to violent crime, according to CIGNA's Carla Ferrara. She notes that employers must also realize that workplace crises that result from traumatic events, such as violence and threats of violence, can cause problems which most businesses are not equipped to handle. The support provided to employees by trained therapists tends to their emotional vulnerabilities and early intervention diffuses many potentially violent situations in the workplace.[22]

While human resources can provide tremendous support toward healing the psyche of employees during and after a crisis, the public relations professionals must deal with the damage inflicted on the company. The importance of maintaining a comprehensive crisis plan tailored to the company is essential.[23]

Robert B. Irvine, president of the Institute for Crisis Management in Louisville, Kentucky, says normal rules of media relations are cancelled when there is workplace violence. "Most law enforcement agencies have public information officers experienced in dealing with the media after violent crimes are committed," he says. "Let them handle that aspect of the problem. With sirens screaming, hand-held radios blaring, people running, shouting and sobbing hysterically, your biggest challenge will be to keep a cool head amid the chaos. Focus your attention on internal communications."[24]

As with any crisis, an immediate response is critical, and as in dealing with many others, there will be an information vacuum. Irvine believes than an immediate response can help alleviate some pressure until the initial chaos subsides. "A statement may only be three or four sentences, but it needs to be written quickly and given to anyone who is answering the phones, manning the reception desk or communicating to the public or media," he says. "Knowing exactly what to say is difficult unless you start with the phrase, 'This is what we can confirm at the present time.' Just give the facts you know and continually update the statement."[25]

Endnotes

1. Janet Zimmerman, "A crime watch for restaurants," *USA Today*, July 10, 1997, pg. 3A.

2. Carla L. Ferrara, *Workplace Violence, Issues, Case Studies & Solutions: A Look To The Future*, paper for master's degree in journalism at Temple University, Philadelphia, 1995 and D. Anfuso, "Deflecting workplace violence," *Personnel Journal*, October 1994, pgs. 66-67.

3. Carla L. Ferrara, *op cit.* and S.L. Smith, "Violence in the workplace: a cry for help," *Occupational Hazards*, October 1993, pg. 29.

4. Ibid.

5. Carla L. Ferrara, *op cit.* and D. Anfuso, *op cit.*

6. Janet Zimmerman, *op cit.*

7. Ibid.

8. Associated Press, *The New York Times*, December 18, 1994.

9. Matthew Fordahl, Associated Press, "Three slain on campus; alleged gunman was defending thesis," *Bryan-College Station Eagle*, Bryan, Texas, August 16, 1996, pg. A3.

10. Carla L. Ferrara, *op cit.*

11. Andrew Stern, speech on crisis management at Texas A&M University, College Station, Texas, 1994.

12. Associated Press, "Government seeks to reduce violence on job," *The Dallas Morning News*, March 1996.

13. Ibid.

14. Carla L. Ferrara, *op cit.*

15. Martin Zimmerman, "Restaurants should prepare for tragedies, expert says," *The Dallas Morning News*, July 8, 1996, pgs. 1-2F.

16. Janet Zimmerman, *op cit.*
17. Ibid.
18. Martin Zimmerman, *op cit.*
19. Ibid.
20. Ibid.
21. Robert B. Irvine, *op cit.*
22. Carla L. Ferrara, *op cit.* and Pamela R. Johnson and Julie Indvik, "Workpalce violence: an issue of the nineties," *Public Personnel Management*, Winter 1994.
23. Carla L. Ferrara, *op cit.*
24. Robert B. Irvine, *op cit.*
25. Ibid.

CHAPTER FOURTEEN

PROFIT BY BEING GREEN

People have become increasingly conscious of the world in which they live since Rachel Carson wrote *Silent Spring* in 1962. Who could argue against wanting clean air, clean water, clean soil or against having a safe and healthy place in which to live, work and play? However, it was nearly a decade after Carson's book that the first Earth Day was held on April 22, 1970, to further stimulate the green movement in the United States. Unfortunately, there are still too many companies who want to be seen as pro-environment while continuing to pollute. A number of examples are cited in the book *Toxic Sludge Is Good for You!*[1]

It cost Ashland Inc. a maximum of $30 million for its 1988 spill of 700,000 gallons of fuel (see Chapter 9) because of the way the company and its CEO dealt with the crisis. The payments alone to settle the suit for Exxon, when it spilled 11 million gallons of oil in Alaska's Prince William Sound in March 1989, was $2.9 billion. To settle the suit filed by the state and federal governments, Exxon paid $2 billion for direct cleanup costs and another $900 million to be used for environmental good works throughout the country. The cost to Ashland was $42.85 per gallon compared to $263.63 for Exxon. "The Exxon Valdez disaster, with its images of oiled birds and devastated landscaped, drove home in mind-boggling magnitude the importance of preventing pollution before it occurs," said Jeanne M. Fox, regional administrator for the U.S. Environmental Protection Agency in New York City.[2]

Environmental Crises Get Big Media Attention

Most environmental crises will become major news stories because of the way they can be dramatically pictured on television and in newspapers and magazines. Laws passed by Congress are very specific about the environmental responsibilities of corporate America, educational and nonprofit institutions, and the military and federal and state governments. Yet when it comes to complying with those laws, many CEOs will bring in lawyers to fight.

Companies gain little support or sympathy from the public in a drawn-out controversy with the U.S. Environmental Protection Agency. Some leaders have found it far more expedient, efficient and economical to discuss needed changes and agree to do them over a bargaining table in a conference room rather than in front of a judge or jury. The employees, shareholders, management, customers, suppliers of the company and the community and its people impacted by the pollution are the losers when a company litigates. In a lawsuit, only the attorneys profit.

Others seek relief from their state governments where all too often political campaign contributions can have an impact on how environmental laws are enforced. Some governors have irresponsibly used a "pro-business" bully pulpit, citing the need for jobs and the economy, to ignore environmental laws. Wiser governors have seen that being pro-environment significantly benefits their state's economy.

Frank F. Mankiewicz, Democratic political adviser and former vice chairman of the Hill & Knowlton public relations firm, said: "The big corporations, our clients, are scared shitless of the environmental movement. . . . The corporations are wrong about that. I think the companies will have to give in only at insignificant levels. Because the companies are too strong, they're the establishment. The environmentalists are going to have to be like the mob in the square in Romania before they prevail."[3]

According to an August 1997 poll of 800 voters, 60 percent say environmental protection is "so important that requirements and standards cannot be too high, and continuing environmental improvements must be made, regardless of cost." The survey was released by Public Opinion Strategies at the Midwest Republican Leadership Conference.[4]

Some companies do believe, however, that being green is not only the right thing to do, but profitable as well. In 1992, 54 companies formed Business for Social Responsibility. By 1995 it had grown to more than 800 companies that included AT&T, Ben & Jerry's, Clorox, Federal Express, The Gap, Home Depot, Honeywell, Levi Strauss, Monsanto, Polaroid Corporation, Reebok, Starbucks Coffee Co., Taco Bell and Time-Warner.[5]

The authors of *Toxic Sludge Is Good for You!* write that the organization's board of directors had difficulty defining its policy on eligibility for membership and believed it would be counterproductive to impose specific standards of social responsibility on members. "The bottom line is that BSR's membership now includes some of the most environmentally destructive corporations on the planet, and more are sure to join," write John Stauber and Sheldon Rampton. "Some of the companies are financially supporting corporate front groups and business associations lobbying to weaken important environmental, consumer protection and civil rights laws, and funding right-wing advocacy groups set up to spread the message that environmental protection is incompatible with a healthy economy."[6] They also blame a number of public relations companies for the way polluters were positioned as proenvironmental.

Sharon Beder, a senior lecturer at the University of Wollongong in Australia believes many companies use environmental public relations to "greenwash" their reputations and play up their most trivial reduction in waste and pollution while continuing to foul the earth. "Green PR builds goodwill in the community to enable companies to head off tough regulations that would force them to install costly anti-pollution measures," Beder says. Companies "depict five percent of their environmental virtue to mask 95 percent of their environmental vice," she wrote.[7]

In a new book, *Global Spin: The Corporate Assault on Environmentalism*, Beder takes on companies and agencies who do environmental public relations. She cites Procter and Gamble, Dow Chemical, Mobil and 3M as companies that rely on public relations to greenwash their reputation. She notes that 3M earned a Silver Anvil, the highest competitive honor given by the Public Relations Society of America, for its "Pollution Prevention Pays" program although the company ranked among the nation's top polluters.[8]

The book attacks Porter-Novelli as being a master of "cross pollination," by building alliances between clients who might otherwise be opposed to each other. And this is the reason the agency does pro bono work for the American Cancer Society. Beder claims when a documentary was to be televised that charged a pesticide made by one of the agency's clients caused cancer in children, the firm managed to get the American Cancer Society to issue a memo criticizing the report. Rob Gould, executive vice president in the agency's Washington, D.C., office, dismissed her work as "error-filled" and denied doing any work for the pesticide industry at that time.[9]

Green, Efficient and Profitable

In 1993, after Interface Inc. lost its No. 1 world ranking for the manufacture and sale of commercial carpeting, its founder and CEO, Ray Anderson, took advice from a book given him by an employee. Anderson adopted for Interface concepts recommended in *The Ecology of Commerce* by Paul Hawken, an entrepreneur and environmentalist. He was stunned to read that toxins accumulate in humans from one generation to the next and how carpet mills sucked up hydrocarbons and spewed out toxins. Anderson's new mission was to create zero pollution and consume zero oil while simultaneously advancing the interests of his investors, employees and customers.[10] Anderson gave bonuses to employees and environmental consultants for ideas. Here are just a few of the environmental concepts adopted by Interface:

- A new tufting method cut nylon use 10 percent by combing old fibers rather than melting them for recycling.

- Hemp and flax are substituted for certain yarns, making a carpeting that is both "harvestable" and compostable.

- Processing water is treated for golf course irrigation.

- The plant is landscaped with wild grasses and black-eyed Susans instead of with a manicured and chemically enhanced lawn.

- The mill is muffled, odor-free and bathed in sunlight from three-story windows.

- Massive electric motors are jump-started with gravity-feed systems rather than with huge jolts of electricity.

The changes saved the company $25 million from 1995 to 1997, and another $50 million is expected before 2000. Interface regained its worldwide leadership with revenues topping $1 billion in 1996. Anderson's goal is to be 100 percent sustainable, but solar power, for example, remains uneconomical compared with today's oil prices.[11]

Energy Diversification

In 1997, British Petroleum PLC, one of the world's leading oil companies, announced plans to invest $20 million in what it says will be one of the largest and most technologically advanced solar cell manufacturing facilities in the world, to be located in Fairfield, California. BP's group chief executive, John Browne, broke ranks with other oil and gas executives in May 1997 when he said he believes the possibility of climate change cannot be discounted and should be acted upon. "We think solar is something which could be a valuable business for us," Browne said, and part of his company's response is to develop alternative fuels for the long term.[12]

Solar power, which represents less than a tenth of one percent of the total market for energy, has long been regarded by many as not more than a curiosity. However, it is rapidly growing and attracting new investment because of concerns over global warming where the burning of fossil fuels is creating carbon dioxide and other "greenhouse" gases that could bring devastating changes in temperature and precipitation worldwide.[13]

While the solar industry is expected to increase by nearly one-third worldwide in 1997, it is worth only a little more than $1 billion a year in the United States, which produces about 45 percent of the world's solar power equipment, most of it for export. Equipment demand is highest in the Pacific Rim, which accounts for 26 percent of the purchases, followed by Europe (22 percent), North America (17 percent) and West Asia (15 percent).

Shell Joins Diversification Movement

In October 1997, the Royal Dutch Shell Group, the world's largest producer of hydrocarbons, announced plans to establish a new business in renewable energy that it expects to account for half of the world's power sources by the middle of the 21st century. Shell committed $500 million over a five-year period to establish Shell International Renewables to tap an expected explosion in demand for environmentally friendly power.[14]

The new company will be a fifth core business along with Shell's traditional oil exploration and production, products, chemicals, gas and coal sectors. It believes that by 2020, sales of renewable energy-wind power, biomass (recycled biological material) and photovoltaic will reach $248 billion, up from the present $10 billion in sales, while fossil fuel use will level off. Shell now has solar cell plants in Japan and the Netherlands and plans more factories in other areas of the world. It hopes to capture 10 percent of the solar energy market by 2005. Jim Dawson, president of Shell International Renewables, predicted demand would grow by 15 percent in ensuing years with manufacturing costs dropping by 4 percent each year. He noted that 50 percent of the world's population has no electricity or grid and sees great potential for solar panel and biomass technologies in rural areas, particularly for driving small engines, home lighting, appliances and small-scale industry.[15]

The Hazards of Transportation

Every year millions of tons of various toxic chemicals are shipped throughout the country by rail, truck, barge and pipeline. "Transportation is the sleeping dog of chemical risks," says Wendy

Radcliff, environmental advocate for the West Virginia Division of Environmental Protection. "Every community is at risk."[16]

A May 1994 report by the National Institute for Chemical Studies notes that very few people live out of range of truck, rail or barge movements of hazardous materials. It also said, "There is more certainty regarding the transport of hazardous materials by barge and rail, because the routes used are more fixed in location than those for transport by truck." It concluded that the volume carried in any one rail shipment is significantly larger, and that a hazardous materials incident involving rail or barge transport could potentially release substantially more dangerous chemicals than an incident with a single truck.[17]

On Saturday evening, June 7, 1997, between 10 and 10:30 P.M., a freight train with chemical cars rear-ended a coal train on the CSX line on the south bank of the Kanawha River in Scary, West Virginia, causing a chemical fire. Hundreds of families in a one-mile radius around the wreck site were told to stay in their homes for much of Sunday. Hospitals and paramedics treated more than 100 people who were exposed to fumes from the fire. Another 80 sought shelter at an elementary school where they were helped by the Red Cross.[18]

The train wreck and fire brought up a number of questions, including "How can residents in isolated hollows escape chemical leaks if their crossings are blocked by derailed trains?" The 250 residents of Ventroux Hollow had no alternate route for emergencies and for years have complained about trains blocking them in. Officials brushed aside criticism saying there is no way to ever do a concrete plan to respond to every possible transportation emergency. "Whenever you plan for a hazardous materials transportation accident, you're planning for a moving target," said Bill White, director of emergency services for Kanawha County.[19]

Being Proactive and Prepared

Many products used today, including food, clothing, beauty products, medicine, fuel and toys, have exotic or formerly hazardous chemicals in them. These chemicals have to get from the manufacturer to another manufacturer to produce the finished product.

Union Pacific Railroad transports nearly a quarter of all hazardous materials moved by rail in the United States and according to it, railroads offer the safest means of transporting environmentally sensitive cargo.[20]

As the nation's largest rail carrier of hazardous materials, the company works with its customers and with federal, state and local emergency response groups to prevent, prepare for, respond to and recover from emergencies involving customers' products. Union Pacific provides hazardous material training to its employees, to the local emergency response personnel along its rights-of-way and to its shippers. During 1996, the railroad trained 20,289 employees.[21]

When Union Pacific has a problem, its public relations department works with all involved company personnel, customers, government agencies and contractors to provide the media accurate information in a timely manner. "Our employees can reach us 24 hours a day," says Mark W. Davis, regional director of public relations for the railroad in Omaha. "It's our responsibility to make sure they know where they can reach us. Because of our unique position in working with all the departments of the railroad and various groups in the 'real world' we are able to make suggestions to improve emergency response plans that may be overlooked. Above all, we are ready to respond at a moment's notice to hazardous material accidents."[22]

Once notified of an incident, it determines if someone needs to be on-site. If it is minor, with no immediate danger to the general public, the department notifies the appropriate media to insure factual reporting without going to the scene. Company personnel will be briefed on how to handle local press inquiries at the scene. If the incident is major, a member of the public relations staff goes to the site while others contact the media. Once on the scene, a series of media briefings are conducted hourly as information warrants. After the initial incident information is provided, updates are done at two-hour intervals, as information warrants, until the situation is stabilized. The briefings continue around the clock unless the media agree to another schedule.[23]

After the incident, public relations works with others to evaluate the incident and suggest ways to strengthen the emergency plan. In one of its company publications, Union Pacific writes: "Why should public relations be proactive when there's a hazardous material release? If we don't tell our story, someone else will and we may not like the results."[24]

Communicating Risk During Chemical Releases

There is no foolproof way to prevent a chemical release according to JoAnna J. Wagschal, public involvement practice leader at Woodward-Clyde Consultants in Denver, Colorado. "By preparing for them, an organization can mitigate losses and the time it takes to resume normal business practice. Swift response and effective communication can minimize the potential loss of life and property and protect the surrounding community. Decisive leadership could make the difference in maintaining your company's positive image even in the worst of times."[25]

Companies, organizations and institutions that have facilities that manufacture, use, store, distribute or handle any of 140 toxic or flammable substances in certain quantities must provide the EPA with a worst-case scenario and five-year accident history for each regulated substance, and a risk management plan. Because this plan is available under the Freedom of Information Act, it is important to consider community relations implications as it is being developed.

Effective June 21, 1999, an estimated 66,000 facilities throughout the country will be affected. This will include chemical manufacturers, wholesalers and retailers of propane, municipal facilities including drinking water systems, wastewater treatment works and public utilities. How the message is delivered to the public is important. No one wants to create a panic situation with a description of a potential catastrophe. And citizens do not want to be reminded of the dangers of living in a community that is susceptible to an accidental release of toxic or flammable substances.

This is where the public relations professional must take the lead, and not an attorney, engineer or chemist. The communicator must consider the best interests of the facility and the community in whatever risk communications plan is implemented. "Many affected companies have been so focused on producing the reams of paperwork required that they haven't begun to consider how the public—and the media—will react when the information is released," says Jeff Braun, general manager of The Ammerman Experience, Stafford, Texas. "Yet this ruling poses some formidable communications challenges. "If handled poorly, the very act of revealing the information could create a public relations crisis if people believe a disaster could occur any minute at the plant down the street," Braun, a former television news director, adds. "That's why it's critical that you convey to your audiences that your company cares about the community, that you've made every effort to minimize risks and that you're prepared to respond effectively if such a worst-case scenario does occur."[26]

Carol J. Forrest of Equinox Environmental Consultants Ltd., Wheaton, Illinois, echoes Braun's concerns. "The communications professional must already know or take time to understand the EPA regulations and the intent behind the risk management program before developing a community outreach program," she says. The author of *The Practical Guide to Environmental Community Relations*, Forrest says, "I consider community assessment to be the cornerstone of effective environmental community relations, but it tends to be underutilized, with few good models for how to perform these studies systematically."[27]

"Cardinal Rules" of Risk Communications

Some tips can be taken from an EPA Superfund publication that lists "The Seven Cardinal Rules of Risk Communications." EPA notes these are basic principles of effective communication developed by the agency and are suggested guidelines and not hard and fast rules.[28]

1. *Accept and involve the public as a legitimate partner.* Involve the community and all other parties that have an interest in the issue early.

2. *Plan carefully and evaluate your efforts.* Successful planning and evaluation entails the following six elements: (1) begin with clear, explicit objectives; (2) assess the strengths and

weaknesses of your information; (3) identify and address the particular interests of different groups you work with; (4) train your staff, including technical staff, in communication skills; (5) practice and test your messages; (6) evaluate your efforts and learn from your mistakes.

3. *Listen to the public's specific concerns.* Do not make assumptions about what people know, think or want done. Take the time to find out what people are thinking by letting all parties with an interest in the issue be heard. Identify with your audience.

4. *Be honest, frank and open.* State your credentials, but do not ask or expect to be trusted. If you do not know an answer or are uncertain, acknowledge that but get back to people with answers as soon as possible. Do not hesitate to admit mistakes.

5. *Coordinate and collaborate with other credible sources.* Coordinate with other organizations or groups and issue communications jointly. Few things make risk communication more difficult than conflicts or public disagreements with other credible sources.

6. *Meet the needs of the media.* Be open and accessible to reporters. Realize that reporters must meet their deadlines. Provide risk information tailored to the needs of each type of media. Prepare in advance and provide background material on complex issues. Keep in mind that the media are frequently more interested in politics than risk; simplicity than complexity; and danger than safety.

7. *Speak clearly and with compassion.* Be sensitive to norms, such as speech and dress. When addressing large groups or individuals, use simple, nontechnical language. Whenever possible, use comparisons to help put risks in perspective, but avoid comparisons that ignore distinctions that people consider important. Acknowledge and respond with words and actions to emotions that people express—anxiety, fear, anger, outrage and helplessness.

Cleaning Up for Tourism

When a Southern Pacific tanker car derailed near the Northern California town of Dunsmuir on July 14, 1991, and spilled 19,000 gallons of toxic pesticide into the Sacramento River, the economic survival of the town and its people were threatened. Dunsmuir, with a population of only 2,300, was almost solely dependent on tourism and watched its tourism economy base die. As the poison flowed downstream, it killed every living thing in its path for 40 miles, including 250,000 trout.[29] Surrounded by a million acres of forest and wilderness areas and in the shadow of majestic Mt. Shasta, the city billed itself as "Home of the Best Water on Earth."[30]

The small community already was economically depressed, with a shrinking number of railroad and timber jobs, and 25 percent of the residents were on welfare. Without tourist dollars to support existing businesses, the survival of the community was at stake.

With funds given it by Southern Pacific, now a part of Union Pacific Railroad Co., the city retained Edelman Public Relations Worldwide to reverse and control negative publicity and increase tourism above previous levels, measured through tax revenues.[31] New income-producing special events were designed and promoted to attract a steady flow of tourism and tourist dollars throughout the seasons. The primary audience was potential visitors to the area—seniors, families, outdoor enthusiasts, fishermen, Interstate 5 tourists, skiers, history and railroad buffs and nature lovers. The secondary audience targeted by the program was the Dunsmuir community, with the goal of increasing community morale and improving relations among the citizens.

The railroad worked closely with the town and the Edelman agency to create special events. It brought down an historical train over Labor Day weekend as a tourist attraction. With the river closed to fishing, it constructed two fishing ponds stocked with rainbow trout at Railroad Park where the public could fish free. This attracted more than 60,000 people during three years.[32]

The community was promoted as a tourist destination emphasizing the river's safety and many water sports, as well as the area's rich history, event offerings, attractions and visitor services. A senior bus tour program was developed to drive senior citizens to Dunsmuir. The aggressive media relations campaign resulted in nearly 30 million overall impressions in some 300 national, regional and local media outlets. Following the spill sales tax figured dropped by 8 percent, but by the end of the second quarter of 1992, tourist traffic and spending had risen markedly, and Dunsmuir experienced, by a wide margin, the largest increase in taxable sales in the North State region with spending up 24.5 percent.[33]

On July 15, the day following the accident, the railroad established a claims office in Dunsmuir to ease the handling of individual claims. By November 1,650 had been opened and more than 500 settled. Within a week following the accident, Southern Pacific prepared a detailed assessment plan. The company employed and assigned to the site recognized toxicologists as well as environmental, engineering and remediation experts to assess potential impact of the chemicals. In addition to continued monitoring and testing, the company provided senior-level liaison with local government officials with the presence of a Dunsmuir-based executive so the community had immediate access to Southern Pacific management.[34]

In February 1992, Southern Pacific pledged its continued support to restoring the Upper Sacramento River and its fish habitat, and to holding meetings immediately with established consensus-building forums of all concerned parties. The company worked closely with the California Fish and Game Commission and California Trout Inc. to speed the recovery of the river's trout fishery.[35]

Just Don't Go Near the Water

The Pagan River winds slowly past pig slaughterhouses in the town of Smithfield, Virginia, and drains into the James River and, ultimately, the Chesapeake Bay. It has been closed to shellfish harvesting since 1970 because of high levels of fecal coliform, bacteria found in animal excrement, and is considered a health risk for swimming and other human contact.[36] In April 1977 the environmental organization American Rivers placed the Pagan on its list of the "20 Most Endangered Rivers in the U.S."

Smithfield Foods, Inc., a $4 billion Fortune 500 company, is the largest pork processor on the East Coast. It has two slaughter-houses on the Pagan River where it packs products under names including Smithfield and Gwaltney. After months of discussion and negotiation, in July 1997, EPA took Smithfield to court charging the company violated antipollution rules 6,982 times between 1991 and 1996, dumping hog wastes into the Pagan River.[37] In asking for a fine of at least $20 million, U.S. Attorney Sarah Himmelhock said: "This company must be penalized to get its attention. The maximum fine, under strict reading of the law, is $174 million."[38]

The suit so irked Joseph Luter III, chairman and CEO of Smithfield, that he called a press conference to label it "extortion" and then ran a full-page ad in *The Washington Post* to put his spin on the issue.[39] He also told a reporter of an offer to settle his case for $3.5 million in exchange for pleading guilty to various violations. "I'll spend $5 million in attorney fees before I'll pay [EPA] $3 million in fines," Luter said. "I'll take my chances in court."[40]

From the beginning of the controversy, Luter and Smithfield had little media or public support. On December 20, 1996, both *The New York Times* and *The Washington Post* published editorials supporting EPA and criticizing the company, Virginia's Governor George F. Allen and the state's handling of environmental polluters.[41] In a follow-up editorial, *The Post* wrote that, "The story behind this case . . . explains why violators deserve tough treatment."[42]

After a five-day trial, U.S. District Judge Rebecca Beach Smith fined Smithfield $12.6 million, the largest fine in history in a federal water pollution case. Smith called the meatpacker's environmental offenses "extremely serious" and said most of the violations "were both frequent and severe, and had significant impact on the environment and the public."[43] Robert L. Harris, an accountant who specializes in the financial analysis of pollution cases, told the court that Smithfield "gained more than $16 million in wrongful profits by failing to install necessary pollution controls in the 1990s" and "would not be seriously hurt by a fine of the same amount."[44]

"This decision sends a strong message that there can be no profit in pollution," said W. Michael McCabe, regional adminis-trator for EPA's mid-Atlantic region.[45] "This is a victory for public health and the people of Virginia," he added. He also noted that federal officials offered to settle the case for "considerably less" than the $12.6 million, but Smithfield declined.[46]

During the controversy, environmentalists and many state legis-lators criticized Governor Allen and his administration as being soft on polluters and being too close to Smithfield Foods, noting that Luter had given Allen's political action committee $125,000 in campaign contributions.[47] "Because water and air pollution re-spect no state boundaries, and because pollution-prone businesses may shop for locations with the weakest environmental protection, the Smithfield case is a good example of the need for more uniform federal enforcement," wrote the editors of *The Washington Post*.[48] As one chapter closed, Smithfield faces a separate state lawsuit in Isle of Wight Circuit Court alleging more than 22,000 pollution violations.[49]

One month after the trial, Smithfield announced a two-for-one split of the company's common stock and strong first-quarter sales and earnings. "Smithfield Foods has outperformed 99 percent of the rest of the [competing] companies out there, regardless of in-dustry conditions," said George F. Shipp, securities analyst with Scott and Stringfellow in Norfolk, Virginia.[50]

The Public Needs to Be Convinced

While leading a global warming conference in October 1997, President William Clinton noted a great deal of environmental problems can be solved by a single energy-efficient lightbulb—a compact flourescent that can be purchased at most major hard-ware stores, costs more than a standard incandescent lightbulb, but lasts 10 times longer and uses far less energy. A typical com-pact flourescent can save as much as $50 in electricity costs over its lifetime compared with a 60-watt soft-white bulb and will consume the equivalent of 200 pounds less coal. These lights are used in fewer than 2 percent of all the residential light fixtures in the United States, and the average home is responsible for more than twice the level of carbon dioxide emissions than the average car.[51]

Businesses often are more willing than consumers to invest up-front expenses if they are likely to produce long-term cost savings. Marriott Corp. saved millions of dollars by replacing incandescent lightbulbs with compact flourescents in its hotels. But many companies want an investment paid back in two to three years, according to Brad Whitehead, head of the North American environmental practice of McKinsey & Co. "It's not that these guys are stupid. With energy, you're talking about big decisions involving their core assets. Even a little bit of uncertainty is enough to make them wary," says Whitehead.[52]

In the early 1990s, Potomac Electric Power Co. mailed its seven million customers in Maryland and Washington, D.C., discount coupons to purchase compact flourescents for as little as $2. The bulbs retail in the $12 range and for as much as $29 in some stores, compared to as little as 69 cents for a standard incandescent lightbulb. At the lower price, the lights could have paid for themselves within a few months. However, only 900,000 coupons were redeemed.[53]

Endnotes

1. John Stauber and Sheldon Rampton, *Toxic Sludge Is Good for You!*, Center for Media & Democracy, Common Courage Press, Monroe, Maine, 1995.

2. Douglas Martin, "Exxon Valdez Money to Aid City Wetlands," *The New York Times*, September 11, 1997, pg. B3.

3. John Stauber and Sheldon Rampton, *op cit.*, pg. 123.

4. Greenwire, "Sixty Percent Want Environmental Protection at All Costs," *National Journal's Cloakroom*, National Journal Inc., September 3, 1997.

5. Ibid., pgs. 71-72.

6. Ibid.

7. "'Green' PR Trashed as Corporate Ruse," *Jack O'Dwyer's Newsletter*, February 25, 1998, pg.7.

8. Ibid.

9. Ibid.

10. Thomas Petzinger Jr., "Business Achieves Greatest Efficiencies When at Its Greenest," The Front Lines, *The Wall Street Journal*, July 11, 1997, pg. D4.

11. Ibid.

12. Martha M. Hamilton, "Energizing Solar Power," *The Washington Post,* August 26, 1997, pg. D1.

13. Ibid.

14. Tony Roddam, "Oil Giant Shell Bets on Renewable Energy Boom," Reuters, London, October 20, 1997.

15. Ibid.

16. Ken Ward Jr., "Report citing danger buried," *The Charleston Gazette,* Charleston, West Virginia, June 9, 1997.

17. Ibid.

18. Linda B. Blackford and Ken Ward Jr., "Crash 'signal or human error,'" *The Charleston Gazette,* Charleston, West Virginia, June 9, 1997.

19. Ken Ward Jr.,"Hazardous payload," *The Charleston Gazette,* Charleston, West Virginia, June 23, 1997.

20. Mark Davis, Public Relations Department, Union Pacific Railroad, Omaha, Nebraska, fax of September 15 to Rene A. Henry.

21. Ibid.

22. Ibid.

23. Ibid.

24. Ibid.

25. JoAnna J. Wagschal, "Communicating Risk During Chemical Releases," Best Practices, *On the Environmental Horizon,* Environment Section of the Public Relations Society of America, May 1997, pg. 2.

26."Making the Most of Your Worst-Case Scenario," *Ethos,* Vol. 20, 1997, The Ammerman Experience, Stafford, Texas, pg. 1.

27. Carroll J. Forrest, correspondence and telephone calls with the author, December 1997 and February 1998.

28. "Risk Communication," *Community Relations in Superfund: A Handbook,* United States Environmental Protection Agency, Washington, D.C., January 1992, pg.84.

29. Public Relations Society of America, Silver Anvil Entrant, 1992.

30. Carole Terwilliger Meyers, "In the shadow of Mount Shasta, Dunsmuir delights," *San Francisco Examiner,* August 16, 1998, pg. T-6.

31. Telephone conversation of September 12, 1997 with Michael J. Furtney, director of public relations, Western Region, Union Pacific Railroad Co., San Francisco.

32. Ibid.

33. Ibid.

34. "Southern Pacific Efforts Since July 14 Derailment," news release, Southern Pacific Public Relations, San Francisco, November 1991.

35. News release, Southern Pacific Public Relations, San Francisco, February 7, 1992.

36. Scott Harper, "Judge fines Smithfield Foods $12.6 million," *The Virginian-Pilot,* Norfolk, Virginia, August 9, 1997.

37. Scott Harper, *op cit.,* July 22, 1997.

38. Scott Harper, *op cit.,* July 26, 1997.

39. Scott Harper, *op cit.,* July 21, 1997.

40. Donald P. Baker, "EPA Went Hog Wild, Pork Baron Says," *The Washington Post,* February 24, 1997, pg. B1.

41. "Environmental Defiance," *The New York Times,* editorial page, December 20, 1996, and "Wishy-Washy on Water Pollution," *The Washington Post,* editorial page, December 20, 1996, pg. A26.

42. "Assault With a Deadly River," *The Washington Post,* editorial page, January 21, 1997, pg. A10.

43. Scott Harper, *op cit.,* August 9, 1997.

44. Bill Geroux, "Smithfield profits criticized," *Richmond Times-Dispatch,* Richmond, Virginia, July 23, 1997.

45. Ellen Nakashima, "Court Fines Smithfield $12.6 Million," *The Washington Post,* August 9, 1997, pg. A1.

46. Bob Piazza and Rex Springston, "Smithfield is fined $12.6 million," *Richmond Times-Dispatch,* Richmond, Virginia, August 9, 1997.

47. Scott Harper, *op cit.,* July 14, 1997.

48. "Smithfield's Dirty Deed," editorial, *The Washington Post,* August 13, 1997, pg. A28.

49. Associated Press, *The Daily Press,* Newport News, Virginia, August 8, 1997.

50. Akweli Parker, "Smithfield Foods sets two-for-one split of common stock," *The Virginian-Pilot,* Norfolk, Virginia, August 29, 1997.

51. Clay Chandler, "The 60-Watt Mind-Set," *The Washington Post,* November 14, 1997.

52. Ibid.

53. Ibid.

CHAPTER FIFTEEN

CLOSING THE BOOK— AFTER AN INCIDENT

Do crises really end? Some people will say no, because the memory of so many will linger on for years. Think of all of the crises that immediately come to mind. Make a list of them. Then write down the date you believe each crisis occurred. Some may have happened 10 or 20 years ago.

This is a quick way to see how a crisis can affect the image, reputation or stature of a company, organization, institution or individual. This also is a simple way to impress a CEO or senior management as to why crisis management and crisis communications plans are so critical. Then review the list and think about why you remembered each particular crisis. Could it have been replayed in a book, a feature film or a television movie? W. R. Grace and Beatrice Foods probably wished their problems in Woburn, Massachusetts, could have gone away in the mid-1980s, not becoming the 1999 blockbuster Disney movie *A Civil Action*.

While the crisis may be ended, the memory of the crisis can remain for decades.

To bring closure to a crisis, so much depends on how quickly the initial incident can be contained and all issues quickly resolved. "After a crisis, people are not interested in your facts," says Sunshine Janda Overkamp, vice president of membership, marketing and communications at the Council on Foundations, Washington, D.C., and former senior vice president of United Way.

"Many still do not know of the changes that have occurred since the United Way crisis began."

However, the reputation of the company, organization, institution or individual needs to be reestablished and its image rebuilt with all stakeholders.

If victims were involved, what has been done to communicate with them or their families? Some practitioners recommend doing an act of goodwill for those impacted by the crisis. This could be during or immediately after the crisis, whenever it is most appropriate and possible.

Whatever the problem, customers must know the problem is now fixed—both the ultimate consumer, to whom the product or service is being sold, and the trade wholesaler, through whom the product is being sold. Shareholders must be given another message. The pride and spirit of the institutional culture must be reinforced with employees. There will yet be other messages to be told to the community as well as to elected and appointed local, state and federal government officials where applicable.

This means reviewing the mission statement and strategic plan and the specific public relations and communications action plan. The public relations plan may need to be reprioritized in the wake of a crisis.

Amanda Spade, senior editor for food safety at *U.S. News & World Report*, believes one PR mistake is not getting back to reporters after a crisis ends to tell them what the company is doing to prevent another situation from occurring.[1]

Learning From the Experience

As soon as the crisis is considered over, it is time to get to work and be prepared for the next crisis. First the company must declare an end to the crisis. The next step is to follow up by staying in touch with the publics involved with the crisis, especially those directly affected. This is time for the community relations program to be further evaluated. Be sure the media is aware of any updates in the situation. And review internal policies to try to avoid a repeat of the crisis situation.

Raymond J. O'Rourke, executive vice president, managing director of crisis communications at Burson-Marsteller, believes the only clear-cut "opportunity" in every crisis is the chance to learn from the experience and thereby minimize the likelihood that another crisis will disrupt your organization sometime in the future. He adds that, unfortunately, most organizations fail to undertake a well-managed effort to learn from the experience.[2]

O'Rourke believes the review can begin within a month of a return to relative normalcy. He recommends the following as indicating when the worst has passed:

1. The media have few or no new developments to report; coverage has shifted from breaking news to wrap-ups.

2. The volume of customer calls to 800 or service lines returns to near normal volume.

3. Intelligence reports from the field and sales reflect less customer concern.

4. For a publicly traded company, stock volume and price volatility have returned to historical seasonal levels.

5. Headquarters crisis management team meetings are down to one a day or less.

6. A field response team determines with local management that it can return to headquarters.

He believes it is important to audit internal actions and perspectives and to explore public opinion research to determine quantitatively whether there has been actual, measurable damage to brand image or corporate reputation. Nearly all of the major opinion research companies run weekly national telephone surveys and questions cost in the range of $1,000 each. A set of 10 to 12 questions can feed back valuable insight to the company.[3]

O'Rourke believes a post-crisis analysis is a critical step to help frame future crisis response strategy. If the company had a crisis management plan already in place, a review should identify which parts of the plan helped and which were extraneous. Where there was no plan, the review should provide source material to create one.[4]

He believes most companies don't learn from the experience because looking back at a crisis is contrary to prevailing corporate culture. "Successful executives look forward; they don't dwell on the past," he says. The initiative for the review should come from the CEO.

He believes no review should begin until the field response team can actively participate. Its views on what field support was available or how the focus of decision making helped or hindered their efforts can be invaluable.

This is a time to carefully review every minute detail. Ask the team if there any potential crises that have not been anticipated? Is there a better way to respond? Was the media fair? Was the affected public forgiving? Develop a new "what if" list and plan frequent meetings of the crisis management team.

What's Next?

There should be no mystery at all about crisis management or crisis communications. In the most basic of terms, it all comes down to using good common sense, applying all of the best techniques of dispute resolution and customer service, and using whatever techniques are in the public relations, communication and community outreach toolbox.

Crisis communications is not for the novice. The CEO and senior management should rely only on a senior, experienced professional for advice in preparing a plan and for taking charge of its implementation and execution if a crisis should happen. If the company does not have a counselor on staff with qualifications and experience in this area, then outside help should be retained.

The last thing a company or organization needs in a crisis is for the person in charge of its crisis communications plan to be getting "on-the-job training" when a crisis strikes. Money spent on the best available professional is like buying insurance. You want the protection if and when it is needed.

Bridging Professional Gaps

Crisis communications and risk communications are primarily courses offered in college by schools or departments of journalism, public relations or mass communications. The subject is not taught at all in law schools. And the subject has not been given priority in businesses schools. There is a need for institutions of higher education to look at this subject as an interdisciplinary course for future businessmen and lawyers, as well as engineers and scientists.

At the least, crisis communications should be no less than a required half-day seminar for all students graduating with degrees in business and law. An education is not complete without giving the student a preview of what can happen in the real world.

The need to understand the media and the public is best expressed by Dr. JoAnn Burkholder, an aquatic ecologist at North Carolina State University. "Scientists are trained to conduct bioassays and take field samples," she says. "We're not trained in how to give congressional testimony, assess the political lay of the land, or respond to reporters' questions. Yet increasingly, that's part of the job."[5] Without any prior exposure to what crisis communications and media relations is all about, it is difficult for anyone to recognize when training is needed.

The Future . . .

During a speech before the Philadelphia chapter of the Public Relations Society of America, Harold Burson talked about two important developments regarding crisis communications. He said Burson-Marsteller had organized a department to develop expertise in how to deal with chat-board rumors and dissemination of true and false information on the Internet during a crisis situation. Since information can be sent worldwide with a keystroke, the professional communicator must know how to respond accordingly in this medium.[6]

Burson, who is considered by his peers to be the dean of public relations counselors, also expected to see challenges to giving the public relations crisis communicator the same privileges an attorney now has with a client, especially in view of the confidentiality needed in developing a strategy involving a crisis. He believes there may be challenges in the courts over allowing the crisis communications counselor to be given the same privilege of confidentiality that lawyers have with their clients. He also noted that several companies that have serious crisis communications situations have public relations executives and spokespersons who also happen to be attorneys and can invoke the client confidentiality privilege.

In crisis communications and many other areas, public relations and law are closely allied. An individual with the double discipline and experienced in both areas may be in the future what the individual with a Harvard M.B.A. degree was in the '70s and '80s.

Endnotes

1. "Honesty Is Best Policy in a Crisis," *Jack O'Dwyer's Newsletter*, June 30, 1999, pg. 2.

2. Raymond J.O'Rourke, "Learning From Crisis: When the Dust Settles," *The Public Relations Strategist*, pgs. 35-36.

3. Ibid., pgs. 37-38.

4. Ibid., pg. 35.

5. "Society loses in clash of science, politics," *Daily News,* Philadelphia, February 18, 1988.

6. Harold Burson, APR, Fellow PRSA, Burson-Marsteller Inc., in luncheon speech at the Public Relations Society of America, Philadelphia, February 18, 1998.

Index

ABC
  Disney and, 15
  Food Lion vs., 74, 76–77
  Philip Morris vs., 75
Aberdeen Proving Ground, 99
Abrams, Floyd, 74–75
Academic institutions. *See* Higher
  education
Adams, Vickee Jordan, 61
Adelman, Richard, 251
Adelphi University, 246
Airline crashes
  TWA, 3, 35, 115–16
  ValuJet, 3, 117–19
Albert, Marv, 204
Alinsky, Saul D., 34
Allegheny University Hospital, 190
Allen, George F., 105–9, 286, 287
Alliance Health System, 270
Almand, O. Hale, 215–16
Aloisio, Monica, 101
Alomar, Roberto, 13
Alta Bates Medical Center, 198–200
Alta-Dena Dairy, 85–90
Altizer, Andrew A., 259
Alton, Travis, 143
Alumni, 241
American Cancer Society, 276
American Red Cross, 14, 148
American Restaurant Association, 13
American Society of Composers, Authors
  and Publishers (ASCAP), 13–14
American University, 111
Anderson, Martin, 238
Anderson, Ray, 276–77
Anderson, Warren, 18

Anger, public, 8–9
Anheuser-Busch, 150–51
Apologizing, 6, 171
Aponte, Jose A., 148
Aptheker, Herbert, 252
Aramony, William, 62
Argue, John, 103–5
Arledge, Roone, 76
Armenia, 149
Armstrong, Neil, 52
ASCAP. *See* American Society of
  Composers, Authors and Publishers
Ashland Oil
  crisis management recipe, 182–83
  as role model, 184
  storage tank collapse, 45, 165–82, 273
  tanker explosion, 183–84
Ashlock, Jim, 137, 142, 143
Astra USA, 10–11
Attorneys
  confidential communication between
    clients and, 59, 295–96
  following advice of, 43, 51, 61
  as poor spokespersons, 42
  as the problem, 53–58
  public relations counselors vs., 43, 45, 53
  public relations counselors working with,
    59–60, 295–96
  Work Product Doctrine, 59
Avis Rental Car, 267
Avtex Fibers, 109
Ayers, Edward, 244

Babyak, Edward, 181, 182
Baby Kerri, 198–200
Baer, William, 63

Bagnoli, Al, 216
Baker, Lisa, 251
Baltimore, David, 256
Banin, Josef, 77
Barnett, Susan, 76
Barrett, Wayne, 63
Barry, Marion, 96
Baseball
  charges against New York Mets, 203
  controversies surrounding George Stein-
    brenner, 207–8
  controversy surrounding Marge Schott, 13
  controversy surrounding Roberto Alomar,
    13
  offensive remarks by Jason Isringhausen,
    207
Basketball, college, 226–28
Basketball, professional
  attack by Latrell Sprewell, 203
  charges against Anthony Mason, 205
  offensive remarks by John Calipari, 207
  suit filed against George Shinn, 205
  tax evasion by referees, 203
Battelle Institute, 180
Beatrice Foods, 4, 291
Becker, J.J., 110–11
Beder, Sharon, 275–76
Bederman, David J., 79
Beef industry, 79–80
Beer Institute, 110
Bell, Roger, 78
Bell, T. March, 106, 109
Benjamin, Burton "Bud," 84
Bennet, Bernie, 52
Benoit, William, 6
Berkey, Edgar, 178
Berkow, Ira, 227–28
Bernsen, Corbin, 249
Beverly, John, 133
Bhopal, 18–19
Bildman, Lars, 10, 11
Bilsky, Steve, 216–17
Birnbaum, Jeffrey, 97
Bivin, Teel, 144
Black, Clint, 80
Block, Philip, 178
Blue Chips, 228–29
Board of directors
  of nonprofit organizations, 58
  as problems, 61–62
Boat collision, 156–57
Body language, 37
Bok, Derek, 238
Bon Vivant soup, 2
Borschoff, Myra, 193
Boston University, 245–46, 257
Bowen, Ray, 69, 125, 132, 143

Boy Scouts of America, 13
Bradley, Tom, 103, 104
Braun, Jeff, 282
Bray, Sarah Hardesty, 244
Brennan, Tim, 80
Bressler, Richard, 63
Brest, Paul, 56
Brill, Steven, 63
British Petroleum, 277
Brown, James, 217–18
Brown, Richard A., 205
Browne, John, 277
Brushy Community, 124, 125, 141, 142
Bryn Mawr Hospital, 190, 191
Bryn Mawr Rehabilitation Hospital, 190
Buczko, Kathleen, 114
Budget reductions, 196–98
Buffalo Creek dam, 151–52
Burkholder, JoAnn, 295
Burnett, Carol, 82–83
Burns, Arnold, 213
Burson, Harold, 25, 60, 295
Burson-Marsteller, 25, 295
Bush, George H.
  interview with Dan Rather, 37
  presidential library, 123–37
Bush, George W., 136, 142
Business for Social Responsibility, 275

Cain, Delmar, 139
California Institute of Technology, 252
California Pacific Medical Center, 194–96
Calipari, John, 207
Calleia, Anton, 103–5
Cannon, Glenn, 166
Carlesimo, P. J., 203
Carnival Cruise, 26
Carpet industry, 276–77
Carroll, Matt, 143
Carson, Rachel, 273
Carter, Jimmy, 103–5
Casey, Robert P., 167, 168
CBS
  General William Westmoreland vs., 84–85
  NCAA contract with, 226–28
Celeste, Richard, 169
CEO
  final decision and, 58, 61
  as spokesperson, 42
Chaffee, John, 178
Charlotte Hornets, 205
Chemical munitions cleanup, 111–13
Chemical releases, 281–82
Chodorow, Stanley, 217
CIA, 96
The Citadel, 10
A Civil Action, 4, 291

Clayton Baptist Church, 123, 124
Clergy, sex and, 16–17, 101
Clery, Ben, 248
Clinton, William, 55, 64, 95, 110, 218, 287
CNN, 238
Coal dams, 151–52
Coca-Cola, 28–29, 81
Cochran, Johnnie, 203
Coking, Vera, 77
Colleges. See Higher education; specific
    schools
Community relations
    blueprint for, 111–13
    University of Miami and, 160–61
    University of Pennsylvania and, 250–51
Conflicts of interest, 209–14, 243
Cornell University, 256
Corning Inc., 51
Costa Rica, 149
Covello, Vincent T., 37
Cox, James, 43, 51
Credibility. See also Reputation
    establishing before a crisis, 24–26
    initial response and, 42
    regaining after crisis, 7–8
Crile, George, 84–85
Crimes
    by athletes, 202–8, 250
    on campus, 247–50
Crisis
    aftermath of, 291–96
    Chinese symbol for, 2
    common to all organizations, 26–27
    definitions of, 2
    determining vulnerability to, 22–23
    first minutes of, 42–43
    origins of, 4–6
    questions to ask in, 6
    resolving, before becoming major, 3–4
    responsibility for, 6–7
    signs of end of, 293
Crisis communications. See also Public rela-
    tions; Risk communications
    building team for, 35–36
    courses on, 294–95
    definition of, 1
    internal, 47–48
    notification priorities, 33, 41–42
    objective of, 3
    preparing plan for, 30–32
    professionals needed for, 294
Crisis management, 40–48
    Ashland Oil's recipe for, 182–83
    definition of, 1
    importance of communications for, 40–41
    necessity of plan for, 25
    preparing plan for, 30–32

Cronkite, Walter, 36–37
Cruise lines, 26
Curry, John A., 246
Cutler, Lloyd, 103

D'Addario, Francis, 269
Dairy industry, 85–90
Dale, Lynn, 76
Dallas Cowboys, 205
Dallas Morning News, 61
Dangerfield, Rodney, 83
Daniel Drake Memorial Hospital, 193–94
Dannemeyer, William, 89
Dartmouth University, 256–57
Davidson, Rachel, 152–53
Davis, Mark W., 280
Dawson, Jim, 278
Dayan, Moshe, 105
Debt collecting, 14
DeCristofaro, Anthony, 61–62
DeFrancesco, John, 43
DeGeneres, Ellen, 15
Dehaene, Jean-Luc, 28
Delaware State, 258
Dempsey, Cedric, 228
DePalma, Anthony, 237
Department of Energy, 102
Department of Transportation, 116–19
Desert Storm, 53
Deterding, Sir Henri, 56–57
Dey, Susan, 249
Diamandopoulos, Peter, 246
Diehl, Bill, 205
Dingell, John, 257
Disney. See Walt Disney Co.
Dodd, Mike, 209–10, 213, 214
Donaldson, Sam, 77
Donoahue, Doug, 143
"Doonesbury," 77
DOT. See Department of Transportation
Doublespeak, avoiding, 46
Dow Chemical, 276
Downsizing, 190–92
Drach, Ann, 99
Dribben, Melissa, 217
Duffy Communications, 101
Duke, 229
Duncan, Donnie, 219, 221, 224
Dunlop, Becky Norton, 108, 110
Durst, Douglas, 53

Earthquakes
    Armenia (1988), 149
    effects of, 41, 154
    indexing risks from, 152–53
    Los Angeles (1994), 155–56
    measuring, 155

New Madrid Fault, 153, 154–55
San Fernando Valley (1991), 155
San Francisco (1906), 151, 155
San Francisco (1989), 150
seismic building codes, 153–54
The Ecology of Commerce, 276
Edelman, Richard, 60–61
Edelman Public Relations Worldwide, 47,
    81, 284
EEOC. See Equal Employment
    Opportunity Commission
"Ego syndrome," 5
Ellis, Ruby, 138
Employees
    assistance programs and counseling,
        47–48, 270–71
    keeping informed, 47
Energy conservation, 287–88
Energy diversification, 277–78
Environmental crises
    Beatrice Foods and W.R. Grace, 4
    chemical releases, 281–82
    global warming, 277–78
    hazardous materials accidents, 278–81,
        284–85
    higher education and, 257–59
    media attention to, 274–76
    oil spills, 165–84, 273–74
    water pollution, 105–6, 285–87
Environmentalism
    dolphin-safe tuna, 81–82
    energy conservation, 287–88
    energy diversification, 277–78
    profitability of, 276–77
Environmental Protection Agency (EPA),
    169, 176, 178, 274, 286
Environmental racism, 123, 137
Episcopal Church, 16
Equal Employment Opportunity Commis-
    sion (EEOC), 9–12
Everitt, Steve, 205–6
Exxon Valdez, 184, 273–74

FAA, 116–19
FBI, 96, 115–16
Federal Aviation Administration. See FAA
Federal Emergency Management Agency
    (FEMA), 161, 162
Ferrara, Carla, 270
Field, Patrick, 8
Fineman Associates Public Relations, 13
Fink, James, 51
Fink, Steven, 29
Fisher, D. Michael, 177
Fitzpatrick, Kathy R., 59
Fitzwater, Marlin, 5, 52
Flinn, Kelly, 99, 100–2

Floods, 148, 151–52
Florida International, 258
Foerster, Tom, 170, 182
Fonda, Jane, 253
Food Lion, 74, 76–77
Foodservice industry, violence in, 268–69
Football, college
    University of Oklahoma, 217–25
    University of Pennsylvania, 216–17
Football, professional
    charges against Dallas Cowboys, 205
    charges against Steve Everitt, 205–6
    legal problems of Lawrence Phillips, 203
Foote, Edward T., II, 157–61
Footlick, Jerry, 215–16, 240
Forgiveness, winning, 7–8
Forrest, Carol J., 282
Fox, Fanne, 96
Fox, Jeanne M., 274
Frazier, A.D., 214
Freedman, James, 256
Freeh, Louis, 116
Friedkin, Bill, 229
Fuhrman, Mark, 113, 114
Funess, Richard, 75

Gage, E. Dean, 125
Gallagher, Jim, 172
Garcia, Dan, 207
Garcia, Gerald, 67
Garland, Tam, 142
Gaston, Jerry, 125, 143
Gates, Daryl F., 252
General Motors, 74
Georgetown University, 258
Georgia Pacific, 14
Gerdy, John, 225, 238
Giamatti, Bart, 207
Gifford, Frank, 203–4
Gilman, Andrew, 43
Gilmore, James S., III, 109
Gipson, Fred, 220
Girl Scouts of America, 13–14
Giuliani, Rudolph, 63–64
Global warming, 277–78
Goldberg, Whoopi, 199
Goltz, Paul M., 174
Goodfriend, Gary, 43
Gorney, Carole, 238
Gough, Russ, 227
Gould, Rob, 276
Government. See also specific agencies
    doublespeak by, 46
    lack of management continuity in, 97
    legal advice in, 58–59
    public's mistrust of, 19, 94–96
Grace, W.R., 4, 291

Grassley, Charles, 116
Greene, Albert L., 198–99
Greenfield, Meg, 52
Greenwood, James, 250
Gretzky, Wayne, 209
Grove, Andrew, 17–18, 56
Guo, David, 178–79

Hack, Gary, 250
Hager, Bob, 140
Haje, Peter, 63
Hall, Gus, 252
Hall, Jim, 118
Hall, John, 45, 165, 167–78, 180, 182
Hamilton, Joe, 82
Hardee's, 269
Harper, Charles, 13
Harris, Robert L., 286
Harris, Thomas, 25, 47
Hart, Gary, 96
Hartman, Lisa, 80
Hartz, Jim, 219–24
Harvard University, 253
Harvey, James, 247
Hasbro/Kenner Products, 47
Hate speech, 254–55
Hawken, Paul, 276
Hawthorne, John, 214
Hazardous materials transportation, 278–81, 284–85
Healthcare facilities, 189–201
    budget reductions and layoffs, 196–98
    checklist for, 200
    kidnappings, 198–200
    mergers and downsizing, 190–92
    murder, 192–96, 267
Hechler, Ken, 152
Heflin, Howell, 96
Helmick, Robert H., 209–14
Helwig, Bill, 140
Henry, Hue, 215
Hewitt, Don, 90–91
Heyward, Andrew, 77
Higgs, Robert, 252–53
Higher education, 234–60. See also specific schools
    accountable for students' work preparation, 246–47
    alumni development, and public relations, 241
    athletics and, 216–28
    controversial speakers, 253–54
    crime statistics, 247–50
    declining public trust in, 237–38
    determining priorities for, 259
    environmental laws and, 257–59
    examples of crises in, 234–37, 259–60

fundraising and, 240
high salaries in, 246, 251
overhead, 255–57
political correctness and, 252–55
problems facing, 241–43
professors' workloads, 244–45
reasons for high incidence of crises in, 238–40
science research, 251–52, 255–57
strategic planning and marketing needed in, 243–44
Hill, Anita, 223
Hill, Robert M., 259
Hill, Tom, 220
Himmelhock, Sarah, 286
Hinson, David, 117, 118
Hirsch, Alan, 62
Holder, Marc, 214
Hollywood
    media and, 52
    sports films, 228–29
Homicides
    in the healthcare industry, 192–96, 267
    in the workplace, 27, 265–69
Honan, William, 244
Hopkins, Thomas L., 106, 108, 109
Hospitals. See Healthcare facilities
Huber, Richard, 238
Humperdink's, 269
Hundrieser, Elaine, 156
Hurricane Andrew, 157–62
Hybl, William, 213

Impel Marketing, 213
Institute for Crisis Management, 23, 27
Intel, 17–18, 56
Interface Inc., 276–77
Internal communications, 47–48
Internet, 45
Interviews, 37–38
Investigative journalism, 76–77
IRS, 97–98
Irvin, Michael, 205
Irvine, Robert, 60, 270–71
Isringhausen, Jason, 207
Issues management, 34–35
Ivester, M. Douglas, 28
Ivy League, 216–17

Jack in the Box, 3
Jackson, Jesse, 11
Jacobs, Martin, 168, 169, 181–82
Jacobwitz, Eden, 254–55
Japan Overseas Enterprises Association, 12
Jereski, Laura, 74
Jewell, Richard, 115, 215
Johnson, Lyndon B., 84

Johnson, Scott, 177
Johnson, Suzen, 204
Johnson & Johnson, 3, 7, 182
Jones, Janet, 208–9

Kamal, Ibrahim, 105
Kamer/Singer & Associates, 198
Kan, Lydia A., 150
Kelly, Charles, 181
Kelly, Tom, 212
Kemp, Jan, 215–16
Kendrick, N.A., 204
Kennedy, Donald, 255–56
Kennedy, James, 77
Kentucky Fried Chicken, 269
Kerber, Fred, 207
Kerrigan, Nancy, 208
Kidnappings, 198–200
Killanin, Lord, 103–5
King, Rodney, 113
Kirkpatrick, Jeane, 252–53
Kirtley, Jane, 75
Kissinger, Henry, 82–83
Klein, Anne Sceia, 196, 200–201
Kolbert, Elizabeth, 63
Koppel, Ted, 223
Korean Air Lines Flight 007 incident, 53
Kornheiser, Tony, 203
Kos, Rudolph, 16–17
Kowet, Don, 84
Kuhn, Bowie, 207

Lacy, Dan, 167, 180, 182, 183
Lade, Brian, 157
Lafayette College, 252–53
Land, Richard, 15
Lankenau Hospital, 190, 191
Lautenberg, Frank, 178
Lawyers. See Attorneys
Layoffs, 196–98
Lazier, Bruce, 171
Lee, Charles, 124
Lee, Kathie, 203
Lee, Spike, 253
Lehigh University, 248
Leo, John, 203
Leonard, John, 15
Letterman, David, 101, 204
Leval, Pierre, 85
Levy, Ron, 53–54
Lewin, Nat, 76
Lewinsky, Monica, 64
Libel. See also Media; Reputation
    British law, 78
    Carol Burnett vs. National Enquirer, 82–83
    definition of, 72–73

ethics and, 73–76
General William Westmoreland vs. CBS, 84–85
McDonald's vs. vegetarians, 77–79
Rodney Dangerfield vs. Star, 83
Texas cattlemen vs. Oprah Winfrey, 79–80
LifeNet, 149–50
Light bulbs, energy-efficient, 287–88
Lindsey, Joe B., 178
Linn, Rick, 219
Lo Frumento, John, 14
Los Angeles
    County Health Department, 86, 90
    earthquake (1994), 155–56
    Olympic Games, 103–4
    Police Department, 113–15
Louis Harris & Associates, 237
Luby's Cafeteria, 268–69
Luellen, Charles J., 167, 172, 183
Lukaszewski, James E., 7, 50, 58, 59
Luken, Tom, 176
Lupica, Mike, 204
Lurie, Jeffrey, 209
Luter, Joseph, III, 286, 287
Lutz, William, 46
Lyman, Howard, 80

MacColl, Wanda, 98
Main Line Health System, 190–92
Majors, Orville Lynn, 192–93, 194
Mandel, Ernest, 252
Mankiewicz, Frank F., 274
Margulies, David, 269
Marriott Corp., 288
Marrow, Mitch, 216–17
Martin, Lynn, 11
Mason, Anthony, 205
Massachusetts Institute of Technology, 256
Massy, William F., 256
Mattel, 14
Mazzullo, Jim, 134
McBride, Tim, 114
McCabe, W. Michael, 287
McCaffery, Seamus, 209
McClure, Fred, 136–37
McCurry, Mike, 64
McDaniel, James L., 109
McDonald's
    alleged rat tail in Happy Meal, 80–81
    British vegetarians vs., 77–79
    hot coffee lawsuit, 7
    workplace violence, 268–69
McKenna, Michael, 106–9
McLaughlin, J.J., 110–11
McSherry, John, 13
Mears, David, 15

Media. *See also* Libel; Television
  being prepared for, 36–38
  center, 44
  communications and operations plan for,
    31
  cooperating with, 43
  ducking, 51
  getting to know, 43
  interviews with, 37–38
  investigative methods of, 76–77
  news releases for, 32, 46–47
  "no comment" by, 62–63
  organizations scrutinizing, 90–91
  providing information to, 44–45
  public's trust in, 19
  relations training, 36
  suppression of stories by, 62–63
Meek, John, 217–24
Mejia, Elaine, 137
Mergers, 190–92
Mexico City, 153
Meyers, Gerald, 169, 171, 184
Miami, 157–61
Military
  problems resulting from rank, 58
  public mistrust of, 95
  sex scandals in, 98–102
  sexual harassment at service academies,
    10
Miller, Howard, 210
Mills, Wilbur, 95
Misinformation, 5
Mississippi Valley, 154–55
Misunderstandings, 6
Mitsubishi Motor Manufacturing USA, 10,
    11–12
MMAR Group, 74
Mobil, 276
Monongahela River, 165, 166, 170, 174,
    177
Moore, Arch, 152
Moran, Mike, 212
Morris, Dave, 78
Morris, Dick, 95
Morse, Rob, 195
Mount St. Helens eruption, 149
Moynihan, Daniel Patrick, 95
Murders. *See* Homicides
Murphy, Donna, 219, 221, 223
Murphy, W. Tayloe, Jr., 110
Murrah Federal Building. *See* Oklahoma
  City bombing

National Enquirer, 82–83
National Institute for Chemical Studies, 279
National News Council, 90
National Organization for Women, 11

National Religious Broadcasters
  Association, 13–14
National Security Agency, 96
National Transportation Safety Board, 118,
    119
Nationwide Mutual Insurance, 15
Natural disasters. *See also specific disasters*
  assessment by satellite video, 149–50
  case studies, 149–61
  death tolls and costs of, 147–48
  importance of communication during,
    148–49, 161
  plan for, 161–62
NBC, 74
NCAA, 226–29, 250
Nedbalek, George, 143
New Madrid Fault, 153, 154–55
New Orleans, 156–57
News releases
  prepared beforehand, 32
  video, 46–47
New York, 40–41
New York Daily News, 63
New York Mets, 203
Nike, 3
"No comment" response
  alternatives to, 42, 52, 55
  implies consent, 64
  implies guilt, 42, 51
  ineffectiveness of, 50–51
  by the media, 62–63
Nolan, Joseph T., 102
Nonprofit organizations, 58
Northeastern University, 246
Northridge Fashion Mall, 155–56
Notification priorities, 33, 41–42

O'Dwyer, Jack, 18
Oglethorpe University, 259
Ohio River, 170, 174, 177, 178
Oil spills
  Ashland storage tank collapse, 165–82,
    273
  Ashland tanker explosion, 183–84
  cost of, 273–74
  Exxon Valdez, 184, 273–74
Oklahoma City bombing, 48, 115, 270
Oklahoma Natural Gas, 48
O'Leary, Hazel, 102
Olympic Games
  Albertville (1992), 212
  Atlanta (1996), 115, 214–15
  early crises in, 202
  ethics conflicts, 209–14
  Los Angeles (1984), 103–4
  Moscow (1980), 103
  Munich (1972), 208

O'Neil, Robert M., 253
Opposition research, 33–34
O'Rourke, Raymond J., 292–94
O'Rourke, Robert L., 252
Overkamp, Sunshine Janda, 61–62, 291
Overy, Julie, 106, 108

Pagan River, 285–86
Paglia, Camille, 252
Paoli Memorial Hospital, 190
Parry, John, 228
Payne, Billy Porter, 215
Peña, Frederico, 117, 118
Penn State, 258
Pentium chip flaw, 17–18
Pepsi
    contest with Harrier jet as prize, 15
    syringe incidents, 7, 80
Perhach, Vanessa, 204
Perlmutter, Marion, 251
Peters, Nick, 46
Peterson, Howard, 212
Philip Morris, 75
Phillips, Lawrence, 203
Phinney, Carolyn, 251–52
Pines, Wayne, 27
Pittston Coal Company, 151–52
Plum, Kenneth R., 109
Pohl, Michael, 105
Political correctness, 252–55
Pork industry, 134–35, 143–44, 285–87
Porter/Novelli, 9, 19, 94, 276
Postal workers, 267
Potomac Electric Power Co., 288
Powell, Colin, 53
Powell, Jody, 104
Pradhan, Dhiraj, 143
Preparedness, 22–38
    checklist, 38
    determining level of, 22–24
    innovation and, 161
    issues management and, 34–35
    lack of, 27–28
    for media, 36–38
    questions to ask, 29–30
Presbyterian Church, 16
Presbyterian Medical Center, 196–98
Press releases, 32
Preston, Paul, 78
Prevette, Johnathan, 12
PrimeTime Live, 76–77
Procter and Gamble, 276
Professors
    affairs with students, 101
    workloads of, 244–45
The Program, 228–29
Psychological counselors, 47–48

Public relations. See also Crisis communications
    counselors vs. attorneys, 43, 45, 53
    counselors working with attorneys, 59–60, 295–96
    environmental, 275–76
    litigation, 60
Public Relations Society of America, 82, 276
Purrington, Roliff H., Jr., 141

R.J. Reynolds, 13
Radcliff, Wendy, 279
Radio communications, 41, 148–49
Radio Shack, 14
Ralston, Joseph, 99, 100
Rampton, Sheldon, 275
Rapes. See Sexual assaults
Rather, Dan, 37
Reebok, 14
Reich, Robert, 267
Rendell, Ed, 209
Reporters. See Media
Reputation. See also Credibility; Libel
    importance of, 19
    management, 24–26
Rice, Donna, 96
Risk communications. See also Crisis communications
    "cardinal rules" of, 282–83
    during chemical releases, 281–82
    courses on, 294–95
    definition of, 1
Risk management, definition of, 1
Riverwalk Marketplace (New Orleans), 156–57
Roberts, Gary, 211
Rodin, Judith, 251
Rogers, Cora, 138
Rogers & Associates, 249
Roman Catholic Church, 16–17
Rosener, Judy B., 34–35
Rossotti, Charles, 97, 98
Rothstein, Philip Jan, 156
Rouse, Cedric, 123, 139, 140
Royal Majesty, 26
Rozell, Mark J., 108
Rubenstein, Howard, 204
Rubin, Robert, 98
Ruby Ridge, 115
Ruffino, Carolyn, 142
Rules for Radicals, 34
Runyon, Marvin, 27

Sabatini, Clare, 77
Sabato, Larry J., 108
Sacramento River, 284–85
Safer, Morley, 135

Sagon, Glenn, 114
Salinger, Pierre, 37
San Diego State University, 266
San Fernando Valley earthquake (1999), 155
San Francisco
  California Pacific Medical Center, 194–96
  earthquakes, 150, 151, 153, 155
Santa Monica Hospital Medical Center, 249
Sawyer, Diane, 76
Saxton, Cathie, 52
Schaffer, Albert, 133, 136, 137, 140, 141, 142
Schaffer, Ruth, 134, 142
Schiavo, Mary, 116–19
Schiller, Harvey, 212, 213
Schott, Marge, 13
Schrum, Roger, 173, 183
Schultz, Gary, 11
Schwarzkopf, Norman, 53
Science research, 251–52, 255–57
Seagren, Bob, 210
Sears, 14
Secondhand smoke, 13
Security on Campus, Inc., 248
Seif, James, 176
Seiz, Allen, 175
Seles, Monica, 208
Sexual assaults, 99, 249–50
Sexual harassment, 9–12, 99–100
Shell, 278
Sherry, Don, 48
Shinn, George, 205
Shipp, George F., 287
Silber, John, 245–46
Silent Spring, 273
Simon, William E., 210, 252–53
Simpson, Alan K., 75
Simpson, O.J., 113
Sims, Billy, 218
Singel, Mark, 179
Sister Souljah, 252
Skinner, Larry, 176
Slade, Margo, 43, 51
Smilnyak, Norman, 181
Smith, James R., 153–54, 155
Smith, Judy, 51
Smith, Larry, 193
Smith, Lloyd, 143
Smith, Rebecca Beach, 286
Smith, Sally Bedell, 84
Smithfield Foods, 105–7, 285–87
Soccer violence, 208
Solar power, 277–78
Soundbites, 37
Southern Baptist Convention, 15–16

Southern Pacific, 284–85
Spade, Amanda, 292
Speakers, controversial, 253–54
Spira, Howard, 207
Spokespersons
  attorneys as, 42
  CEO as, 42
  media relations training for, 36
  questions about, 22, 23, 24
Sporkin, Stanley, 56
Sports, 202–3. See also specific sports and individuals
  charges and controversies, 202–8
  college, 216–28
  ethics conflicts, 209–14
  films about, 228–29
  security concerns, 208–9
Sprewell, Latrell, 203
Springston, Rex, 108
St. John, Burton, III, 47
Stanford University, 255–56, 257
Star, 83
Starbucks, 269
StarKist, 81–82
Stauber, John, 275
Steel, Helen, 78
Steil, David, 250
Steinbrenner, George M., 207–8, 212
Stern, Andrew, 29, 33
Stone, Robert J., 42
Stonewalling, 4, 171
Student Right-to-Know and Campus Security Act, 247
Stueve, Harold J.J., 85–89
Suckenik, Harold, 55
Sunshine Consultants, 14
Susskind, Lawrence, 8
Swank, David, 217–24
Swayze, Patrick, 80
Switzer, Barry, 205, 217–24
Swoboda, Frank, 12, 64
Sykes, Charles, 238

Television. See also Media; specific networks
  impact of, 46–47
  spots for NCAA, 226–27
Tenure, 243
Texaco, 61
Texas A&M University
  Houston Post editorial about, 64–70
  Open Records Act and, 61
  other lawsuits against, 142–43
  pig farm, 123–42, 144
  sexual harassment at, 10
Theodosius (Roman emperor), 103, 202
Thomas, Clarence, 223

Thomas Jefferson University Hospital, 191
Thompson, Fred, 6, 29
3M, 276
Tietze, Matthew S., 150
TIVI Amsterdam, 211
Tobacco industry
  Philip Morris vs. ABC, 75
  public's mistrust of, 19, 94
  secondhand smoke and, 13
Tokyo, 153
Tomlinson, Don, 46
Tornadoes, 156
TransSports, 212
Travis, Galen, 135
Trudeau, Garry, 3, 77
Trump, Donald, 77
Tuition, 242–43
Tuna industry, 81–82
Turner, Ed, 42
Turner Broadcasting, 210
TV Guide, 84
TWA airline crash, 3, 35, 115–16
Tylenol, 3

Union Carbide, 18–19
Union Pacific Railroad, 279–81
United Church of Christ, 16
United Way of America, 61–62, 292
Universities. See Higher education; specific
  schools
University of Cincinnati, 258
University of Georgia, 215–16, 257
University of Miami, 157–62
University of Michigan, 251, 257
University of Missouri, 258
University of New Hampshire, 257
University of Oklahoma, 217–25
University of Pennsylvania
  crime at, 247–48
  hate speech policy, 254–55
  ineligible player, 216–17
  property sale, 250–51
University of Pittsburgh, 256
University of South Carolina, 229
University of Texas (Austin), 241, 256
University of Virginia, 258
Uplinger, Harold, 149–50
U.S. Army Corps of Engineers, 40–41,
  111–13
U.S. Military Academy at West Point, 10
U.S. Naval Academy, 10
U.S. Park Police, 110–11

ValuJet airline crash, 3, 117–19
Vance, Cyrus, 105
Van Horn, Richard L., 223
Van Sauter, Gordon, 84–85
Ven den Bossche, Luc, 28

Vermillion County Hospital, 192, 193
Vessey, Robert D., 148
Video news releases, 46–47
Vincennes, 53
Vincent, Fay, 207
Viniski, Janet, 174
Virginia Military Institute, 10
Virginia Tech, 258
Voltaggio, Thomas, 178

Wachter, Michael, 217
Wade, Catherine, 134
Wagshal, JoAnna J., 281
Wallace, Mike, 84, 90
Wall Street Journal, 74
Walt Disney Co., 15–16
Warner, Harland (Hal), 6–7, 22
Washington, D.C., 111, 269
Washington, Joe, 218
Watkins, Jack, 104
Watkins, Rev. James M., 16
Watts, J.C., 218–19
Weaver, Randy, 115
Weber, Gary, 80
Webster, David, 148
Werlein, Ewing, Jr., 74, 136, 138, 139, 140,
  142
West, Mary Nan, 136
West Central Community Hospital, 194
Westling, Jon, 246
Westmoreland, William C., 84–85
West Point. See U.S. Military Academy at
  West Point
Wheeler, Tim, 52
White, Bill, 279
Whitehead, Brad, 288
Widnall, Sheila, 100, 102
Will, George, 253
Williams, Etta Ruth, 138
Williams, Willie, 113–14
Winfield, Dave, 207
Winfrey, Oprah, 79–80
Wiseman, W. Tom, 171
Wixted Pope Nora Associates, 27
Woodrum, Pearl, 152
Woods, Tiger, 206
Workplace
  students' poor preparation for, 246–47
  violence in, 27, 265–71
Work Product Doctrine, 59
Wright, Richard N., 175

Yale University, 257

Zanakis, Michael, 80–81
Zigo, Marc, 102
Zoeller, Fuzzy, 206
Zuckerman, Mortimer B., 95

RENE H. HENRY, Fellow PRSA, is director of the Office of Communications and Government Relations for the mid-Atlantic states region of the U.S. Environmental Protection Agency based in Philadelphia. He has had diverse careers in public relations, sports marketing and management, housing and construction, television and entertainment, politics, higher education and as a trade association CEO.

In the mid-70s, he co-founded ICPR which became the second largest international public relations firm in the West with headquarters in Los Angeles and offices in New York, Washington and Paris. It was the first PR or advertising agency in the U.S. to establish Hispanic Marketing and Sports Marketing Divisions. He has counseled *Fortune 500* companies, leaders in entertainment, sports and politics, and even foreign governments, on a myriad of issues and crises.

Henry also was president and CEO of the National Institute of Building Sciences (Washington, D.C.); worked with Mayor Tom Bradley and his team to direct international media activities to help Los Angeles get the 1984 Olympic Games; and was a senior member of George Bush's 1988 presidential campaign staff. He later served in the Bush Administration and was a member of the team at the U.S. Department of Labor that researched and wrote *The Glass Ceiling Initiative*.

Prior to joining EPA, he was executive director of university relations and on the president's executive cabinet for more than four years at Texas A&M University. He has also advised the Chilean government on manufactured housing and how to create a secondary mortgage market.

He has created and produced award-winning videos and television documentaries and authored books on land investment, utility cogeneration, sports and public relations. His *Marketing Public Relations—the hows that make it work!!* is used by professionals, professors and students. *Offsides,* a book about referee Fred Wyant's 27 years of officiating in the National Football League, is scheduled for publication in mid-2000. His other books are *How to Profitably Buy and Sell Land; Bears Handbook—stories, stats and stuff about Baylor University Football*; and *MIUS and You—the developer looks at a new utility concept.*

His honors include three *Silver Anvils* from the Public Relations Society of America, two CINE *Golden Eagles,* three Creative Excellence in Black Advertising awards, the *Clarion Award for Human Rights* from Women In Communications, *Distinguished Citizen Award* from the PRSA Los Angeles chapter, "Best In Texas" *Silver Spurs,* a silver and two bronze medals from World-Fest Houston International Film Festival and numerous awards and citations from professional organizations for campaigns and excellence in public relations.

He also is a member of the Academy of Motion Picture Arts & Sciences and the Academy of Television Arts & Sciences. He has judged the Primetime Emmy awards eight times as well as international film and TV festivals in Italy and Hungary. He is chair-elect of the College of Fellows of the Public Relations Society of America.

He received his A.B. degree in economics from The College of William & Mary and did graduate study in marketing at West Virginia University.